12·20·79

College Degrees for Adults

College Degrees for Adults

A Comprehensive Guide to Over 120 Programs featuring Options for Self-Directed Learning, Credit for Learning through Life Experience and Off-Campus Learning

WAYNE BLAZE

JOHN NERO

with an Introduction by Barbara Lazarus

Beacon Press   Boston

Library of Congress Cataloging in Publication Data

Blaze, Wayne.
    College degrees for adults.

    Includes bibliographical references and index.
    1. Adult education--United States. 2. Degrees,
Academic--United States. 3. Nonformal education--United
States. 4. Self-culture. I. Nero, John, joint author.
II. Title.
LC5251.B57   374.9'73   78-53779
ISBN 0-8070-3156-9
ISBN 0-8070-3157-7 pbk.

For our parents:

    Charles Blaze
    Evelyn Blaze
    Anthony Nero
    Catherine Nero

    who guided our learning of order,

and for Len Krimerman,

    who guided our learning of disorder

Preface and Acknowledgments

This book is based on an earlier publication entitled External Degree Study: A New Route to Careers, which we had prepared with Barbara Lazarus under the sponsorship of the Career Education Project of the Education Development Center. The Career Education Project was a national model funded by the National Institute of Education to develop new ways to deliver career information and counseling to adults.

We would like to thank Juliet Brudney, the project director, under whom the interest in the external degree project was initiated, and Vivian Guilfoy, who was project director at the time of the completion of the first manual. We are also very grateful to the entire staff of the Career Education Project, all of whom in one way or another contributed to that original effort. Special thanks are due Barbara Lazarus, who was the immediate supervisor of the project, and to Richard Landon and Beth Gerber, who assisted in the information gathering.

We are grateful to all of the authors whose work is cited in Part I of this new version and are grateful not only for the passages that have been quoted but for the inspiration we have gained from all of their work. We would also like to thank Richard Bolles, H. B. Gellat, Mardy Grothe, Morris Keeton, and James O'Toole for their comments along the way. We hope we have represented them fairly.

Much credit for the descriptions in Part II goes to the schools themselves, who were cooperative in sending materials and verifying our descriptions. Space limitations, however, required additional editing after this verfication and we hope that our summaries remain faithful to each program's image of itself. We apologize for any confusions that may result from our interpretation of the materials we used. We also regret any possible oversight of schools that should be included but weren't.

The development of this book took about a year from start to finish, during which time we received support, assistance, direction, advice, and critical comments from many people. We would like to thank the following people, with apologies to those whose names may have been omitted accidentally: Peter Armitage, Josh Bell, Claudia Buzzi, Susan Farstrup, Sam Goodyear, Clyde Ingle, Fran Macy, John Mandryk, Linda Mastrodicasa, Don McCreight, Angela Nero, Orchitecture, Steve Samuels, Jeff Smith, Bob Stump, Nancy Tobin, Peter Woodberry, and John Valentine.

And extra-special thanks due to our editor, Luna Carne-Ross, the unsung heroine of the project, whose editing is surpassed only by her patience.

Contents

Introduction

Recent times have seen dramatic changes in the role of education in the lives of adults. More than a third of today's college students are 25 years of age or older. In the words of K. Patricia Cross, "Lifelong learning now outranks motherhood, apple pie, and the flag as the universal good."[1]

Institutions of higher education all over the country are adapting to the growing clientele of adult learners by developing new approaches to teaching adults. Existing programs are being reexamined and new programs are being undertaken to provide educational concepts and delivery systems suitable for adult learners. There are innovations ov every variety: flexible scheduling opportunities, new delivery systems, new degree programs, and holistic programs which attempt to incorporate the entire spectrum of change.

At the heart of this activity is a consideration for the adult as a self-directed learner. Despite, or perhaps because of, the numerous options available, many adults are confused about which institutions offer the best alternatives. In light of the explosions in programs and processes, adults seeking further education are in real need of more and better information.

This book offers answers to key questions facing adults considering further education. Focusing on the more nontraditional new degree programs, those which allow maximum opportunity for self-directed learning, the authors describe the variety of programs that exist and provide suggestions for planning a program of study within them. College Degrees for Adults is a particularly valuable resource for adults interested in exploring new alternatives but raises issues that must be confronted by anyone who is planning to enter or reenter the world of formal education.

The book is divided into two major parts. The first part written by John Nero, consists of five chapters that combine an overview of the new learning options with suggestions for making the most creative use of these options. Chapter One begins with the discussion of the range of options available. By defining unfamiliar terms such as "credit for learning from life experience," and "experiential learning," the chapter provides a concise introduction to the major questions today's adult learner must face. Chapter Two helps the reader deal with the uncertainty that is often associated with learner-centered programs by describing planning techniques that have been developed by business consultants and psychologists. In Chapter Three, the author confronts one of the major problems of nontraditional degree programs: evaluating new learning opportunities. In this chapter, the criteria developed by the institutions themselves are summarized for student use.

Fully aware that many students need further education for an end other than the learning itself, Chapter Four deals with difficult questions about relating nontraditional education to graduate school or jobs. This chapter draws upon the pioneering work of Richard Bolles and James O'Toole in order to establish a real link between self-directed learning and survival in the work world.

Chapter Five covers another item of real interest to adult learners: financial aid. The chapter makes the point that most financial aid comes from only a few large sources, which can be easily located, and that many adults have a good chance of obtaining aid.

Part II, coordinated by Wayne Blaze, provides detailed descriptions of over 100 college programs through which adults can undertake a major portion of their learning off-campus or earn a major portion of their degree for learning that occurred prior to enrollment. Readers can turn here to find out what local programs are available and to link their own interests and needs with the programs described. In this part, the philosophy and goals of the programs are enumerated and degrees and certificates listed. Part II also includes information on the calendar, residency requirements, the general pace of the program, and the costs. Admissions requirements are given in detail, and information on how the program assesses prior learning is also available. Finally, the descriptions include degree requirements and information about supportive services, including financial aid.

College Degrees for Adults contains important information for any adult who is considering some form of college education. It is information that most people are not likely to encounter anywhere else. Those who have abandoned college, or felt abandoned by college, may find new hope within these pages.

Dr. Barbara Lazarus
Director of Career Services
Wellesley College

College Degrees for Adults

I DESIGNS FOR SELF-DIRECTED LEARNING

1. New Options for Older Learners

. . . there is no one best system of education.
Only one characterized by a wide variety of
opportunity and choice can meet the needs of
American citizens and the [demands] of an
unpredictable future.

James O'Toole
Work, Learning and the American Future

Education can be viewed as a trail of decisions . . . decisions about what, where, and when to study, how and with whom. For more than half of your school life most of these decisions were made for you. Your first chance for input came at age sixteen, when you could have decided that those who had been directing your education would not be allowed to continue to do so. But because such a choice would probably have meant leaving school entirely, you really didn't have much choice after all.

Upon obtaining a high school diploma, you had another choice to make—the choice of continuing beyond high school or not. The decision to continue your schooling meant finding a new group of people to direct your learning. Although you had more options from which to choose, once you selected one, the result would be similar, except that new people would be in the driver's seat.

If at some time you decided that more schooling was not the best solution, your need to make learning decisions did not stop. While organizing your home, earning your living or working in your community, you were faced with daily decisions which had immediate bearing on your life and the lives of others. Each success and failure resulted in new skills and knowledge that would affect later decisions and would contribute to the creation of your personal learning style.

Because you are now reading this book, we assume that you are reexamining the role that further schooling can play in your life. If you've been looking at college programs, you have probably already discovered that most are geared to people who are accustomed to having much of their learning shaped by others, and those who can make themselves available for such shaping on a full-time, daily basis.

Many older students who have found themselves in such situations have taken refuge in adult education and evening division programs, and some have been able to arrange their affairs so that they could attend on-campus classes during the day. More and more capable learners, however, are having difficulty finding college programs which adequately meet their needs.

Listed below are learning needs commonly expressed by adults who are continuing their education. As you read through them, you will notice that though some can be, and have been, effectively met through existing educational structures, most require the creation of new learning structures. How many of these needs do you share?

The need
- to design and direct your own studies
- to work independently
- to set your own learning pace
- for recognition of the skills and knowledge you already have
- for a degree to advance in your current job or to enter another

- for a study schedule that is compatible with your work schedule
- to reflect upon the learning you are gaining from your job
- to pursue in-depth study of a subject that interests you
- to develop specific learning skills, rather than just memorize facts
- for more theory in an area in which you have already had some practice
- for more practice in an area in which you have already had some theory
- for more practice or theory in an area which is new to you
- to study in an area in which courses or training programs are not readily available
- to pursue creative work according to your sense of the direction it should take
- for support and encouragement to carry out your college plans
- for help in exploring career options
- to work with others in group projects
- for personalized attention and direct feedback on your work

Recently, most colleges have become more sensitive to the learning needs of adult students and are reviewing their courses and programs in this light. Some are making their regular programs more available to adults by modifying scheduling, by adding special adult-oriented seminars or by allowing more credit for learning done independently. A number of colleges, however, have built new programs from scratch, using their understanding of adult learning needs as the blueprint. It is these programs which are the major topic of this book.

Five years ago, half of the programs described in Section II did not exist. Now most are well on their way to providing ongoing assistance and accredited degrees to adults who are studying at the college level. Through these programs you can earn credit toward a degree for study done in your home, on your job, in field work situations, in part-time courses as well as in campus-based course work. This is all possible because of a number of new approaches which have been refined in the past few years, mostly as a result of the increased demand for education by older learners. Among these features are the following:

- External degree study: the opportunity to earn a degree primarily through off-campus study

- Self-directed study: the opportunity to design and direct your own study program

- Competency-based education: the opportunity to view your learning in light of skills developed rather than just facts memorized

- Credit for learning from life experience:
  the opportunity for recognition of the
  college-level learning you've gained through
  your life experiences

- Expanded classroom and independent study:
  the opportunity to take classes from a
  number of different schools, or to study on
  your own

- Holistic planning: the opportunity for
  personalized education and career planning.

Some of the new programs may offer only one
of these opportunities, some a few, and some may
attempt to provide them all. It may take a bit
of searching to find a program which provides
the right blend for you, but such opportunities
are now within the reach of residents of almost
every state.

To select a program that meets your needs,
you will have to face a host of new questions
about how you want to go about getting your
education.

In this chapter we discuss how these new
opportunities are realized in the colleges
described in Section II, and the new issues
they raise.

SELF-DIRECTED LEARNING
How much direction is really necessary?

Self-directed learning is learning in which
most of the responsibility for designing and
directing studies rests with the learner. In
carrying out a self-directed study plan, you
must continually draw the line between what you
can and want to learn on your own and what you
could learn better from others. Self-directed
learning rests on the assumption that any learning
activity—whether it be in a highly structured
classroom setting, a field work situation, or
independent reading—will mean more to you if it
is part of a program of your own design.

In adult-oriented degree programs, you can
expect to play a major role in determining which
of your learning activities will be directed by
you, and which will be directed by others.
Different schools, however, will put different
emphasis on the portion of your study program
they will allow or expect you to direct: some
programs will limit your power to decide what
subjects you should cover, but will allow
unlimited freedom in how you study them. In such
a program you would have a defined choice of
subject areas, such as programs in a standard
college catalogue (e.g., psychology, sociology,
business management). Within each subject
area, you might also be required to learn
something about very specific components of the
field. In psychology, for example, you might be
expected to have some exposure to the psychology
of personality, of perception, of development,
of the child, of the family, and so on. These

requirements would be clearly stated, and then
you would be given free rein to fill them in any
way that is convenient for you. This could mean
reading on your own or obtaining private tutoring.
It could mean enrolling in courses, or even just
sitting in on courses; such courses might be
offered by the school itself or might be available
to you at other schools in your region.

In other programs, you might encounter a
situation which is almost the reverse. You can
study almost any subject that interests you, but
must do so in a prescribed manner. You may, for
example, be required to get a portion of your
learning in structured classes, and get a portion
off campus.

Degree programs in which you have complete
responsibility for all aspects of your learning are
rare. In most programs you will have the major
responsibility for defining what and how you will
be learning, while the school itself will take
most of the responsibility for determining whether
or not you have succeeded.

Information which will help you to determine
how much opportunity for self-direction exists
at each of the schools summarized in Section II
is presented with the description of each
school under the headings "Curriculum/
Learning Options" and "Degree Requirements."

EXTERNAL DEGREE STUDY
How much campus contact do you need?

External degree study is study in which most
of your learning can occur outside a college campus.
It is now possible for you to earn a degree
with no campus contact at all; with campus contact
a couple of hours a week, a couple of weeks a
year, or as much of it as you like.

Currently, there are at least three programs
from which you can earn a legitimate college degree
almost entirely through the mail. These programs,
the Regents External Degree Program in New York
State, Thomas Edison College of New Jersey, and
the State Board for Academic Awards in Connecticut,
do not even have campuses. They are, in fact,
not colleges at all, but degree granting agencies
who have the job of "certifying" learning done
at any point in one's life.

The basis for the degree is a set of learning
requirements that must be completed in one of
a number of specified majors. These requirements
form the shell of a degree program, which can
be filled with courses you have taken at other
colleges, courses taken in relation to work,
courses taken in the military, study done on
one's own, or knowledge gained from life
experiences. Courses sponsored by approved
colleges, in subject areas which match program
degree requirements, are usually accepted
immediately upon the presentation of a transcript.
Courses and learning completed in business and
industry are accepted for credit on the basis of
guidelines established by the American Council
on Education and the New York State Department
of Education.[1] Learning gained from military
experience and training is assessed on the basis

of standards also developed in conjunction with the American Council on Education.[2] Learning done on one's own, before or after enrolling in the program, is measured on the basis of performance in proficiency tests. These could include tests administered by the College Level Examination Program (CLEP), tests developed and administered by the agencies themselves, or other tests which measure college-level learning, such as graduate record examinations or advanced placement tests. Learning (including learning on the job) which is not sponsored by other agencies or is not covered by existing tests is credited through a process called *special assessment*. In this process, learning is judged through an interview with a number of experts, usually professors from nearby colleges.

Except in the case of knowledge gained directly from life experience, there is no limit on the number of credits that can be earned in any of the above ways, and no limit on the amount of time it takes to earn the degree. The Regents External Degree Program, for example, has awarded associates' and bachelors' degrees to students almost entirely on the basis of learning they had done before enrolling in the program. An example of a person who might qualify for such advanced standing would be a member of the armed forces who had taken a wide range of courses while in military service, but had previously lacked a degree framework in which to apply the credits earned. In most cases, however, past learning experiences will not match so neatly with the degree requirements, and students will have to take a number of tests to fulfill the requirements.

Although these three programs are in the East, many of the tests are offered throughout the nation. At present, however, students needing special assessment are still required to appear at one of the three programs based in the East. These programs are best for people who have already amassed a number of college credits and are looking for a degree structure into which they might fit. They are also best suited to those who can study independently, guided primarily by a reading list and a study guide; and to students whose interests are directly in line with the content areas covered by traditional degree programs.

These three programs represent <u>external degree study</u> in its truest form. However the phrase is also applied to many other programs which award credit for life learning and which allow a good portion of off-campus study but will require more campus contact than the three programs described above. Most of such programs grant up to three fourths of the necessary credits for learning done prior to enrollment, and will require less than one semester's worth of credit to be earned through campus-based activities. Campus contact of this sort usually involves meetings with an adviser in which each student's work is planned and progress is assessed. It could also mean a required residency period. At programs offered by the Goddard College Adult Degree Program and the Syracuse University Independent Study Degree Program, for example, the only contact with the campus occurs during one- to two-week live-in sessions which

are sandwiched between each learning period. At such residency sessions, old work is evaluated and new work is planned. Students may thus spend three to six months working on their own between residency sessions.

Other adult-oriented degree programs prefer not to be thought of as external degrees at all, even though they grant credit for prior learning and off-campus study. At Minnesota Metropolitan State University, for example, students have a great deal of leeway in structuring their own programs, both on and off campus, but program organizers feel that the classes, workshops, and other meetings that occur on campus are an essential part of the learning experience.

Information about the amount of campus contact that is required by the schools described in Section II is found under the heading "Residency/Required Contact with Program."

COMPETENCY-BASED EDUCATION
Do you need information and facts about specific subjects, general skills, or both?

Competency-based education is education which stresses the development of skills, rather than just the gathering of information. Throughout your education, the development of *competencies*, or skills, will occur hand in hand with the gathering of specific *facts*. Until recently, learning in most colleges has been information-based rather than competency-based. Competencies were generally regarded as silent partners which developed automatically in the quest for information. As a result of this assumption, most scholars spent their time defining and redefining information areas (e.g., biology, molecular biology, astrobiology, sociobiology) while all but ignoring definitions of competency areas. This has led to the conclusion that information itself is the end product of education, rather than only one of its parts. An example of such confusion could be liberal arts majors completing college with reams of information about their subject but having only a foggy notion of how their learning skills might be applied to gain new information in other areas.

A competency-based approach seeks to avoid such confusion by seeking to highlight the relationship between skills and information. The first step in bringing about such a balance is to find a method that will name areas of competency in much the same say as academic disciplines are named (e.g., humanities, social sciences, hard sciences). One basis for such a method has been used by the Department of Labor for over thirty years, primarily to simplify record keeping.[3] In this approach, competencies are divided into three major areas—competencies in working with <u>ideas</u>, competencies in working with <u>people</u>, and competencies in working with <u>things</u>. Examples of such competencies are as follows:

Competencies related to ideas:
● Planning

- Goal setting
- Decision making
- Problem solving
- Researching
- Investigating

Competencies related to people:
- Teaching
- Negotiating
- Managing
- Leading
- Helping

Competencies related to things:
- Using tools
- Operating machinery
- Drawing
- Constructing
- Measuring

In these examples, competencies cut across information areas. Competencies such as planning or researching, for example, have broad applications in any information area. It is also possible to apply this ideas-people-things method within specific areas of information. In the study of psychology, for example, one would be working with ideas, but might also develop competencies in dealing with people (for instance, through group experiences) or things (through test administration or using video equipment).

Likewise, a marketing major might learn skills in dealing with ideas (figures) and things (computers) while a management major might work with ideas and things, but would in addition focus more heavily on skills in working with people.

Competency-based education, to which we will return in later chapters, is not featured in all adult-oriented degree programs, but most of them are moving in this direction. Those which do will require the student to define his or her learning in ways that show the relationship between skills and information.

Information on how the schools described in Section II view the relationship between information and competencies may appear under the headings "Curriculum—learning options" or "Degree requirements."

as college-level. Most programs will agree that any learning covered in the courses of established colleges or by the questions on established college-level examinations should be considered college-level. And more colleges are recognizing that learning obtained in any sponsored programs, such as courses in the military or business world, should also be considered college-level if it is equivalent to that usually obtained in college courses.

New areas will be judged on the basis of at least two factors. The first will be the student's ability to relate that area to currently established information and skill areas. Meditation, for example, may be considered college-level if approached by the scientific method, or if accepted techniques in logic are used to illustrate its relation to the scientific method, or if techniques of sociology are used to explore it as a social phenomenon, etc.

A second criterion that might be applied is an assessment of how well the new area matches learning goals. If the student is judged to have college-level learning goals, and can demonstrate the relationship between the new area and these goals, then chances are good that the area will be considered college-level. Thus, in the example just given, meditation techniques might be considered college-level learning if it can be demonstrated that the goals achieved were similar to those of accepted college learning, such as increased awareness of the world, self-understanding, or problem-solving abilities.

As will be seen in Chapter Three, the fact that learning is considered college-level doesn't guarantee that it will be accepted for credit in any program. The final decision will usually be made on the basis of how well the learning fits into an overall learning program.

Information on the policies by which the schools described in Section II award credit for prior learning is found under the heading of "Assessment of Prior Learning."

CREDIT FOR LEARNING FROM LIFE EXPERIENCE
What college-level learning have you gained from your life experience?

Any significant event in life can be a source of college-level learning. This can include learning gained on the job, in personal life, family activities, travel, hobbies, or even from extensive conversations with experts. In most programs, the emphasis is on what is learned from the experience, not the experience itself. Thus, a person who had written a book on gardening would not earn credit for having written a book, but only for the skills and information gained in the process of preparing the book.

Program philosophies begin to differ, however, in which kinds of learning will be recognized

EXPERIENTIAL LEARNING
How much theory is needed? How much practice?

Although all learning is experiential at some level, when used to discuss adult-oriented education programs, the term usually refers more specifically to learning done outside the confines of the traditional classroom. Experiential learning, in this context, focuses on the practical application of knowledge rather than on its theoretical underpinnings.

This is not to imply that one aspect of learning is in any way more important than the other. As Alfred North Whitehead puts it:

"Every subject of study should be presented in the abstract and the concrete. Both sides are wanted. We learn them in the abstract and feel them in the concrete."[4]

In the traditional sequence of learning, the abstract theory is first presented in the classroom and later put into practice. In many subject areas, students do not get any practical experience until they have entered the world of work. Since 1876, when Johns Hopkins Medical School revolutionized medical education by actually allowing students to perform autopsies and observe _real_ patients receiving treatment,[5] practical experience has become an essential part of college programs such as law, allied health, and laboratory sciences. To most students, however, especially undergraduate students, the opportunity for practical learning is denied. It is denied not because it is not thought important, but because learning outside the classroom is difficult to organize, difficult to maintain, and difficult to measure. It was not until the recent growth of competency-based education, and its elaboration by the CAEL project (about which more will be said later), that schools have had any real help in operating such programs in other areas of learning.

If you feel your practice in a certain area has been extensive, but you lack the theory, some programs will allow you to focus on reading, research, and reflection. If, on the other hand, you've been spending time reading and thinking about a subject, there are programs which will encourage you to gain more practical experience. Most schools are striving toward programs in which theory is supported by practice and practice is supported by theory.

Information on the opportunities for experiential learning in the programs described in Section II is found under the heading "Curriculum—learning options." To locate options for experiential learning at other colleges, see the introduction to Section II on page 43.

EXPANDED CLASSROOM AND INDEPENDENT STUDY
How much classroom learning do you need? How much independent study?

If you do have the need to learn theory, what is the best way to go about it? A regular course on the subject can certainly be one good way. If you can find a topic that interests you, having the information arranged in course outline by an expert is a luxury that is hard to pass up. Most adults who have found classroom learning to be inconvenient have had problems, not so much with the classroom structure itself, but with the availability of the _right_ classes. This is one reason why adult-oriented programs now allow you to take courses almost anywhere you can find them. This includes courses at other colleges, in continuing education programs, or in agencies offering college-level courses.

If you can't easily locate courses on the

topics you want to study, or if you just prefer to study on your own, a number of other alternatives are now open, most of which fall under the general heading of independent study. Probably the next best thing to a course perfectly tailored to your needs is a one-to-one tutorial with an expert in the field. Some programs now maintain a staff of faculty members who are available for this purpose. Others maintain working relationships with experts throughout the country, and will arrange opportunities for you to work with these people. Still others allow you to work with anyone from whom you feel you can learn.

In the most external of the external degree programs, you may find yourself working entirely on your own, guided only by the program's degree requirements and a study guide. Many students preparing for proficiency tests in external degree programs, however, often sit in on classes at area colleges. In some cities public libraries have begun providing special services to help students prepare independently for such proficiency tests.

If you cannot attend classes, it is possible to have the classes come to you. Most schools described in Section II give you the opportunity to earn a good portion of your degree through correspondence study. Although correspondence courses often receive bad publicity, many established colleges offer excellent ones.

In some parts of the country, it is also possible to obtain college credit through televised courses. The city college system of Chicago, for example, makes it possible to earn an associate's degree entirely by means of such courses.

Other sources may be businesses and the military. The American Council on Education and the New York State Department of Education have prepared a number of guides from which you can learn how courses taken from corporations or during military training might translate into college credit. Through their work, they have discovered that there are many such courses in which the content is equivalent to that covered in regular colleges.

Another learning option which is a combination of independent and classroom learning is known as a study group. Some schools organize a number of people with common interests into a study group.

Information on opportunities for independent study and classroom learning at the colleges described in Section II can be found under the heading "Curriculum—learning options." To locate information about options at other schools, see the introductory comments to Section II on page 43.

HOLISTIC PLANNING
How do your education plans relate to your other life plans?

Earlier in this chapter, when we asked how

much direction you needed, we were referring mostly to direction in planning and carrying out specific learning activities. Here, we ask you to shift gears and think about how much help you need in sorting through this entire process. Since most of the questions raised in this chapter did not even exist until very recently, it is expected that determining how much self-direction, campus contact, or other help you actually need will take you a considerable amount of time.

A good place to begin examining these issues is at an educational brokering agency. These agencies, which are usually free or low-cost, perform the same function for students about to invest in education as a stockbroker performs for those about to invest in stocks. Many of the two hundred agencies which are now operating have developed side by side with the adult degree programs in their regions and are thus familiar with the options these offer. These agencies can help you sort through your learning needs a. match them with the resources that are available. Other counseling agencies may not be as familiar with specific issues raised by self-directed learning programs, but that doesn't mean they won't be helpful. As we will discuss in later chapters, the basics of self-directed learning are the decision-making and problem-solving skills which you use throughout your life. Thus, any counseling agency with which you feel comfortable can be of great help.

You will also find that many of the colleges to which you apply will provide help in determining how well their offerings might meet your needs. Since it is always difficult for program staff members to be completely unbiased, however, it is important that you approach several programs before reaching any final conclusions. One thing you must be certain to clarify in your discussions with the staff of each program is the nature of the support services that will be available once you've enrolled.

In the most common arrangement, the major source of support is a learning adviser assigned to you. The adviser will be responsible for helping you plan your program. This will include setting long- and short-term career goals, planning learning activities, locating learning resources, and planning evaluation procedures.

In some programs this kind of planning can be a part of your overall study. You might work on this task only with an adviser, or in special workshops sponsored by the college. In schools that offer such workshops, the focus is on helping to develop the skills and information you need in your education and career planning. There are usually weekly projects related to that goal, and you share the results with other class members involved in the same process.

One variation on such workshops is seminars designed to help ease the shock of reentry for students who are returning to school after an extended absence. Such seminars are designed to help students overcome obstacles such as math blocks or feelings that they are too old to study again.

Information on educational brokering agencies and other educational information centers in your area can be found by using the Educational and Career Information Services for Adults: 1978 Directory published by the National Center for Educational Brokering in Washington, D.C. (the cost of the directory is $2.00).[6] A directory of special counseling services for women is included in What Color Is Your Parachute? by Richard Bolles. Information regarding the support services available at the colleges described in Section II can be found under the heading "Supportive Services—financial aid."

2. Planning Your Learning Experience

or a few seconds Moon-Watcher stood
ncertainly...
ow he was master of the world, and
e was not quite sure what to do next.
ut he would think of something.

                        Arthur C. Clarke, _2001_

s every good coach knows, when things
tart to get out of hand it's time to go
ack to the basics...save the fancy stuff
or later.

              Ned Tibbe, at CEEB Conference,
                    December 1977

New learning options may pose new learning problems, but the solutions to such problems are rooted in principles that have been in use for ages. The basics of education and career planning are not the three Rs but the process of setting goals and spelling out the steps by which these will be reached. Too often, in our attempts to find creative solutions to planning problems, we assume that a method so matter-of-fact could not be the route to the solutions we desire. However, a good plan is the very foundation of a successful learning experience. Every person has his or her own approach to planning. Once one's planning style is developed, it is usually applied to situations at all levels, from long-term career goals to immediate learning projects. In this chapter, we hope to help you refine your planning style by introducing the planning approaches of a number of writers on the subject. In doing so, we will discuss these three aspects of the planning process:

1. Designing a plan
2. Dealing with obstacles in the planning process
3. Making planning decisions

1. Designing a Plan

Dr. Robert Mager, a consultant to industry and education, has detailed his planning system in the highly readable book, Goal Analysis.[1] In a very lively discussion, Mager describes his system for removing what he calls the "fuzziness" that so often characterizes goal-setting situations. He suggests that one should always begin a plan with a written statement of one's goal. This statement is then followed by a list of the performances which would define the goal more precisely. To help the reader describe these performances, he recommends asking questions such as the following:

- How would I recognize success in achieving the goal?
- Thinking of someone who has achieved the goal, what is it they do or say that makes me think so?
- Given a room full of people, on what basis would I determine which of them might have achieved this goal, and which might not have?

Thus, if your goal was stated as "a satisfying career," Mager would have you list the things that would have to occur to enable you to recognize the fact that you had actually attained a satisfying career. You might, possibly, respond as follows:

I will know I have a satisfactory career when

- I am working in a job which is using the potential I feel I have
- I am earning more money than I now earn
- I am helping others in clearly definable ways
- I have the respect and support of my coworkers

In Goal Analysis, Mager provides guidance and support for the task of clarifying responses to

such questions, identifying those which are most immediately attainable, and formulating a plan by which to bring them about.

A person who has found Mager's approach valuable in developing his own system is counseling psychologist Mardelle Grothe. Dr. Grothe has the following comments about phrasing goal statements:

A goal statement should describe the end result of a process rather than a process itself. The statement, "to develop an understanding of the fundamental principles of management," for example, is not a goal statement because it describes a process. The goal statement that would be derived from the same desire would simply be "an understanding of the fundamental principles of management."

This may seem like a minor modification, but making it can help reduce the frustration that almost always results from shooting for a goal which you have defined as a moving target.

What Robert Mager terms performances Dr. Grothe terms objectives, and says the following regarding the distinction between goals and objectives:

Goals usually sound important, while objectives may sound trivial . . . . The goal "recognition as a poet," for example, sounds much more glamorous than the related objectives such as "a regular writing schedule," "research on topic areas," or "communications with publishers." Goals which are not accompanied by realistic objectives are little more than pipe dreams.[2]

A clear statement of goals and objectives is the essence of planning, but as Grothe also reminds us, it is only the first step. The real work is defined in an action plan. For each objective identified, one must develop a list of very specific tasks that are to be completed over a specified time period.

The application of similar planning techniques to the problems of self-directed learning is presented by Malcolm Knowles in his book, Self-Directed Learning (Guidelines for Students and Teachers.[3] For Dr. Knowles, often called the father of adult education because of his pioneering work in the field, goals are defined in terms of very specific learning projects. Each learning project is then further divided into learning objectives. To aid in identifying specific learning objectives Knowles suggests consideration of the following:

- The knowledge that might be gained from the learning project
- The specific skills that might be developed in the learning project
- The new understandings that might be had from the learning project
- The attitudes that might be formed during the project
- The values that might be affected by the project.

Like Mager and Grothe, Knowles feels that it is important to put plans on paper, and uses the term learning contract to describe such a presentation.

Learning contract seems to be the most popular of the many terms which are currently being used to refer to learning plans. We will use this term throughout this book. The learning contracts we will illustrate, however, will be somewhat simplified in comparison to those presented by Dr. Knowles. When you are at the point of actually writing your plan, you should look at his format as well as at the format that might be used by any colleges with which you may have been in touch.

For the purpose of illustration, we will use learning contracts representing three basic elements which characterize most approaches to planning:

a. A clear statement of what is to be accomplished— this we will refer to as the goal
b. A description of some events which must occur that will indicate to you that the goal has been attained—these we will call objectives
c. A listing of some specific tasks which must be carried out over a period of time— these we will call activities.

We will thus be referring to goals, objectives, and activities as they exist in the relationship illustrated below.

GOAL
What you want to accomplish

OBJECTIVES	RELATED ACTIVITIES
What conditions must be present for goal attainment?	What specific action must you take to complete each objective?
Objective 1	Activity 1a (time period)
	Activity 1b (time period)
	Activity 1c (time period)
Objective 2	Activity 2a (time period)
	Activity 2b (time period)
	Activity 2c (time period)
	Activity 2d (time period)
Objective 3	Activity 3a (time period)
	Activity 3b (time period)

2. Dealing with Obstacles in the Planning Process

Most planning approaches can be viewed as systems for organizing responses to a series of questions. Once you answer the question What do I want to accomplish? you might, for example, immediately follow with the question How do I go about doing it? or How can I tell when I've done it? Such a line of inquiry flows almost naturally until it is interrupted by a question for which you do not have an answer. For many, the inability to produce instant answers to planning questions is a major source of frustration which too often leads to an end of planning and an abandonment of goals.

Keeping the planning wheels turning depends as much on asking the right questions as it does on having the right answers. We will draw from the work of writers in various fields who provide suggestions as to how special attention to your questions can help keep your planning in motion. These suggestions will be presented within five separate approaches for dealing with a question you can't answer.

A. The divide and conquer approach

Divide and conquer is perhaps the most common way of dealing with a difficult question. Rather than try to cope with a large complex question, you identify the component parts of the question and ask simpler ones regarding each. In Chapter 1, for example, we used the technique to help you approach the question, What role can new learning options play in helping me to meet my learning needs? Among the smaller questions asked were: How much direction do you need? How much campus contact do you need?

The planning approaches described above represent another example. In order to help you approach the question, What do I do next? the planners to whom we referred suggest that you ask yourself more specific questions: What do I want to accomplish? How do I know when I've done it?

Success in using the divide and conquer approach depends upon your ability to identify the parts of the question that you can't answer, and build questions that relate to these parts.

B. The Hawkshaw approach

We have named this after the detective in Thomas Taylor's play, The Ticket-of-Leave Man.[4] It involves prefacing the question that you cannot answer with words such as How can I learn? or How can I find out? Instead of asking, What do I want to accomplish? you might ask, How can I learn what I want to accomplish? Or, instead of asking: What steps must I take to reach my goal?, you might ask How can I find out which steps I must take in order to reach my goal? Just as a detective might put off naming the culprit until after having completed a thorough search for evidence, a careful planner might put off naming a goal or objective until after a thorough information search has been done. In doing so, the search itself then becomes a short-term goal or objective.

C. The rocking chair approach

Bob Hope once said that John Kennedy liked his rocking chair because it provided "motion without danger."[5] This technique is called the rocking chair approach because it helps you keep your planning in motion without the "danger" of immediate commitment to a specific goal or objective. Here, you phrase answers in what psychologist George Kelly terms the "invitational mood," a mood that invites exploration. In doing so, each possible answer is prefaced with the word suppose. Thus, if the question that stumps you is What do I want

to accomplish?, and you can think of a number of
possibilities, you might try each out by including
it in the sentence, Suppose I wanted to accomplish X
what do I do next? In this way you can map out
related objectives and activities and then make
your later decision on the basis of a complete
proposal rather than just an idea.

A good example of this technique is the
scientific method. An engineer might ask:
How can we get energy from the sun?—a topic
about which s/he may already have a few ideas he'd
like to explore. To do so, he might say:
Suppose we use giant mirrors, what would we do
next? Without committing himself to the use of
giant mirrors, he will continue to map out
objectives and activities that relate to the
use of giant mirrors. Having a sense of the
objectives and activities, he will then have more
information upon which to decide whether giant
mirrors would be a feasible means of collecting
energy from the sun.

D. The backdoor approach

In this particular method, attention is turned
away from defining what it is you want to happen
and toward defining that which you do not want
to happen. We may not always have a good idea of
what we would like to see happen, but can often
clearly define what it is we want to avoid.

The lifestyle of the Balinese people, as it
is described by Gregory Bateson in Steps Toward
an Ecology of Mind,[6] provides us with a working
example of the backdoor technique. Bateson tells
us that the Balinese seldom set very specific
goals for things they would like to see happen
in their future, but gear their daily activities
toward the avoidance of specific events.

Planning to avoid the worst rather than
shoot for the best may or may not be a useful
approach to all of your planning problems, but
it can be helpful in situations in which you
are having difficulty specifying precise goals.

E. The Koko dodge

This approach is named after Koko, a female
gorilla who is learning sign language from Penny
Patterson, a Stanford University graduate student.
Her progress is described in a New York Times
Magazine article as follows:

> Like...other chimpanzees, [Koko] puts learned
> words together to devise appropriate names for
> new objects: "finger bracelet" for ring,
> "white tiger" for zebra, "eye hat" for mask,
> "elephant baby" for a "Pinocchio doll."[7]

Later in the article Ms. Patterson describes the
following incident:

> Once a reporter was here and he asked [Koko]
> whom she liked best, me or my assistant. Koko
> looked at me, looked at my assistant, looked
> at me, looked at my assistant, and then gave
> the sign for "bad question!"[8]

If all your attempts to answer a planning
question have failed, chances are that further
struggles will do more harm than good. Edward
DeBono might compare pursuing a bad question
to digging oneself deeper into a hole. In The
Use of Lateral Thinking, he says the following:

> Logic is the tool that is used to dig holes
> deeper and bigger, to make them altogether
> better holes. But if the hole is in the
> wrong place, then no amount of improvement
> is going to put it in the right place....
>
> The disinclination to abandon a half-dug
> hole is partly a reluctance to abandon the
> investment of effort that has gone into the
> hole without seeing some return. It is also
> easier to go on doing the same thing rather
> than wonder what else to do: there is a
> strong practical commitment to it.[9]

The writers of the U.S. Constitution recognized
the value of the Koko dodge by including the
fifth amendment. In planning, rather than
refusing to answer on the grounds that answering
would incriminate you, you can refuse to answer
on the grounds that attempting to answer is not
getting you anywhere.

3. Making Planning Decisions

The planning approaches discussed thus far are
essentially techniques for stalling your decision-
making until you have more and better information.
Regardless of how well you search, however, you
will seldom be able to gather perfect information,
and at some point will have to make a decision
based on the data you have. This may mean having
to decide on the basis of what you feel to be
inadequate information or it may mean having to
select from among several alternatives which may
have been generated by your search.

The importance of understanding the ways in which
people approach the decision-making process is
only beginning to be recognized, as is the fact
that decision-making is a problem which is common
to almost everyone. In the following passage,
Arthur Chickering, of Memphis State University,
provides a glimpse of the decision-making predica-
ment in which many adults find themselves:

> Persons with the most diverse, rich, and
> meaningful interests often seem to have
> difficulty in settling on future plans and
> in developing clear purposes that provide
> motivational power. For it is difficult
> to recognize, and more difficult to accept,
> that every affirmation is 90 percent renuncia-
> tion, that every choice to do one thing is a
> choice not to do ten others. It is hard to
> give up becoming an expert skier, an accom-
> plished musician, and a successful entrepre-
> neur, in order to pursue a profession. It is
> likewise hard to give up reading contemporary
> literature, dabbling with mobiles, lying in
> the sun, building with wood, gambling. All
> interests provide satisfaction and stimulation.
> Who wants to surrender them for the abstract,
> hazy, and unexperienced rewards that may
> reside down some vocational path? Small

wonder that many secure, able, and creative persons put off such decisions and spend prodigious ingenuity and energy keeping as many options open as they can.[10]

A useful guide to the decision-making process is the book Decisions and Outcomes, by H. B. Gellat and Gordon Miller.[11] Gellat and Miller define decision-making as a process for "using what you know to get what you want." The result of a good decision, they feel, is a course of action which has both the payoff possibilities of having bet on the long shot in a horse race, and the security of having bet on the favorite. This combination can be attained only after a careful search for information, coupled with a realistic assessment of your values.

To guide you in this search, Gellat and Miller provide a series of steps which describe the ground that must be covered in any well-thought-out decision. The questions presented below are derived from these steps:

a. What is the decision that needs to be made?
   What is the question that you are having difficulty answering? Are you able to clearly state your problem?

b. Why is it important that the decision be made?
   What is at stake? Your health? Your self-image? Your relationships with others?

c. What information do you now have that relates to the decision?
   What solutions have already been attempted? Why were they unsuccessful? Of what value were they? What sources of help and information do you now know of?

d. What new information do you need?
   What are the new questions that need to be answered? What are the new questions that need to be restated?

e. What are your alternatives?
   Has the questioning process yielded new alternatives? New short-term goals? New objectives?

f. What are the risks and gains?
   What do you have to gain or lose from each alternative? How much of your time is at stake? How much money? How much physical or emotional stress?

g. What is your course of action?
   Having organized the information you have, gathered any new information you might need, and examined your alternatives, which course of action will you take? Which goals, objectives and activities will you carry out?

On another occasion, Gellat also referred to the work of Irving L. Janis, a psychologist who is conducting research on how people make decisions. In the May 1978 issue of Psychology Today, Janis and Dan Wheeler describe some of the decision-making strategies that they have been studying. Among them is a technique called the balance sheet, which represents a new twist to the standard approach of weighing the pros and cons of each alternative that is being considered. In this method, you list the practical gains or losses that might be associated with each alternative, and you list them not only for yourself, but for others who might be affected by your decisions. You then write down statements about the extent to which you approve or disapprove of each option and repeat this step for each other person that may be involved in the decision. A sample balance sheet is given in the Psychology Today article and a detailed description of the approach is included in the book Decision-Making, by Janis and Leon Mann.[12]

While working on decision-making skills with adults who were studying independently for the CLEP tests, H. B. Gellat found that those who were working entirely on their own had difficulty following through in their planning and decision-making despite the fact that they understood the underlying principles of the strategies they had been taught. For this reason, he suggests that learners try to enlist a friend to help them in the process of asking questions and staying on the track.

If you are not used to planning and decision-making on your own, it might be wise to begin working on these issues with a counselor. Understanding the information presented in this chapter will help you to grasp what role a counselor might play in helping you concentrate on the decisions that you need to make. Whether you are planning on your own, with a friend, or with a counselor, we think it would be well worth your while to take a closer look at some of the references mentioned in this chapter.

CASE STUDIES

The remainder of this chapter will be devoted to an in-depth case study of a woman who applied many of the techniques discussed here to her education planning, and a number of shorter case studies of students who used adult-oriented degree programs to plan learning experiences in line with their specific goals.

In-depth study

Laura is a twenty-eight-year-old woman who is currently completing three years of employment as a dental assistant in a health care program at a public school. Five years ago she left college after earning three years of credit toward a degree and teaching certificate in English literature.

Since leaving college she has been doing a little reading on her own, dabbling a bit in real estate, and working at various clerical jobs in order to supplement her income.

For the past year, Laura's concern over the lack of direction in her career had been growing steadily. She was feeling stagnant and helpless. She couldn't make any plans to get herself out of the situation because she didn't know what she really wanted out of life.

She was, however, doing a lot of thinking. At times she felt that her experience as a dental assistant might be a basis for a career in public health, while at other times she thought that the fact that she had been successful in helping her friends deal with their problems might be an indication that she would be comfortable in a counseling career. Through her clerical jobs she had a great deal of exposure to the business world and often considered that a direction in which she might like to move. And when she was thinking about business, she also thought more about pursuing her interest in real estate more intensively.

To all of these considerations she added the need to complete her college education, both as a way of dealing with "unfinished business," and as a way of applying some pressure to "begin using my mind again."

At first she tried to integrate all of these interests into an overall learning scheme, but even if she could have found a degree program with adequate resources and flexibility, she would still have been plagued by the problem of extending her planning beyond the question, What is my goal?   None of the options she had been considering emerged as the thing to which she wanted to devote the rest of her life.

After mulling over these issues for several months, she was able to reach a partial resolution and even generate a working plan. Her planning process was much more haphazard than the step-by-step approaches recommended by professional planners, but at one time or another she solved various planning problems, using techniques similar to those discussed in this chapter.

She divided her major question into a number of smaller questions: What have I found enjoyable? How do I like to spend my time? What things bore me? Which activities am I best at? What are my strengths? Am I motivated by money? Challenge? Variety? Is a family more important than a career?

She used the Hawkshaw approach by talking to counselors, friends, and coworkers in order to get more information that would help her to clarify her goals.

As in the rocking chair approach, she "tried on" each of the alternatives she was considering by asking questions like: Suppose I wanted to enter the health field, exactly how would I do it and what would it mean if I succeeded? or Suppose I wanted to do nothing but get a degree, how would I go about it?

She used the backdoor technique and asked herself what she definitely didn't want to give up over the next few years, and used the Koko dodge in allowing herself to begin planning before she answered the question, What do I really what to do with my life?

As a result of this deliberation, the first decision she made was to exclude the possibility of pursuing a career in public health. "It was time to do something completely different." The decision as to how to incorporate the other elements into her life was slightly more complicated, but after another somewhat traumatic period of deliberation, in which she also haphazardly employed basic decision-making strategies, she designed the following plan:

GOAL
A comfortable, organized approach to my career

OBJECTIVES	RELATED ACTIVITIES
Objective 1: the comple-tion of my English degree	1a. Enroll in the New York State Regents External Degree Program

and complete five tests
1b. Prepare for tests by devising a learning contract based on the study guides

Objective 2: Directed activity toward becom-ing a licensed realtor	2a. Enroll in real estate course 2b. Sign on as a part-time realtor with a major real estate organization 2c. Prepare independ-ently for real estate exam
Objective 3: Support my-self and explore oppor-tunities in the business world	3a. Work as a temporary typist and keep my eyes open for any good jobs I might encounter while doing so 3b. If something doesn't occur over the summer this way, I will begin a serious job search in the fall
Objective 4: Explora-tion of interest in counseling	4a. Read The Art of Counseling, Human Relations in Counseling, and other books 4b. Concentrate on my own interactions in helping others deal with their problems.

In addition, her work toward the completion of her college degree required a second plan by which she would prepare for the Regents tests. Her first thought was to take one test which would award her her thirty-nine credits, the equivalent of her entire last year of school. With that in mind, she devised the following learning contract, using College on Your Own by Gail Thain Parker and Gene Hawes,[13] as a guide.

Learning Contract: Preparation for Proficiency Examination in Literature

GOAL
A score on the Graduate Record Examination in Literature which will be acceptable for credit toward a degree from the Regents External Degree Program

SPECIFIC OBJECTIVES	RELATED ACTIVITIES
1. A review of American literature	1a. Read sections of A Literary History of the United States by Robert E. Spiller, et al., which cover areas I feel I need to review 1b. Read Understanding Poetry and Understanding Fiction, by coauthors Cleanth Brooks and Robert Penn Warren

2. A review of English composition	2a. Read <u>Elements of College Reading and Writing</u>, by P. J. Canavan
	2b. Read <u>The Complete Stylist</u>, by Sheridan Baker
	2c. Read <u>The Elements of Writing</u>, by Robert Scholes
3. A Review of English literature	3a. Read appropriate sections of <u>A Literary History of England</u>, by Albert Bough et al.
	3b. Read <u>The Discarded Image</u>, by C. S. Lewis
	3c. Read the introduction to each play in the Pelican Shakespeare Series, and reread any play that still seems fuzzy
	3d. Read Boswell's <u>Life of Johnson</u>
	3e. Review Harold Bloom's <u>English Romantic Poetry</u> according to plan set out in <u>College on Your Own</u>, by Parker and Hawes.

She has since decided, however, that she would rather earn credit through five smaller tests. Her learning plan for this will now be adapted from the study guides which the Regents program provides for each test, supplemented by suggestions from <u>College on Your Own</u>. The most important thing about Laura's decisions is not the specific elements of the plan, which may or may not eventually lead to her goal, but the fact that in having a plan she was actually able to feel that she was dealing with her problems in an organized manner. "Now that I have this plan," she says, "it'll be a lot easier to change direction later on, if I want to. It's kind of a reference point. You have to start somewhere!"

The remaining case studies are of students who used some of the programs described in this book in order to work out their own career plans. As you read through them, try to imagine how their learning contracts might have looked, and to think about the kinds of decisions that had to be made.

1. A young woman interested in pursuing a career in the field of accounting became disenchanted with the course requirements of the junior college which she was attending and enrolled in a program which allowed her to choose learning options that interested her. Her new learning program consisted of private tutoring by a faculty member from a nearby business college, a few regular courses at a local liberal arts institution, and independent study in the area of psychology. She received work-study financial aid, which involved keeping the books for one of the social service agencies associated with the school.

2. A student who had been unable to get a double major at her state university enrolled in a program which would allow her to prepare for a career in music therapy. She received some advanced standing for demonstrating applicable learning from regular and continuing education courses at her state university, her volunteer work at a hospital, and her experiences as a professional singer. The remainder of her program centered around library research and supervised field work in a mental hospital. Twice a week she met with her mentor (adviser), who evaluated her work on the criteria agreed upon at the outset—the presentation of short reviews of applicable readings, a log of her daily learning activities, and a final essay synthesizing all of her work in the program.

3. A student enrolled in an external degree program after having served in the U.S. Navy. He was awarded forty-five credits for previous college work done through the U.S. Armed Forces Institute, the University of Hawaii, and the State University of New York. An evaluation of his record showed that these courses met nearly all of the requirements for an associate's degree. He fulfilled the remaining requirements, in mathematics and the natural sciences, through the College Level Examination Program, and then pursued a bachelor's degree in business administration through the Regents program.

4. A mother of eight enrolled in an adult degree program after most of her children had left home. Her main interest was working with children who had learning disabilities; but she felt she should also explore other options. Since she planned to concentrate primarily on the field of education, she hoped to receive some advanced standing credit for her job as a teacher's aide.

Her first semester's work included supervised reading in the area of learning disabilities, some field work in the school at which she had served as a teacher's aide, reading in general liberal arts areas, and keeping a journal of her experiences. She maintained contact with her adviser, a faculty member who specialized in child development, through a regular exchange of letters. Her external degree study enabled her to explore one area of interest and gain experience that helped decide her career direction.

5. A woman enrolled in a program which featured classroom study, but allowed students the leeway of selecting classes that interested them. She planned to take courses in art, psychology and social work, all areas in which she was interested. She hoped that by doing so, she would be better able to define a career direction for herself. After a four-hour interview, she was awarded a semester's worth of advanced

standing for past experiences, which included volunteer work for the heart fund and a part-time job in public relations. She pursued a basic liberal arts study program, choosing courses in the subjects mentioned above from the college's regular offerings, as well as from a series of special classes designed specifically for adults. She found the approach attractive because she earned credit for some learning she had already had, was able to participate in special classes offered at convenient hours, and had the flexibility to select courses that interested her.

6. A rehabilitation counselor felt that she needed a degree to advance in the field of counseling. Expecting to receive about one year of advanced standing for her work experience, she structured most of her program around the group counseling she had done in her job. Her progress was evaluated on the basis of her reports on the knowledge and skills she felt she was acquiring. Through the program this student was able to build on her experience as a rehabilitation counselor, while obtaining credentials she felt she needed to stay in the field.

7. Another student augmented her job-related learning with study in specific academic areas. The director of a community human services center, she wanted to get more skills, knowledge, and advanced credentials. She received a good deal of credit for her past experiences and incorporated the following job-related activities into her study program: planning and developing a program on the problems of mental retardation, and conducting workshops on various issues in human services for elementary school teachers. She also enrolled in a biology course taught by her adviser (to obtain a background in genetics for her work in psychology), in a child development course at a nearby college, and takes a private tutorial in statistics. Since she planned eventually to enroll in a doctoral program in psychology, she designed her program with the admissions requirements of graduate schools in mind.

8. An engineering technician, because of his irregular work schedule, was unable to take a traditional university curriculum to become an engineer. Therefore, he enrolled in a program which would allow him to earn his B.S. by combining regular course work in engineering at a local university with correspondence study in engineering and liberal arts sponsored by other universities. He has graduated and reports that responses from prospective employers have been favorable. This student used the flexibility of the UWW program to pursue what is basically a traditional educational program.

9. A registered nurse felt she was underemployed and used one program to prepare independently for graduate work in sociology. She received no credit for her past experiences, since they did not relate to her career goal, and did independent study in classical philosophy, sociology, literature, and science. To prepare for a new career, she covered traditional content areas through independent study.

10. A manager of the fabrication division of a large electronics corporation had been interested in obtaining a master's degree in business administration ever since he had earned his bachelor's degree in business management several years earlier. After surveying the opportunities that were available to him from traditional colleges, he felt that most of the programs required course work in areas which he had already covered in his work experience. Still, he felt the need for additional study beyond the bachelor's level. Through the personnel office of his firm, he learned of an accredited college program which would grant credit for the learning he had gained from his work experience, and would at the same time help him design a study program in the areas in which he felt he needed more work.

He enrolled in the program and on the basis of a 250-page document which described the learning he had acquired through his work as well as by studying on his own, he earned thirty of the sixty credits required for the M.B.A. degree. The remaining credits will be earned on the basis of independent study in relevant areas and the completion of a thesis on a topic related to inventory control.

3. Degree Requirements, Grades, and Credits

And time yet for a hundred indecisions,
And for a hundred visions and revisions.
                              T. S. Eliot,
            "The Love Song of J. Alfred Prufrock"

In order to develop programs for self-directed learners, colleges had to change or eliminate many of the structures usually associated with college education, but they could not entirely eliminate the need for some structure. Degree requirements, grading systems, crediting systems of any sort, can be grimly stifling to the learner; or, from another perspective, unusually liberating. Like a rhyme scheme in poetry, degree requirements, grades, and credits are only useful anchors for otherwise free-floating ideas. In Swann's Way, Marcel Proust reminds us that poets are often driven to new insight through the requirement of rhyme.[1] In the above quotation, for example, if Eliot had not been searching for words that rhymed, he might not have discovered the insightful relationship between indecisions, visions, and revisions. Problems arise, however, when such details are afforded more attention than they deserve—for example, when a study program is planned only around degrees, grades, and credits. The result is like that of a nonsense poem in which the lines rhyme, but are otherwise meaningless.

Just as there are many different structures to help the poet (some rhyme-based, some not), there must be many structures to help the learner. Most higher education in this country, however, has been dominated by one set of structures which, as noted in Chapter 1, is heavily information-based. In order to earn a degree in sociology, for example, you would be required to know 60 to 70 percent of the information presented in a set number of sociology courses, such as social problems, sociology of religion, or sociological methods. This is said to be your major. In addition, you must likewise pass a somewhat smaller number of courses in a related area, such as anthropology or psychology. This is your minor. And finally, in order to attain a "well-rounded" education, you must also know the information presented in other, less related, courses, such as the sciences and the humanities.

On the opposite end of the spectrum is the competency-based program. Rather than earn a major in an information area, you earn a major in a competency area, such as communications skills, analytical skills, or problem-solving skills. At Alverno College in Alverno, Wisconsin, for example, you can select your major from eight such competency areas. Each of these competency areas has six levels of achievement. To earn a B.A. degree, you must reach the sixth level in one of the areas, and the fourth level in each of the other seven. The sixth level in the analytical skills area, for example, might be achieved by having a research paper published in a journal. (We refer to the Alverno program only by way of illustration; it is not included in this directory because it is an essentially campus-based program.) Most programs in this directory could not be called totally information- or competency-based, but stress the relationship between the two. For example, the B.S. in business administration from the Regents External Degree Program, requires you to demonstrate knowledge of business-related subjects as well as of general education areas. The business area is further classified into majors, such as marketing, finance, and accounting. You must then demonstrate competencies at three different levels within your major area and two levels in related areas.

Minnesota Metropolitan State University describes the mix of skill and information it expects as follows:

> The University recommends that each student receiving a degree demonstrate a high level of competence in each of these areas of life: communications and basic learning; the responsibilities of being a member of a self-governing community; work; recreation; and personal development and social awareness. To achieve competence in the areas listed means that students must know and employ many of the arts, sciences, humanities, and applied disciplines. It also frequently means that students will require types of knowledge and understanding—particularly experientially-based knowledge and affective knowledge—which vary significantly from the types usually associated with higher education. The University seeks to broaden the concept of what it means to be learned.[2]

In order to assess your learning in a way that is useful to you in setting your learning goals, and useful to the schools in determining whether you've met them, it is necessary to understand the questions upon which assessment procedures are commonly based. The extent to which you understand these questions and the reasons for which they are asked, is the extent to which you can profit by the methods used to answer them.

Much of the credit for identifying these questions, and organizing them so that new methods could more easily be developed, belongs to a project known as the Cooperative Assessment of Experiential Learning (CAEL).[3] Originally started by the Educational Testing Service, and now operating independently, CAEL is an effort to coordinate its 304 member colleges in the development of new procedures for the assessment of learning. The six questions upon which the CAEL procedures are based are listed below. Following each, in parentheses, are the terms which represent each question in CAEL talk.

1. What was your college-level learning? (Identifying.)

2. How does it relate to your learning goals? (Articulating.)

3. When, where, and with whom did you learn? (Documenting.)

4. How well did you learn (Measuring.)

5. How much was your learning worth? (Evaluating.)

6. How will your learning be presented? (Transcribing.)

These questions follow almost naturally from each other. The learning that is being considered must first be clearly identified, then it must be determined how useful it is to you by articulating, or matching it to your learning goals. Once it is identified as useful, you must somehow document, or prove, that you had the experience you claim, and then the quality of the learning you extracted from these experiences must be measured. Once the quality of the skills and knowledge has been established, it is necessary to evaluate it in terms of academic credit or some other standard, and finally the whole process must be summarized in a transcript or other means of making your learning experience more portable.

In most traditional, information-based programs, these questions are answered as follows:

What is college-level learning? All learning which is listed in the college catalogue is defined as college-level learning.

How does it relate to your goals? It will be useful to you in that it fulfills the requirements for covering major, minor, and related information areas.

How will it be documented? It will be documented primarily on the basis of your class attendance and papers submitted.

How will it be measured? Multiple-choice and essay tests, research papers, and oral presentations will be graded in the following manner: excellent: A; good: B; average: C; passing: D; and failing: F.

How will it be evaluated? A passing grade for each semester will earn you three credits. Each credit is worth about 1/120th of a college degree.

How will it be presented? All of your learning will be recorded on a transcript which lists the name of your degree, the names of each course you took, the grade in each course, and the number of credits you earned.

The answers to these questions will be quite different, however, when asked in relation to student-designed programs, to programs which include the development of skills, and to learning which is not done in the classroom.

We will now discuss these questions in more detail, primarily as they relate to the learning you have gained from your life experiences. Most of the following will be based on a CAEL publication entitled A Student Handbook for Preparing a Portfolio for the Assessment of Prior Learning, to which we refer you for a more detailed treatment of the subject.[4] Although all programs which assess prior learning or experiential learning do not subscribe to the CAEL approach, it is likely that this approach will in some way resemble the procedures used in them.

STEPS FOR ASSESSING PRIOR LEARNING

Step One: What was your college-level learning? (Identifying.)

The purpose of this step is to identify the learning which will be looked at in later steps. When completed, you should have a personal catalogue of the information and competency areas for which you could potentially earn college credit. CAEL provides the following guidelines to give you some idea of the kinds of learning that could be considered college level. These are as follows:

1. The learning should be publicly verifiable. You should be able to demonstrate to an expert in the field that you possess the learning which you have claimed, and such an expert should be able to objectively measure and evaluate the learning which has occurred.

2. The learning should be equivalent to college-level work in terms of quality. Some colleges even require that the prior experiential learning be related directly to courses in the catalog or requirements for graduation.

3. ...You should not expect to receive college credit or recognition for mere application of a manual skill or a narrowly prescribed routine or procedure. You should understand why you are able to do what you do.

4. The learning should have a general applicability outside of the specific situation in which it was acquired. For example, most colleges will not award credit or recognition for knowing the specific procedures for processing personnel applications which apply to only one company.[5]

Step Two: How does your learning relate to your goals? (Articulating.)

The purpose of this step is to determine how the college-level learning for which you are seeking recognition relates to your educational goals. Since learning goals are generally associated with your major area of study or career plans, you should, at the completion of this step, have a clear idea of how each of the skills and information areas identified in Step One fits into your overall educational plan. If a learning activity relates directly to your goals, it is likely that it will fulfill major degree requirements. If it is indirectly related, it could be applied to general requirements. If it is not related at all, it is likely that it would receive no further consideration, regardless of whether it has already been judged college-level.

An example of the first possibility would be a person whose learning from work as a copy writer in an ad agency would be applied toward a marketing major; an example of the second possibility would be that person's same learning being accepted as part of a general education requirement for a degree in English literature; and an example of the third would be the learning not counting at all toward a degree in music history.

Step Three: Where, when and with whom did you learn? (Documenting.)

The purpose of this step is to document the fact that you had the learning experiences which resulted in the college-level learning identified in the first two steps. When completed, you should have a file filled with printed (or taped) evidence that you had actually engaged in a learning experience. Some of your learning, of course, will already have been fully documented. In these cases it is only necessary to include transcripts of courses you have taken and notifications of your scores on college-level proficiency tests. For all other learning, the most common form of documentation is letters of verification from people with whom you worked, or people who in some way witnessed your study. The CAEL handbook, however, also states that, according to the requirements of each program, any of the following forms of documentation may be used:

Certificates, commendations, newspaper articles, job descriptions, course outlines or syllabi, artistic works and accomplishments (photographs, art work, speeches, publications, designs, etc.), examination reports, bills of sale, military records, audiovisual presentations (audiotapes, slides, videotapes, recordings, etc.), programs of performances, mementos, work samples, exhibits, writing samples, awards, honors, and licenses (pilot, brokers, real estate, cosmetology, daycare, etc.).[6]

Step Four: How well did you learn? (Measuring.)

The purpose of this step is to measure the quality of your learning, as judged by experts in the appropriate field. Learning will be subject to review by experts who may be on the staff of the program from which you are seeking credit, or who may be brought in especially for the occasion. The end product of this step will be ratings and statements by these experts which attest to the quality of your work. These ratings may be made on the basis of any of the following situations:

1. Direct observation of you engaged in the activity in which you are claiming learning has occurred.

2. Presentation of an audio- or videotape of you in the actual situation.

3. Presentation of a product you have developed, such as a sculpture or a computer program.

4. Participation in an oral interview.

5. Performance on a multiple-choice test, such as the CLEP test, or other test offered by the school.

6. Performance on essay test.

Step Five: How much is your learning worth? (Evaluating.)

The purpose of this step is to express your learning in terms of a standard which can help both you and the school measure your progress toward your goals. In most schools credits are still used, although an increasing number of schools are beginning to think in terms such as learning blocks, learning units, or even years

of study. The end product of this step will be a number of credits or equivalents which you will be awarded toward the completion of your degree. The following guidelines for estimating how many college credits a specific learning experience might be worth are adapted from the CAEL handbook:

1. Learning which has been sponsored by approved schools and is judged relevant to your goal is generally accepted directly as a transfer credit.

2. Learning which has been done in military service is accepted as it is interpreted by the American Council on Education.[7]

3. Learning which is done in business is credited according to guidelines set forth by the American Council on Education and the New York State Department of Education.[8]

4. Some schools count the number of hours it took you to learn and translate this into credit by figuring out how much credit you might have earned had you spent that time in related classroom learning.

5. Another approach is to estimate how much classroom time or regular college attendance would have been required to attain the levels of knowledge and competency you have demonstrated. This is estimated primarily by looking at others who have now graduated or are already working in a related field.

6. Other institutions may not deal in credits at all, but may only award advanced standing. That is, rather than try to make any credit award at all, you may just be allowed to enter the program as something other than a first year, first semester student.

Step Six: How is your learning to be presented? (Transcribing.)

The purpose of this step is to develop a method for recording your learning in a way which is clear and descriptive, yet succinct and easily used by the graduate schools to which you may be applying or others to whom you must communicate your learning. The end product would be a transcript which might reflect your learning in any of the following ways:

1. As regular course credit, just as if your prior learning has been sponsored by the school.

2. As a listing of information areas in which the school has rated you proficient, accompanied by the methods of measurement used.

3. As a listing of competency areas in which you have been judged proficient, and the method by which that was measured.

4. As advanced standing, with a brief explanation of why advanced standing was awarded.

ASSESSING LEARNING THAT OCCURS ONCE YOU ENROLL
IN A PROGRAM

Once you have enrolled in a degree program similar
steps would be applied to assess your learning,
though the order in which they occur might
be somewhat different:

The major difference will be that once you
have enrolled, you will <u>know</u> which methods will
be applied to you at each step, since you will
have had a hand in deciding what they were.
When you set out your learning activities with
your adviser, you will thus go through the
following steps:

1. <u>Identify</u> the college-level skills and
    information you expect to cover during
    one semester.

2. <u>Articulate</u> it to your learning goals by
    creating learning plans in which goals,
    objectives and activities are clearly
    stated.

3. Agree on the method by which your
    learning experience will be <u>documented</u>.

4. Develop a plan for <u>measuring</u> how well
    you learned.

5. Agree on the <u>evaluation</u> method by deciding
    on the range of credits (or equivalent) you
    will hope to earn.

6. Have an idea of how the learning will be
    recorded on a transcript or similar form.

In this chapter we presented only a brief
overview of the ways in which you might expect
your learning to be assessed. Once you have
enrolled in a program, you will find that a
slightly different method will be employed,
but even then, it will be to your advantage
to use the CAEL publications as a guideline.

4. Jobs, Graduate School, and Lifelong Learning

...the absolute first lesson to learn in the
job-hunting process is that there are no
short-cuts.

John Crystal

As the practical benefits of self-directed learning are becoming more widely appreciated in the world of education, similar benefits of self-directed job hunting are breaking new ground in the world of work. Although it is usually assumed that the way in which we look for work is to some extent directed by others, it was not until Richard Bolles so clearly presented the situation in What Color Is Your Parachute?[1] that we began to realize just how much of the job search is defined by others. The choice of what jobs you apply for is at least partly defined by the listings in newspapers and employment agencies. The choice of who can apply for these jobs is again partly defined by the qualifications stated in the ads. The choice of how you apply for them is defined by standardized resume and application forms. The choice of when you apply is dictated by application deadlines. And the choice of to whom you apply is limited to a P.O. box, telephone number, or personnel office. There is no doubt that some direction of this sort is needed to orchestrate the movement of some ninety million people through the world of work; just as there is no doubt that scheduled classes provide useful direction for the twelve million people passing through the world of higher education. The question which Bolles raises for the job search is the same question that the influx of adult learners raised for higher education: who is being helped by such direction, and who is being hindered? According to Bolles, such techniques only haphazardly direct anyone to jobs that are truly in line with their interests and abilities. As he puts it:

> ...the number of people who turn to any one of them (employment agencies, classified ads, job banks, etc.) without getting a job as a result, is simply mind-blowing.[2]

And more and more research is beginning to support this. More than half of all jobs are not obtained through ads or employment agencies, but through direct contact with the employer. Direct contact in these cases might have been made through having heard that an opening was planned, having been in the right place at the right time, or through having an "in" of some sort. Bolles offers us an alternative that concerns the last method of contact—not having an in, however, but creating one. What he gives us is not a new technique, but the clearest description ever of a technique that has probably been used successfully for centuries. It involves these three basic steps:

1. Take stock of your skills and interests

2. Define the problems that you can solve, or would like to help solve

3. Find someone or some organization that has these problems and will pay you to help solve them

The key to the approach is in directing your attention to the solution of very specific problems, rather than to the more nebulous task of "finding a job." By doing so, you are defining yourself and your value on the job market rather than trying to force-fit yourself into a predefined slot.

The ability to carve out your own space in the work world might be an element of what David Riesman and his associates termed the "inner-directed" character in The Lonely Crowd.[3] On the book's cover the inner-directed person is described as "the pioneer, the individualist; [while] the other-directed persons are those whose character is defined chiefly by the example of their peers and contemporaries..." In the text, the authors continue as follows:

> ...inner-direction is the typical character of the "old" middle class— the banker, the tradesman, the small entrepreneur, the technically oriented engineer, etc.-- while other-direction is becoming the typical character of the "new" middle class--the bureaucrat, the salaried employee in business, etc.[4]

Thus, it is the inner-directed persons who bring fresh insight to the solution of problems, while it is the other-directed ones who earn their living carrying out the solutions developed by others. There is certainly nothing terrible about being other directed. The major difficulty lies in the fact that new problems develop much faster than we can learn other people's theories for solving them. If we are dependent upon such solutions for our bread and butter, then our value as a worker and the satisfaction we derive from our work will only be as good as the quality of the solutions we know how to apply.

Self-directed learning should be an excellent means of preparation for self-directed job hunting. If approached with careful planning it can provide the opportunity to understand your skills and problems to which they apply, and the time to test some of your own solutions. The steps described below are from introductory material to What Color Is Your Parachute?[5] and are presented in relation to some of the features of adult-oriented degree programs.

1. Inventory your achievements and pick out your strongest skills, those which you do best and enjoy most.

In most adult-oriented programs, this process begins with the assessment of your prior learning and continues throughout your program as you design and revise each of your learning plans. This process will be of particular value to you in programs which emphasize competency-based learning, in that you will have a better understanding of the skills and information you now have and the skills and information you will be gaining during your enrollment. In some programs, taking stock of your skills, interests and abilities can itself constitute a portion of your study plan.

2. <u>Research different fields to identify what career can use your strongest skills best.</u>

Experiential education options can help you research a career from the inside. By beginning this process <u>during</u> your education rather than at the end of it, you will not only have the opportunity to determine how your current skills match a career area, but you will also learn of the new skills you might be developing.

3. <u>Determine where you would most enjoy working, and begin to research the field.</u>

If you begin a file of potential employers and maintain it faithfully, through your field work and library research, by the time you complete your degree you should have a decent number of places in which to begin your job search. Through the technique of "interviewing for information" (invented by John C. Crystal), you contact potential employers not only for employment, but for information about other potential employers; thus you can steadily increase future job possibilities.

In addition, through experiential learning programs, you will have the luxury of experiencing the rewards and demands of many careers on a firsthand basis. This can be invaluable in helping you to decide whether it is an area you want to pursue further.

4. <u>Research each organization that interests you. Focus on organizations you like, that have problems you can solve.</u>

By having the opportunity to concentrate on both practice and theory, you will be in the position of learning firsthand what the problems of a certain field are, and then have the opportunity to do some thinking about better ways to solve them. From those who work in the field on a day-to-day basis you can learn of current unresolved problems. This will guide you in your reading and planning.

5. <u>In each organization identify the top person responsible for solving these problems; go to that person and explain how you can help solve them.</u>

In order to succeed at this stage, you must first be confident of your ability to solve the problems you've identified. But even if you are very confident, you may fail unless you develop a track record of preparing and implementing successful problem-solving plans. Practice in this area begins early in your education, with careful attention to the process by which you are formulating learning contracts and learning plans.

Likewise, understanding the relationship between information areas and competency areas will help you to direct your attention to the development of each. Thus you will be able to avoid situations like that of an English major trying to sell him or herself on the basis of information (e.g., knowledge of medieval studies) to an employer interested only in general competencies (e.g., ability to think and write clearly).

Now, assuming you have developed the necessary competencies and know that you can solve the employer's problems, you are about halfway there. The next step is <u>convincing</u> the person that you actually have the <u>skills</u> necessary. You are essentially going through the entire CAEL assessment process defined in Chapter Three but this time for employment rather than education purposes. You must <u>identify</u> the skills and knowledge you have to offer, <u>match</u> them to the goals of the employer. <u>document</u> the fact that you have gained the skills; provide products and logic that will help <u>measure</u> the quality of your skills, <u>evaluate</u> what you think your solutions are worth, and make it easy for the employer to <u>present</u> your proposal to others who might have a say in the hiring.

What About the Job Market?

The essence of self-directed job hunting is creating work, rather than waiting for it to be created for you. Thus to Bolles the "job market" and the "unemployment rate" are but popularized myths.

> When he/she (the job hunter) starts into the supposed single job market, to conduct his/her own job search campaign, the job hunter sooner or later discovers that he/she actually faces seventy million or more separate job markets.... Every business or organization has its own way of going about the process of hiring— separate, independent of, and uncoordinated with, other businesses or organizations.[6]

> Prominent press coverage is always given to this one statistic for the whole country: the unemployment figure. The human mind is staggered by the thought of almost five million people being out of work...[7]

> But then, the unemployment figure doesn't really tell us anything about vacancies— as, upon sober reflection, we must realize. It only tells us how many people we are competing with (sort of) for whatever vacancies exist. That is, assuming we all possessed the skills that the vacancies call for.... But how many vacancies are there?[8]

After taking into account the number of new jobs created by business people, by those who start their own business, and by new vacancies that open through advancement or other departure of workers Bolles estimates that about four million job openings occur each month. He then tells us that competition for the jobs among the unemployed is not balanced, mostly because these jobs, for one reason or another, never get publicized; or because they demand special skills which most of the unemployed do not have.

Hence, if you take control of your job search, or at this point, your education, you may have a better chance of ensuring that one of the jobs that opens each month will go to you.

It cannot be denied that chances are better for finding an organization, or enough people, to pay you to do your own thing when the economy is booming. But it does not necessarily follow that the reverse is true when the economy is in a slump.

It could just as easily be reasoned that a slumping economy means that there are more problems around that need creative solutions. Employers who are faced with maximum problems and minimum budgets may be more willing to listen to a student or recent graduate.

Even if self-directed job hunting is not your bag, bringing practical experience to your job search is more, not less crucial during low employment periods. Planning some experiential learning activities into your learning scheme will help you avoid joining the chorus in the familiar "Catch-22 Job Search Blues":

How can I get a job,
When I ain't got no 'sperience...
How can I get 'sperience
When I ain't got no job? [9]

The following quotation illustrates the need for the integration of practice and theory in the planning of your studies:

...much has been made of a recent poll of employers conducted by the College Placement Council that shows liberal arts and sciences students at a disadvantage on the current job market....

These findings might be interpreted in the following light:

First, conditions in the world of work are changing, ...and we should not view the current opinions of employers in a buyer's market as predictive of future attitudes.

Second, other polls show that employers who hire specialists often complain that these young people can't read, write, spell, deal with people or solve problems independently, And third, almost all the employers surveyed by the council said they would hire liberal arts students if only they had some practical or experiential activity on their record, such as a couple of business-related courses (including economics), or a co-op or work-study experience. Thus, employers may not be saying that they favor specialization, but that liberal education should be more practical and experiential. If they can find a broadly educated person who also has some real world experience, they will provide any needed specialized training.[10]

What About Credentials?

Although in self-directed job hunting the emphasis is on your skills, knowledge, and how well you present them to employers, it cannot be denied that credentials will play some role in your job-finding success. This is especially true for professions such as law and medicine; but in an increasing number of other fields, the college degree is being listed as a minimum entry-level requirement or a basis for salary increases. It is also becoming clear, however, that the primary role credentials play in the job market is not one of helping people enter jobs, but of keeping people out of jobs.

Most hiring is not done on the basis of the fact that you have a degree, but on the basis of the fact that employers think you have the skills and knowledge to solve their problems. Having a degree may mean that you won't get bumped during the initial screening of applications or that an employer might think twice about discriminating on the basis of sex or race; but it will have little or nothing to do with whether you finally get hired. Thus, in many career areas, an undergraduate degree has become a necessary but not sufficient qualification.

The next question is what impact a degree from a college featuring off-campus study, experiential learning, and other options which are judged as nontraditional will have on a person's chances for finding work. The results of follow-up programs are now beginning to appear, and studies of the graduates of such are all reaching similar conclusions: students who hold degrees from nontraditional institutions are having no more difficulty obtaining employment than graduates of traditional colleges. This has been verified by studies conducted by the schools themselves as well as by outside researchers. The largest of such studies has recently been completed by the Bureau of Social Science Research, under contract from the National Institute of Education.[11] In this study over 3500 graduates from many of the programs described in this directory were interviewed regarding the role of their education in advancing in their careers. Most of the graduates were older and were employed throughout the time they were enrolled. There were slightly more men than women, and a good portion of them were studying in business-related subject areas. The greatest portion of women focused their attention on the health professions. Typically, the graduates seemed to encounter little difficulty because of the fact that their degrees were earned through assessment of prior learning or off-campus study; and the majority felt that their degree was good preparation for some aspect of their career.

Those who were employed at the time of the survey felt that the following job-related changes occurred after they had completed their degree programs:

- 72 percent reported increased status or respect from their coworkers
- 59 percent reported an increase in job responsibilities
- 55 percent reported a promotion or increase in pay or benefits
- 46 percent reported an increase in job security
- 46 percent reported a change to a different job

Eleven percent of the graduates were not in paid employment at the time of the survey. Of them, less than 2 percent gave employer concern over the validity of their degree as a reason for their not being employed.

The researchers also surveyed employers in the public and private sectors to learn of their attitudes toward nontraditional college degrees. On the basis of responses from eighty-one recruiting and personnel officers, the authors drew the following conclusion:

> ...for many employers the finer nuances of college prestige and quality take a back seat, compared to other criteria. While we do not want to generalize to "all" employers concerning their attitudes toward holders of all types of college degrees, our survey data do strongly suggest that employers—although favorably disposed toward college degrees in general—as a group are not overly concerned with institutional reputation and that external degree holders should not find themselves denied opportunities in employment settings because of the nature of the degree.[12]

Although the study did not deal specifically with the questions of employer attitudes regarding unaccredited versus accredited degrees, they did find that the employers surveyed agreed with the following statement slightly more often than not:

> An external degree granted by an accredited institution is accepted on the same basis as a traditional degree when evaluating a prospective applicant's educational background.[13]

This would imply that accreditation is an issue for at least some. If you are considering a school which is not yet accredited or is in the process of becoming accredited, you should find out exactly what their status is. Some new programs may not be accredited only because they are still young and the accreditation process generally takes several years to complete. Other schools may not even be interested in accreditation because of their educational philosophy. Whatever the case, if you feel that an unaccredited program can meet your learning needs, be certain from the outset that you are comfortable with the reasons they give for the accreditation status.

One should, however, be cautious in putting too much stock in the foregoing study or any others as predictors of how well nontraditional degrees will be accepted on the job market, in part because the total number of students who have used such programs is so small. Laure Sharp and Carol Sosdian remind us of this in their introduction to another part of the study from which we have been quoting:

> To put our target population in proper perspective, one should note that the fall 1976 enrollment in the external degree programs we identified totalled slightly over 54,000, compared to over 11 million persons enrolled in U.S. postsecondary institutions in the fall of 1975. Clearly, to date, this number is a mere drop in the bucket.[14]

However, although these studies give us some indication that a nontraditional degree may not

itself present a major barrier to employment, it will not become an asset unless you approach it with a problem-solving focus.

Graduate Study: Concerns for Graduates and Undergraduates

Study beyond the bachelor's level assumes that your undergraduate education has provided you with the fundamentals for dealing with skills and information of a more complex nature. One way to learn what is expected of you by graduate schools is to look at the tests they require for admission. These test your understanding of language and mathematics, your capacity for abstract thinking, and your knowledge of the content of specific disciplines. Graduate schools also assume that your undergraduate education has prepared you for self-directed study. You will find more emphasis on the development of competencies, more opportunity for field work and practicum learning, more chance to select the classes you want, and more opportunity for independent study and special projects. In most graduate schools you will have more opportunity to mix and match your studies, but must still do so within a highly defined system of requirements. The culmination of your graduate experience, however, either on the master's or doctoral level is your ability to demonstrate your skills as a completely self-directed learner. This final hurdle is measured by your ability to complete a master's thesis or doctoral dissertation.

Yet many come to the task ill-prepared for the demands of self-directed study. A sizeable number of plans to obtain an advanced degree have been thwarted by inability to complete the requirements for the thesis or dissertation. There are many people who have finished all of their course work, but have deferred the completion of their degree for two, five, ten years or, in many cases, indefinitely. Dr. Mardelle Grothe, a counseling psychologist who has offered an advisory service for such people, feels that in some cases the work has been deferred for understandable reasons, such as legitimate interest shifts, but for most, he tells us, the procrastination can be traced directly to a lack of planning and time management skills.[15]

A few graduate schools are now offering programs in which more emphasis is placed on the development of self-directed learning competencies. These graduate programs differ from most in that they allow more flexibility in the design of the learning program, and more opportunity to fill degree requirements through independent, off-campus study. Some offer assessment of prior learning, but it is likely that most of the work would be done under the sponsorship of the program.

Graduate Study and the Job Market

The self-directed job hunt is especially well suited to those who have completed graduate study. As a graduate student you are more likely to come into contact with students who have already been working in a field and who have returned to school in search of solutions to problems they may have encountered. Through advanced study in any area, you will be better able to identify current problems and better prepared to propose solutions to them. A self-directed approach to the job search may in fact be a necessity for most students holding graduate degrees, since the actual value of the degree itself varies so much from profession to profession. It is generally assumed that a graduate degree is the minimum requirement for teaching in the academic professions, and that students with advanced degrees in the sciences or the applied professions (business, allied health, engineering) will have a better chance of getting jobs than those with only bachelor's degrees.

People who aspire to high-level teaching and research positions should find their entry easier if they have doctoral degrees, but even for them, the number of university positions which usually shelter such activities is rapidly shrinking, and new doctorate holders may have to find other avenues through which to apply their expertise.

Those trained in medicine, dentistry and law will have little difficulty marketing their skills. Lawyers who have not graduated from the top law schools, or at the top of their classes, however, may not enjoy as much mobility as they might have in the past.

Looming above all of these considerations is the specter of overqualification, the fear of being too qualified. This is a common reason given for not continuing one's education. The fear of being rejected for being too qualified is viewed by many as the worst possible outcome of an education. Some part of this overqualification syndrome may have been generated by employers who find it easier to say "you are too qualified," than "we don't want you." But even if this were the case, it would explain only a small part of the problem. The real problem, as James O'Toole points out, is not overqualification at all, but under-employment.[16] It is not the possession of too much skill and knowledge that keeps people out of work, but the lack of jobs that require that skill and knowledge. There are at least two approaches to this problem. We can work passively at jobs demanding less skill and knowledge than we have to offer, hoping that the economy will pick up soon and lift us from our troubles; or we can apply our talents to the creation of new jobs and the new solutions to problems, problems of businesses, social service organizations, government organizations, individuals, families, and the like.

Graduate School Admission

Admission to graduate programs depends upon a combination of scores on tests, your academic record as an undergraduate, the way you present yourself in your application and interview, and "something else."

The kinds of tests usually required were mentioned earlier, in our discussion of the skills and knowledge usually expected of those about to pursue graduate study. These tests include the following:

Graduate Record Examinations (GREs)
Miller Analogies Tests (MATs)
Law School Admissions Test (LSAT)
Medical College Admissions Tests (MCATs)
Graduate Management Aptitude Tests (GMATs)

Most schools require you to take only one or two tests, some will waive the requirements in special cases, and others will require no testing at all. If you think there is a possibility that graduate study is in your future, and you think it might be in a discipline in which testing would be required, the self-directed thing to do is to buy the study guides now for the tests you might be taking. Planning your learning experiences in light of an awareness of what might be expected of you in graduate school admissions tests will help relieve the anxiety of last-minute cramming which is felt by many who approach these tests.

For the attitude of graduate schools toward those holding degrees from nontraditional schools, we turn again to the Bureau of Social Science Research study. Of all of the graduates surveyed who applied to graduate school 89 percent were accepted for admission. Those who were not accepted mentioned the following as possible reasons which had some relation to the nontraditional nature of their undergraduate program:

- The transcript did not contain grade point average or information easily converted to something like a grade point average
- The institution (or the program) from which the "nontraditional" degree was obtained did not have full accreditation
- The form or the wording of the transcript made it impossible for the admissions office to judge the amount or type of work that was done
- The admissions office staff did not take the time to read the transcript [17]

If upon beginning your undergraduate studies you feel that you may go on to graduate school, you should check with the program in which you are enrolling to learn how students have approached problems such as those cited above in the past.

Your test scores and undergraduate record will play an important role in your graduate school admission, but it is likely that most graduate schools will have many applicants whose performance in these areas is similar. Thus, like a college degree in the job market, these factors are becoming a "necessary but not sufficient" qualification. The slack is taken up by that "something else" about which we know almost nothing. It could be age, race or sex; it could be the amount of work experience you've had or the brightness of your eyes; or it could be the fact that an influential faculty member decides to sponsor you. Whatever the reasons, they are not much different from the undefinables that ultimately affect employment. An undefinable situation is just another bad question. You can let it frustrate you, or you can define it in a way that allows you to answer it. And the tool for the task is the basic technique of spelling out your goals, objectives, and activities. The same technique can be applied to graduate admissions and to job searching. You should find the program whose interests parallel yours, construct a proposal of what you want to learn and how you intend to do so within this program, and present it to those who can affect your admission.

Lifelong Learning

A college degree can be viewed either as a train ticket or a driver's license. Viewed as a train ticket, you book passage to a job or further schooling and you have little else to do but relax and enjoy the scenery; not a bad deal until we remember that many people get bored on trains. Viewed as a driver's license, however, it means that you've got the basics to be on the road, but you must pay attention at all times. Most of the decisions you'll have to make will be in situations not covered in the driver's manual and probably not even covered in your driver training. Likewise, a college degree should not signify the culmination of a learning experience, but the completion of one phase and the beginning of another.

Throughout this book, we have presented a number of questions which might be raised in relation to various learning concerns you might have during most of your life. These questions, which we summarize below, might be viewed as the core curriculum for what Ron Gross calls "the invisible university" in The Lifelong Learner.[18]

- What method do you use in planning for the goals you want to attain?
- How do you deal with planning questions you can't answer?
- How do you approach difficult decisions?
- How do you know how well you are learning?
- How do you keep track of the learning in which you have been engaged?
- How much direction do you need in continuing your learning?
- How much campus contact do you need?
- Do you need information and facts about specific subjects, general skills, or both?
- What new learning are you gaining from your job, your family life, your hobbies, your community work?
- How much more theory do you need, how much practice?
- How much classroom learning do you need? How much independent study?
- Do you need some kind of standard against which to compare your learning?
- Is there a need for you to present your skills and knowledge to others?
- Do you need college level credentials to advance on your job or enter another?

The way in which you answer these questions, or approach answering them, will help you to decide whether you need a traditional degree program, a self-directed degree program, an external degree program, or no degree program at all.

5. Costs and Financial Aid

We would frequently get calls from students
who would give financial reasons for not
attending particular schools. When we told
them we would provide assistance to cover
the difference, however, other reservations
began to surface.

     Dan Vechitto Speech, August 1977

...More than half of the postsecondary
student population pays less than the full
price of education. Student aid in various
forms makes up the difference.

       Sandra Willett
    Unpublished report, March 1976

Earlier, when we mentioned educational brokering, we spoke of education as an investment. This is an analogy not to be taken lightly. Sandra Willett, the consumer researcher cited above, reminds us that for the average consumer the purchase of education can be the largest single expense, second to buying a house, they may make during a lifetime. Yet it is probably the only expense that must be made without knowledge of the real price. She arrived at this conclusion after completing a study in which she posed as a student requesting admissions-related information from seventy-seven schools and colleges in the Boston area. Only a small percentage of the schools provided her with information upon which she could realistically estimate costs and financial aid.

We sent a letter aimed at getting similar information to many of the schools listed in Section II of this guide, and are pleased to report that most of the institutions who received it responded well in terms of providing information on tuition and fees, and the names of the general financial aid programs in which they participate. There is, however, much more information about costs and financial aid that a student needs in order to make an informed choice of a school. A discussion of some of these factors will form the subject of this chapter.

Costs

Depending on the amount of college-level learning you now have and the kinds of services you require to continue your study, the cost of a bachelor's degree could range from $75.00 to several thousand dollars. At the lower end of this cost spectrum would be the most external of the external degree programs. At Thomas Edison College, for example, the cost of transferring any college credits you've already accumulated is included in a $50.00 enrollment fee. If you require a special assessment for learning which you've done on your own, or for course work that is in question, there is an additional fee of $100.00. The costs for each test you must take to complete your degree requirements will range between $15 and $50. In addition to your test fees there is a $25.00 graduation fee. Since it is possible for 100 percent of your degree to be awarded on the basis of learning you have done prior to enrolling, you could conceivably earn a degree from the program for $75.00, the cost of your enrollment and graduation fee. Of course, the number of students who are able to do this is small, and for most students the average cost is around $500.

The cost benefits of the assessment of prior learning also apply to programs which are less external. At New York's Empire State College which provides its students with a full range of advising and instructional services, the cost for a B.A. degree to an in-state student with no advanced standing is $5400. If three fourths of the student's program was completed through the assessment of prior learning, however, the cost could be reduced to $1380.

In other programs your cost may depend on how much you choose to spend on your education. At Campus Free College, for example, a base rate of $1200 is charged to each student for each year of study. Half of this tuition goes toward the operation of the program, the other half is applied directly to the salary of the student's adviser. If you need additional courses from other institutions, or want to hire mentors to work with you, you arrange this on your own. Thus your total cost can vary widely. Most CFC students spend between $1400 and $1700 per year on their education.

A variation on this model is that used by some members of the University Without Walls system. One program, for example, charges all students a set tuition, but makes special grants available to cover the cost of additional learning resources.

Two other factors should be considered when thinking about costs and both relate to employment. Most of the students who have used these programs thus far remained employed throughout their enrollment. By arranging your studies around your job, you can continue to learn and earn at the same time. The second point is that it is possible in some programs to earn both money and credit for the same activity.

Financial Aid

For many students, costs are only half of the story; financial aid is the other. If you can estimate your need for financial aid well in advance, your chances of being able to receive it are better now than they ever have been.

In 1965, when the first external degree program was born at the University of Oklahoma, the amount of financial aid available to students in the entire country was an estimated $9 million. Today, that figure is estimated at $12 billion, and most of it comes through four major sources: The federal government, state governments, schools and colleges, and employee benefit programs. Most of this money is awarded in the form of grants, loans, and work-study options, and on the basis of need. Age and academic potential play little, if any role. There are, however, four factors which could limit the amount of financial aid you might receive:

1. Enrolling in a school which does not participate in major government financial aid programs.

2. Enrolling on a part-time basis

3. Missing major application deadlines.

4. Lack of information about what is available to you.

Below, we briefly discuss each of these factors.

School participation: there are at least two reasons for which a school might not participate in major programs. The first is that it may not be approved by a state or regional authorizing agency; the second is that they may choose not to do so.

Most of the schools described in Section II are approved or in the process of becoming approved by state and federal agencies. Some, however, are only approved for federal funds, but not state funds; others may be approved for both, but not for veteran's benefits, and so on. Most of the descriptions in Section II name the financial aid programs available to those who attend each school.

Some schools may choose not to participate in financial aid programs even though they may be able to obtain approval. Such schools might prefer to keep their tuition lower and avoid all the red tape associated with these programs.

Part-time enrollment: technically all major federal financial aid programs are open to students who are attending on at least a half-time basis, but in practice, many schools give preference to full-time students. There are essentially two major types of federal financial aid programs: those in which awards are made on the basis of a formula applied evenly to all applicants, and those which are awarded at the discretion of a middle-person, such as a college financial aid officer. In the first type, which includes the BEOG program, there is no problem at all with half-time study; in the second type, however, many financial aid officers use the funds they have to meet the needs of full-time students before even considering half-time students.

Missing deadlines: missing a deadline doesn't always guarantee that you will be excluded, but it severely diminishes your chances. Since financial aid funds are limited and students need to know the size of their awards in advance, financial aid offices must set a cut-off date at which they can begin making decisions about who gets what. In some programs, late applications are ruled out immediately, in others they are put on a waiting list for any funds that may be returned. The general rule to follow is: when in doubt, apply!

Lack of information: information on exactly how much financial aid you can get is almost impossible to come by until you have actually enrolled in a school. But this doesn't mean that "good" information that can help you while you are still deciding is not available. Finding such information is simply a matter of directing your attention away from the search for a jackpot lying in the drawer of some obscure foundation and toward the task of understanding the few procedures you must follow that will put you in touch with 99 percent of all the financial aid that is available to you. In the remainder of this chapter, we will help you answer the following questions:

What financial aid is available?

What programs are open to you?

How do you estimate how much you might receive?

How do you apply?

What financial aid is available?

- A federal grant distributed by the federal government itself (the Basic Educational Opportunity Grant)

- Federal grants, loans, and work programs distributed by schools: the Supplemental Opportunity Grant (SEOG), the National Direct Student Loan (NDSL), and the College Work-Study Program (CWS)

- School-sponsored grants and loans

- State-sponsored grants and loans

- Government-guaranteed loans from banks

- Monthly benefits from the Veterans Administration

- Employer-sponsored tuition reimbursement and payment plans

- Privately sponsored grants and loans

What programs are open to you?

- Basic Educational Opportunity Grants (BEOGs) direct from the federal government are open to you
  - if you are attending an approved school on at least a half-time basis and show limited ability to pay.

- Supplemental Grants (SEOGs), National Direct Student Loans (NDSLs), and College Work-Study (CWS) from the schools themselves
  - if you are attending participating schools on at least a half-time basis and show need.

- Grants and loans from the schools themselves
  - if you attend a school which operates its own financial aid program and have a need which cannot be met by available state and federal funds.

- Grants and loans from your state
  - if you attend a state-approved school and comply with additional requirements of the state. You can learn what these are by contacting the appropriate agency in your state, usually the State Department of Education.

- Monthly benefits from the Veterans Administration
  - if you are attending an approved school and have had military service after January 31, 1955, and before January 1, 1977;
  - or if you are the dependent of a deceased or disabled veteran, or a service person forcibly detained or missing in action.

- Guaranteed Student Loans (GSLs) from banks or schools
  - if you attend an approved school and participating lenders in your state are willing to make the loan. Because the repayment of the loan is guaranteed by the federal government, most lenders will make such loans more easily than regular consumer loans. In some cases cosigners are required, but this is generally rare.

- Tuition reimbursement from employers
  - if you are fortunate enough to be working for some organization that sponsors such programs.

- Vocational rehabilitation benefits
  - if you live in a state which operates such programs and have emotional or physical handicaps which interfere with your normal pursuit of employment.

- Scholarships, grants and loans from private donors
  - if you are really lucky. Privately sponsored aid makes up less than 10 percent of all financial aid, and most is restricted to younger, full-time students attending traditional residential colleges.

How do you prove that you have a need for financial assistance?

- For the BEOG, NDSL, SEOG, CWS and school-sponsored funds, and for most state-sponsored financial aid
  - you must submit verifiable information on your income and assets and show that the amount you can realistically afford to spend on your education is less than the total cost (including living expenses).

- For Guaranteed Student Loans
  - the school you are attending is often asked by banks to verify that your need cannot be met through other programs.

- For veterans' benefits, need is not a factor.

- For vocational rehabilitation benefits
  - you must usually show that you have exhausted all other sources of funding.

- For tuition reimbursement from employers, need is seldom a factor.

- For assistance from private donors
  - need is determined similarly to the way it is determined in schools, although the process may be less standard.

How do you know how much money you can get?

- BEOGs range from $200 to $1600 depending upon your need, the cost of your schooling, and whether you are a part-time or full-time student.

- SEOGs range from $200 to $1500 per year, NDSLs can reach up to $2500 per year

The college work-study program awards jobs at wages of up to $3.50 per hour, depending upon your qualifications.

The school financial aid officer will use these and other funds from the school to compose a package to meet your need.

To estimate your possible award in advance, do the following:

1. Write the school using the questions on page 43 as guidelines.

2. Dial the BEOG toll-free number (see below), and request a copy of the information booklet which shows you how to determine your eligibility index.

3. Write to the College Scholarship Service of the College Entrance Examination Board and request a copy of the "Meeting College Costs Worksheet for Independent Students."

- Guaranteed loans can range up to $2500 per year, depending on the policies within your state. Repayment begins nine months after you graduate or leave school, and the interest rate is 7 percent. If your family income is below $25,000, the federal government will pay all interest which accrues until the time you must begin repaying the loan.

- Veterans' benefits in 1978 ranged up to $311 per month for full-time study, with additional allowances for dependents.

- State-sponsored programs vary considerably from state to state, but generally fall in the $200 to $1500 range.

- Vocational rehabilitation benefits vary from state to state, and from client to client. It is impossible to give a fair estimate. Contact your local office for more details.

- Tuition aid from employers generally covers the full cost of tuition and fees, although some reimburse only a set portion.

How do you apply for financial aid?

- If the BEOG is the only program for which you are applying, you can pick up an application at almost any school, library, or federal office, and mail it, without money, directly to the federal government. If you are applying for financial aid from schools as well, then the application process is combined. (See below.)

To apply for SEOG, NDSL, CWS and other campus-based aid, you must contact the financial aid office of the school, let them know that you need aid, and complete any forms they require. In most cases this will be a brief application form and a somewhat longer financial statement. This statement is then mailed, with a small fee, to an independent agency (the CEEB or the ACT), who will process the information and return it to the school. There is a box on the form which you can check if you want the agency to send your financial information to the BEOG program. If you check that box, no other application is needed for the BEOG.

- Some state-run programs have also combined application procedures with the schools and the BEOG, but most still require a separate application form of their own. Contact your state government to find out the details.

- You usually apply for a Guaranteed Student Loan after you are sure you have exhausted all other possibilities for loans. Applications are made directly to participating lenders. To locate those in your state, ask at the bank with which you do business.

- For veterans' benefits and vocational rehabilitation benefits, apply to the appropriate agency in your state.

- For employer-sponsored aid, review any statement which describes company fringe benefit policies. If you work for a public agency, or one which receives federal funding, ask your employer if they participate in federally-sponsored staff development programs.

- For aid from private donors, refer to the directories available in most public libraries.

Sources of additional information on financial aid

- General Information
  Most of the educational brokering agencies and counseling services will provide financial aid-related information as well as help in estimating awards and completing applications.

- Basic Opportunity Grant
  Toll-free telephone lines:
     1-800-555-6350
     1-800-638-6700

- Campus-based programs (SEOG, NDSL, CWS and School-sponsored)
     Write to the financial aid office of each school in which you are interested. Use the consumer information requirements listed on page   as a guide in the kinds of information you request from each school.

- State-sponsored financial aid
     Locate the appropriate agency in your state for information.

- Guaranteed Student Loans
     Locate the guaranteeing agency in your state for information. Ask at your bank.

- Veterans' benefits
     Contact the closest office of the Veterans Administration.

- Vocational rehabilitation benefits
     Look in the telephone book under the listings for state agencies.

- Employer-sponsored aid
     Contact your employer or the personnel office of the company in which you work.

- Privately sponsored aid
     If you are a woman
        contact
        Clairol Loving Care Scholarship Program
        345 Park Avenue, 5th floor
        New York, NY 10022,

     for the latest copy of "Educational Financial Aid Sources for Women." The 1977 edition of this brochure included descriptions of financial aid programs sponsored by the following organizations:

        Altrusa International, Chicago
        American Association of University
           Women, Washington, D.C.
        Business and Professional Women's
           Foundation, Washington, D.C.
        Clairol Corporation, New York City
        Council of Southern Universities, Atlanta
        General Federation of Women's Clubs,
           local chapters
        National Association of Bank Women, Boston
        Phillip Morris Corporation
        Sears-Roebuck Foundation
        Soroptomists Club, Philadelphia

     If you are a minority group member
        read the Directory of Special Programs for Minority Group Members.[1]

        This book will give you names of the major financial aid programs targeted toward minority group members, as well as the names of organizations from which you might learn of funds available in your community.

     Otherwise, go to your public library and ask for the directories of financial aid programs. A particularly good one is The Grants Register, by Roland Turner.[2]

Foreword to Part II

These descriptions contain information which will help you to compare programs of different institutions offering special opportunities for adult learners.[1] Included are only those schools which allow for a considerable amount of off-campus study or which award a considerable amount of credit for learning gained from life experiences. It is important, however, to compare the opportunities afforded you by these programs with the opportunities available in other programs.[2]

All of the information in these descriptions was taken from the promotional material which each institution will send to any student who requests information. Thus, if you plan to write for additional information, please be sure to request a complete catalogue of offerings. The list which appears below might also be used as a guideline for requesting additional information that is not included in these descriptions. This list describes information that colleges receiving federal funds are required by law to provide to prospective students who request it:

1. what student financial aid programs are available through that institution;
2. how student aid is distributed among students at that institution;
3. how to apply for the student assistance programs and what standards are used to determine eligibility;
4. the criteria used at that institution to determine whether a student is maintaining satisfactory academic progress and the procedures by which a student who has failed to maintain such progress may reestablish eligibility for federal student financial aid;
5. the rights and responsibilities of students receiving financial assistance;
6. the means by which financial aid will be disbursed and the frequency of disbursements;
7. the terms of and schedules for repayment of student loans;
8. the terms and conditions of any employment which is part of the financial aid package;
9. the cost of attending the institution;
10. the refund policy of the institution;
11. the academic programs available at the institution and the faculty and facilities available for those programs;
12. data regarding retention of students at the institution;
13. the number of precentage of students completing each program if such data are available; and
14. where and from whom information on student assistance at the institution may be obtained.[3]

Schools are listed by state and then alphabetically within state. Throughout each description, initials are frequently used in reference to the name of the program. Other sets of initials are used in reference to financial aid programs and testing programs, about which further information can be located by using the glossary at the end of this book.

II DESCRIPTIONS OF SELECTED ADULT-ORIENTED DEGREE PROGRAMS

ALABAMA

UNIVERSITY OF ALABAMA
New College
P.O. Drawer CD
University, Alabama 35486
(205) 348-6010

Philosophy and goals. External degree program is
a response to the growing needs of a nontraditional
clientele—homemakers, servicepersons, minorities,
businesspersons, and others who have not completed
an undergraduate degree, as well as those whose
needs cannot be met through traditional university
programs.

Degrees and certificates offered. An interdisciplin-
ary program of the New College with the Bachelor of
Arts (B.S.) or Bachelor of Science (B.S.) by the
University of Alabama.

Accreditation. Fully accredited by the Southern
Association of Colleges and Schools.

Academic calendar. Students may enroll in New
College as vacancies occur.

Residency—required contact with program. No
residency requirement. Student must attend
orientation program; occasional presence on
campus for advising is helpful.

Part-time enrollment—pace. Part-time enrollment is
possible. The pace at which students work is set
entirely by the students themselves.

Costs. Annual registration fee: $25.00. The
student pays for traditional course work at the
rate per credit hour of the University of Alabama
or the school in which enrolled; correspondence
studies and CLEP exam fees are charged independently.
Out-of-class learning experiences are charged
by regular university credit hour fee; fee for
prior learning is $50.00 to assess a portfolio of
9 hours or less, $75.00 for 10 or more hours.

Admission requirements. Applicants over 22 years
of age will be given preference; a minimum of a
high school diploma or equivalent necessary; those
whose educational goals may readily be facilitated
by program will be given high priority; priority
given to citizens of Alabama, without excluding
qualified nonresident applicants.

Assessment of prior learning. Academic credit for
demonstrated past learning experiences, travel,
attendance at workshops and conferences, on-the-
job learning, and similar activities may be
awarded after documentation is reviewed by a
committee of staff and faculty. Program utilizes
challenge exams prepared by faculty members and
departments at the University of Alabama, as well
as national standardized tests such as the CLEP
and PEP tests. CLEP includes general examinations
in the five basic areas of liberal arts: humanities,
social sciences, mathematics, natural sciences, and
English composition, as well as a wide assortment
of subject matter tests. Program also uses the
Evaluation of Education Experience in the Armed
Services (the CASE book) and other resources for
evaluation of military credits upon presentation
of discharge papers (DD-214) or other documentation.
Demonstrated prior learning, previous academic
credits transferred from an accredited college,
passing of national tests such as CLEP, out-of-
class contract learning, military training, correspondence study, weekend or evening seminars,
educational television courses, and, when feasible,
classroom work, can be applied toward attainment
of a degree.

Curriculum—learning options. Students may design,
with assistance from staff and advisers, an
interdisciplinary program which does not have to
conform to any specific departmental "major"
program, but is based on obtaining the knowledge
needed for learning goals. Curriculum will be
organized approximately along the following
blocks:

Humanities	12 semester hours
Social sciences	6 semester hours
Natural sciences	6 semester hours
Depth study	32 semester hours
Electives	32 semester hours
Final project or major	
piece of work	12 semester hours

The remaining 28 hours may be distributed within
the curriculum to meet the individualized goals
of the student. Acceptable work completed at any
accredited college or university may be transferred
to the external degree program curriculum. A
maximum of 64 semester hours may be transferred
from a junior college. Also, one fourth (32) of
the required hours must be completed under the
auspices of the University of Alabama.

Degree requirements. To be eligible for graduation,
students must complete a minimum of 128 semester
hours of work with an overall Q.P.A. of 1.0 (C), or
better, as outlined in the above-mentioned course
areas.

Supportive services—financial aid. External degree
program staff, other faculty members and students
are available for conferences and planning. The
University of Alabama is approved for participation
in major state and federal aid programs, including
BEOG, SEOG, NDSL, and CWS.

Enrollment in program. 231

CALIFORNIA

THE CONSORTIUM OF THE CALIFORNIA STATE UNIVERSITY
AND COLLEGES—THE THOUSAND-MILE CAMPUS
For addresses of individual colleges, see Additional
Information.

Philosophy and goals. The program is designed for
adult Californians who are unable to attend

45

regularly scheduled on-campus classes to earn bachelor's and master's degrees. Consortium consists of 19 accredited campuses.

Degrees and certificates offered. The program offers B.A., B.S., and M.A. programs either by Consortium, for certificate or degree from Consortium, or in collaboration with a participating CSUC campus, for degree through that campus.

Also offered are professional certificates in several of the fields listed under Curriculum—learning options.

Accreditation. Fully accredited by the Western Association of Schools and Colleges.

Academic calendar. Classes normally begin in September, January and June.

Residency—required contact with program. Although a minimum of 24 semester hours must be completed through Consortium, students may petition in advance for approval to meet this requirement out of residence.

Part-time enrollment—pace. Most Consortium students are enrolled on a part-time basis.

Costs. Tuition: $50.00 per semester hour (approximate)
$60.00 per semester hour for advanced tutorials, directed study, and supervision of internships (approximate)
Application fee: $20.00.
Graduation fee: $15.00.

Admission requirements. For upper-division undergraduate program, student must have completed a minimum of 56 semester hours equivalent in transferable credits from an accredited institution; minimum grade point average of 2.0. Special admission criteria may apply for selected groups, such as the military.

For a graduate program, a student must have B.A. or B.S. degree from a regionally accredited institution, and grade point average of 2.5 or higher on the last 60 transferable semester units. There are certain additions and exceptions, depending on program. Applicant is responsible for having all transcripts and test scores sent to school applied to.

Assessment of prior learning. Credit granted for all courses completed at accredited institutions. Up to 70 semester hours of community college work is acceptable toward the bachelor's degree. Six hours of credit in the lower division is awarded to students who have been in active military service for at least a year. A maximum of 24 semester hours of extension and/or correspondence credit completed in accredited colleges or universities may be awarded toward the bachelor's degree, including credit from the United States Armed Forces Institute. Advanced placement examinations can be taken and credit granted to students who receive a score of 3.0 or higher on each examination. The program also awards credit for completion of certain CLEP examinations.

Curriculum—learning options. Traditional classroom work as well as less traditional modes of learning. The students may work in directed, individual home study courses, or may parallel the work of an ongoing campus class. Several or all of these options can be combined into a single program. Fields of study available: liberal arts, health care administration, business administration, public administration, vocational education, environmental planning, early childhood education, humanities.

Degree requirements. 124 semester hours for bachelor's degree with at least 40 in upper division. A minimum of 30 hours must be taken through Consortium schools, of which 24 must be at upper division level. Minimum grade point average of 2.0.

Requirements for the master's degree may vary among disciplines. In general the requirements are:
a) Advancement to candidacy. After 15 or more semester hours toward requirements with a grade point average of 3.0 or higher, students may, subject to approval, be advanced to candidacy.
b) At least 30 semester hours of approved upper division and graduate course work taken after the baccalaureate.
c) At least 21 hours must be completed in residence.
d) At least 15 hours of graduate courses.
e) All course work for the degree must be completed in seven years.
f) A grade point average of 3.0 or better.

Supportive services—financial aid. Contact the Dean of Continuing Education on the campus through which Consortium courses will be taken for the most recent information on financial assistance.

Faculty advisers are available to students to discuss any questions regarding the program.

Additional information. Additional programs leading to campus degrees have been added and information regarding these programs can be obtained through the Office of the Dean of Continuing Education from the nearest campus.

The member campuses of the Consortium are:

Humboldt State University
Arcata, CA   95521

California State College, Sonoma
1801 East Cotati Avenue, Rhohnert Park, CA   94928

California State University, Sacramento
6000 J Street, Sacramento, CA   95819

San Francisco State University
1600 Holloway Avenue, San Francisco, CA   94132

California State University, Hayward
25800 Jillary Street, Hayward, CA   94542

San Jose State University
125 South Seventh Street, San Jose, CA   95192

California State College, Stanislaus
800 Monte Vista Avenue, Turlock, CA   95380

California State University, Fresno
Shaw and Cedar Avenues, Fresno, CA   93740

California State College, Bakersfield
9001 Stockdale Highway, Bakersfield, CA   93309

California State University, Northridge
18111 Nordhoff Street, Northridge, CA 91324

California State University, Los Angeles
5151 State University Drive, Los Angeles, CA 90032

California State College, Dominquez Hills
1000 E. Victoria Street, Dominquez Hills, CA 90747

California State University, Long Beach
6101 E. Seventh Street, Long Beach, CA 90840

California State Polytechnic University, Pomona
3801 West Temple Avenue, Pomona, CA 91768

California State University, Fullerton
Fullerton, CA 92634

California State College, San Bernardino
5500 State College Parkway, San Bernardino, CA 92407

San Diego State University
San Diego, CA 92182

San Diego State University, Imperial Valley
720 Heber Avenue, Calexico, CA 92231

INTERNATIONAL COLLEGE
Independent Study Program
1019 Goyley Avenue, Westwood
Los Angeles, California 90024
(213) 477-6761

Philosophy and goals. Nonresidential tutorial
degree program, to bring mature and able students
into close association with gifted and established
leaders in a wide variety of disciplines.

Degrees and certificates offered. B.A., M.A.,
Ph.D.

Accreditation. Licensed by the State of California.

Academic calendar. The academic year—a period
of eight months—can begin at any time of the calendar
year. One academic year is the minimum period of
instruction for a program of independent study; may
be extended by additional academic years, or half
years (four months), with or without interruption,
all as desired by the student and agreed to by the
tutor. Sabbatical programs can be arranged for
periods of either four or eight months.
    International College grants 32 units of
undergraduate credit or 28 units of graduate
credit for each eight-month academic year of
independent study.

Residency—required contact with program. Designed
as an independent study program; students have
virtually no direct contact with the College itself.
Contact with tutors is an individually contracted
agreement between intern and tutor.

Part-time enrollment—pace. Part-time study is not
possible, but academic program is sufficiently
flexible so that a student can work part-time or
even full-time.

Costs. Tuition for one academic year: $2,824.00;
for four-month sabbatical: $1,500.00.
    Application fee (nonrefundable), submitted
with application for admission: $20.00.

Enrollment fee, applied as part of tuition,
payable upon acceptance by tutor: $200.00.
    Examination fee for master's degree: $100.00.
    Examination fee for doctoral degree: $200.00.

Admission requirements. Students usually have at
least two years of college or its equivalent.
    Each tutor has specified qualifications and
noted conditions under which he will accept
students. Eilgibility is determined by tutor,
not the college administrative office. Prospective
students without stated prerequisites may present
to the tutor a written defense of their application, stating their reason for requesting admission.

Assessment of prior learning. Assessment of
prior learning is made through personal interviews,
supplemented by other evidence of claimed accomplishment (bibliographies, letters of attestation,
examples of research and writing done, etc.), to
determine whether the prior learning is viable, has
been integrated, and is related to a well-defined
goal. The assessment is made not in terms of credit
but of an equivalent academic standing. Specific
deficiencies that result in an assessment lower
than that claimed or expected are pointed out.

Curriculum—learning options. Each undergraduate
or graduate student accepted for independent study
will work with a single tutor in the student's major
field of interest for at least one academic year.
Ph.D. degree requires study for at least two
academic years with no less than two tutors.
    Program of studies and method of evaluation
will be proposed by tutor and, once agreed to
by student, will be submitted to a dean of the
college for approval. These conditions will be
incorporated into a written and signed plan of
study, a copy of which shall go to all three
parties. Each plan of study provides for creation
of some exemplary work of excellence, and the
college shall retain a copy as permanent evidence
of the student's demonstrated capability. A plan
of study may also be prepared for several (but no
more than twenty) students under the direction of
one tutor. Residency requirements vary according
to the needs of the plan of study and location
of tutor.

Degree requirements. Requirements for graduate
degrees will be determined on an individual basis,
through consultations among the student, the tutor,
and the college deans.

Supportive services—financial aid. Student
financial aid may be available in special cases
and most independent study programs can be arranged
so that the student can work part-time or full-time.

UNIVERSITY OF SAN DIEGO
The Tutorial Degree Program
University Extension
LaJolla, California 92093
(714) 452-3410

Philosophy and goals. Program designed for mature,
highly motivated adults who have an awareness of
their educational needs and the persistence to

pursue long-range goals. Flexibility allows for maximum personal fulfillment. For the individual who requires a more convenient schedule or format than that furnished by traditional degree-earning process or who wants to pursue in depth a topic or field not included in conventional major/minor programs.

Degrees and certificates offered. Bachelor of Arts. TDP is sponsored and administered by University Extension, and the degree is granted by the Union for Experimenting Colleges and Universities.

Accreditation. Institution is a formal candidate for accreditation by the Western Association of Schools and Colleges.

Academic calendar. Students may enroll in the program at any time.

Residency—required contact with program. The program is designed to minimize the amount of on-campus contact necessary. Students may design study programs with little required campus contact.

Part-time enrollment—pace. Students may proceed at their own pace.

Costs. There is a $30.00 nonrefundable application fee. Tuition is $200.00 per month, payable in monthly installments; first payment due when student receives provisional acceptance. Fee entitles student to four one-hour meetings per month with Core faculty member and/or tutor; to biweekly seminars on the degree-earning process, the meaning of academic requirements, self-directed learning, documentation, and other subjects; to meetings with counselor as necessary; to the use of libraries of UC San Diego and other learning resources of the campus. In most cases, it also covers the fees of courses taken at UC San Diego which are approved for the student's program.

Admission requirements. First interview: student meets with counselor to discuss educational objectives and obtain further information on program. Counselor conducts initial screening of program's suitability for student and student's readiness for program.

Second interview: student discusses educational objectives and intentions in greater detail with counselor.

Application: student submits application form, biographical summary, description of educational background, and statement of educational and personal goals as they relate to the program. Application fee of $30.00 is payable at this time.

Students whose preparation for the program is judged sufficient will be promoted to provisional acceptance and assigned to a Core faculty member.

Assessment of prior learning. All learning acquired prior to the student's entrance into program—both formal and informal—will be examined for its relationship to the student's current degree goals and TDP requirements for graduation. Prior learning is assessed in a variety of ways, in the first one to three months of a student's program: with transcripts of record from other schools, or by any suitable means of documentation: student

essays, standardized or specially prepared examinations, art works, published articles or other student products which demonstrate learning acquired Key concepts are documentation and demonstration: prior learning must be judged by the Degree Committee to be suitably demonstrated and documented before credit toward the degree is granted.

Curriculum—learning options. Students are assigned a Core faculty adviser upon provisional admittance to the program. Together they draft both long-term and short-range educational goals, develop degree plan and individual learning contracts for each phase of degree plan.

Tutors direct individual phases of the student's work. They are selected jointly by the student, Extension staff, and Core faculty member; meet with student an average of four times per month for review and dialogue, help arrange internships or research projects, suggest areas of further study, and prepare written evaluation of the student's work after each meeting; and may be UC San Diego faculty, faculty of other institutions, or working professionals in the community.

Program culminates in a final project which relates to the central thrust of student's degree plan and must incorporate a review of student's work, identification of accomplishments, and an indication of direction; may be submitted orally, in writing or other media, and is presented to the Degree Committee.

Degree requirements. Bachelor of Arts degree from the TDP requires clear and accurate written expression; clear and effective oral expression; critical, analytical and creative skills; knowledge in a general area of study (major) approached broadly so as to include at least two other interdisciplinary areas.

The student will demonstrate mastery of these skills through interaction with Core faculty and tutors, and through documentation. Where appropriate, learning through direct participation and experience should be a part of each student's program. Reading, and papers or oral reports which analyze and synthesize the reading, will be a standard method of achievement. Prior learning and experience may be used to fulfill many degree requirements.

Supportive services. The counselor—a professional psychologist permanently assigned to the program—is the first person the potential student talks to when applying for the program. Counselor conducts the initial screening, oversees the application process, and locates a suitable Core faculty member for the student. Counselor is available for further consultation after student enters program.

CONNECTICUT

BOARD FOR STATE ACADEMIC AWARDS
340 Capitol Avenue
Hartford, Connecticut   06115
(203) 566-7230

Philosophy and goals. Established by the Connecticut legislature to enable independent, adult learners to earn academic degrees based on foundations of achievement in arts and sciences. A constituent unit of the Connecticut state system of higher education, the BSAA was created to expand opportunities in higher education by establishing valid alternatives to the traditional mode of earning credits and degrees only on campus. Credit is awarded by a faculty of examiners on the basis of tests, evaluation of performance and classroom credit. The BSAA holds no classes. Therefore, students are identified as external students who earn external degrees.

Degrees and certificates offered. Associate in Arts, Bachelor of Arts, Associate in Science, and Bachelor of Science.

Accreditation. BSAA has state accreditation from the Connecticut Board of Higher Education and is a candidate for accreditation with the New England Association of Schools and Colleges, Inc.

Academic calendar. Students may enroll any time during the year.

Residency—required contact with program. After initial evaluation, students plan courses of study with a BSAA adviser. This may be done by letter, phone or personal appointment. Candidates for a baccalaureate degree must design a program proposal, outlining course work with the Dean of Faculty.

Part-time enrollment—pace. Candidates proceed at their own pace. A degree is awarded when necessary credits are accumulated.

Costs.

Enrollment fee	$50.00
Records maintenance fee	25.00
(for updating of active records payable annually beginning with third year)	
Graduation fee	25.00
Nonresident processing fee	100.00
(payable in addition to enrollment fee by all persons residing outside of Connecticut)	
Baccalaureate program planning and evaluation fee	100.00
Foreign credential processing fee	50.00
(payable by all persons presenting credentials from institutions or agencies outside the United States)	

Fees for standardized proficiency examinations range from $20.00 to $75.00 and are payable directly to the supplier. Special examinations are more costly and are usually arranged when no standardized examination is available and a significant amount of credit seems assured.

Admission requirements. Enrollment open to anyone ready to demonstrate college-level achievement regardless of age, sex, race, creed, citizenship, residence or level of formal education. Persons considering enrollment first discuss plans with a BSAA adviser. Actual enrollment should come only after personal goals have been set.

Assessment of prior learning. Although the BSAA holds no classes it does administer the American College Testing Proficiency Examination Program (ACTPEP) four times yearly, and the College Level Examination Program (CLEP), Undergraduate Program Field Tests (UP), Graduate Record Advanced Examinations (GRE) and the Modern Language Association Examinations (MLA) by appointment in the BSAA office. Special examinations for which no college-level proficiency examination is available may be arranged during a predesignated spring and fall examination period.

Curriculum—learning options. BSAA offers no instruction of its own. A faculty of consulting examiners establishes degree requirements and reviews candidates' programs. Credits toward degree may be earned by completing: courses for regular college credit in accredited institutions; approved military training programs while in service; college-level proficiency examinations with acceptable scores; special examinations that assess college-level learning acquired through work experience, independent study and other activities outside the classroom; courses offered by noncollegiate organizations which have been evaluated for credit by the American Council on Education or by the Office of Noncollegiate Sponsored Instruction of the University of the State of New York. CLEP and ACTPEP are principal examination programs utilized. CLEP tests are administered the third week of every month at testing centers throughout the state or by appointment at the BSAA office; ACTPEP is administered four times yearly at various centers throughout the state. In addition, the BSAA offers the following examination programs by appointment only at the BSAA office in Hartford:

UP field tests and GRE tests	Designed to measure achievement in a particular field of undergraduate study at the basic, intermediate and advanced levels. Up to 27 credits may be earned per exam.
MLA tests	Designed to measure achievement in French, German, Italian, Russian and Spanish. Up to 24 credits may be earned per exam. Special tests in other languages may also be arranged.

Degree requirements. A candidate for an associate degree must complete 60 credits; at least 30 of these must be in the category of arts and sciences. A candidate for a baccalaureate degree must complete 120 credits; at least 60 of these must be in the category of arts and sciences.

For all degrees there must be a basic distribution of studies in the three areas of the Arts and Sciences (humanities, social sciences/history, and mathematics/natural sciences). Candidates for bachelor's degree must show evidence of significant achievement in depth and breadth of learning at advanced level by completing an approved program of 36 credits in an identified area. A 2.0 average must be maintained.

Supportive services. Academic advisement is available at the BSAA Hartford office and at various locations throughout Connecticut.

For exact times and locations, contact the BSAA office. Study guides for college-level proficiency examinations are available from the BSAA office.

TRINITY COLLEGE
Individualized Degree Program
Hartford, Connecticut 06106
(203) 527-3151, ext. 397 or 470

Philosophy and goals. The IDP at Trinity College offers an academically rigorous liberal arts curriculum which introduces students to a wide range of general learning in the humanities and the sciences. Develops ability to think critically and objectively about the basic ideas and experiences of mankind; does not train for specific profession.

Degrees and certificates offered. B.A. and B.S. degrees.

Accreditation. Accredited by New England Association of Schools and Colleges, Commission on Institutions of Higher Education.

Academic calendar. Program operates year-round.

Residency—required contact with program. Because students are expected to contact professors and to make use of the Trinity library somewhat regularly, work in the IDP cannot be done only through correspondence. Study is mostly independent and self-directed, but each department sets it own requirements and some may require classroom attendance.

Part-time enrollment—pace. Part-time study is possible; students proceed at own pace.

Costs. Tuition per year: approximately $2,650.00. IDP students are required to pay the equivalent of four years of tuition; however, the student may take as long as six to ten years to complete the program, and upon prior arrangement with Trinity College, may pay tuition over that period. Tuition may be reduced on the basis of advanced standing. A student may be granted more tuition credit than academic credit.

Admission requirements. Candidates may apply at any time. Materials to be submitted: application form, an essay, two recommendations, all available academic scores and records. Appointment with IDP office to discuss program recommended. An interview may also be required, and students may be asked to complete one or two study units before acceptance.

Trinity undergraduates may apply to transfer into the IDP after first freshman semester and before first junior semester.

Assessment of prior learning. Credits from courses completed at an accredited college may be transferred into nonmajor phase of IDP at discretion of college registrar; maximum 16 nonmajor study units, the equivalent of 12 course credits. Credit in major phase of IDP on the basis of previous course and/or project work completed elsewhere is possible.

Courses used as credits toward the major may not count toward the completion of the nonmajor study unit requirement.

Curriculum—learning options. Major concentrations available in classics, economics, English, history, intercultural studies, modern languages, philosophy, political science, psychology, religion, sociology, and urban studies. Student also needs to complete 24 nonmajor study units, each in a particular area of knowledge, as drawn up by a Trinity faculty member. Units not currently offered may be requested; granting of request depends upon availability of faculty. In addition, students may create their own study units with approval of IDP coordinating committee and faculty member.

Degree requirements. Completion of specific departmental requirements in the major field, of 24 nonmajor study units in which twelve linkages (based on either content or concept) can be demonstrated, and of a nonmajor project (research papers, portfolios of artistic work, laboratory experiments) fulfill the criteria for an IDP degree.

Supportive services—financial aid. Each student is assigned an adviser, who remains the student's primary contact with the program, and also works with a number of faculty advisers. Only limited amount of financial aid is available, and candidates should explore other sources. Information can be obtained from the IDP or Financial Aid Offices. The IDP program is approved for benefits by the Veterans Administration.

Additional information. Library resources, lectures, concerts, theatrical performances, athletic events and facilities at Trinity are available to IDP students. Special IDP events are scheduled throughout the year, and an IDP newsletter is circulated.

DISTRICT OF COLUMBIA

CAMPUS FREE COLLEGE
Central Office: 1239 G Street NW
                Washington, D.C.   20005
                (202) 347-0721
New England Regional Office: 14 Beacon Street
                Boston, Massachusetts
                                   02108
                (617) 742-3060

Philosophy and goals. CFC believes that learning occurs in a wide variety of classroom and nonclassroom settings and that learning should be self-initiated. Provides maximum flexibility and individualized guidance for students, so that they can pursue studies in line with their immediate interests and needs.

Degrees and certificates offered. A.A., B.A., and M.A. from Campus Free College.

Accreditation. Degree granting authority from Washington, D.C., Board of Higher Education. Candidate for accreditation with the Middle States

Association of Colleges and Secondary Schools.

Academic calendar. Program operates year-round. Student's may begin their studies at the beginning of any month.

Residency—required contact with program. No residency is required. Contact with the program is maintained through meetings with a program adviser (PA), located throughout the country.

Part-time enrollment—pace. Students may enroll on either a full- or part-time basis.

Costs. Tuition (college service fee)
Full-time study $300.00/quarterly
Half-time study $200.00/quarterly
Full-time noncredit $200.00/quarterly
Half-time noncredit $125.00/quarterly
Students are expected to hire outside resource persons or enroll in courses at other institutions. Thus, the total cost of a CFC education may range from $900.00 to $1900.00 for a nine-month period, depending on cost of other instruction.

Admission requirements. Admission open to anyone who can interest PA to support his or her study program. A brochure describing the interests and qualifications of all PAs is available from main office. Enrollment limited only by the number of students each PA can work with at any given time.

Assessment of prior learning. All prior learning assessed according to its relationship to the student's academic goals. Assessment coordinated by PA, who makes recommendation for final award of credits to academic council composed of CFC staff.

Transfer credits from traditional institutions or from testing agencies usually accepted if formally validated. Prior learning gained entirely on one's own or from professional experience must be thoroughly documented to show amount, quality, and kind of learning by statements of evaluation from instructors, job supervisors, tutors, or others qualified to comment on student's learning; products, such as reports, papers, diaries, letters, creative writings, film, publications, tapes, or artworks; examinations of any type that are fair tests of the learning for which the student is seeking credit.

Curriculum—learning options. Student's program coordinated by PA, who does not usually offer instruction but assists student in locating resource persons, courses at other institutions, or opportunities for field work. Student and PA devise a contract for a set study period, from a few weeks to many months. Students can study in any area within scope of local resources and background of PA.

Degree requirements. When student and PA feel that learning goals have been reached a degree request is submitted to the academic council. Student must spend a minimum of one academic year in the program. No specific content area requirements, but students are encouraged to gain both a general education background as well as achieve a high level of proficiency in a specific area.

Supportive services—financial aid. The student's program adviser is the main source of guidance for the CFC student.

Additional information. CFC has no campus or resident faculty. The central administrative office is located in Washington, D.C., and regional offices are located throughout the country. Program advisers are resident in more than 150 cities, towns, and rural areas in 34 states.

HOWARD UNIVERSITY
University Without Walls
P.O. Box 662
Washington, D.C.   20059
(202) 636-7660, 7661

Philosophy and goals. Offers an alternative approach to a baccalaureate degree. Aim: to produce life-long creative learners, not "finished graduates." Provides training for students in classroom and through self-direction in learning without spacial and temporal limits of traditional programs.

Degrees and certificates offered. B.A. from University Without Walls at Howard University, reflecting the college of school of enrollment, e.g., College of Fine Arts, School of Communications.

Accreditation. Fully accredited by the Middle States Association of Secondary Schools and Colleges.

Academic calendar. Semester (four and one-half months).

Residency—required contact with program. Regular dialogues with advisers, bimonthly seminars, admissions and orientation workshops required. However, the program is flexible and available to the long-distance learner.

Part-time enrollment—pace. Part-time not possible.

Costs. Cost consistent with the tuition cost of Howard University. Application fee is $20.00. Student enrolling in the university for the first time must pay an enrollment fee of $60.00. Full tuition for each semester is $882.50. Deferred payment plan available: half of total expenses during registration, one-fourth the month after classes begin, and the remaining one-fourth the following month.

Admission requirements. Criteria for acceptance are varied and multi-dimensional. These include:
1. Good follow-through.
2. Ability to articulate educational objective(s).
3. Attendance at an admissions workshop which also includes an interview.
4. A balance between the need for the alternative approach to learning and the desire for a degree.

Assessment of prior learning. Student's faculty advisory team evaluates data on prior education and experience related to a student's stated goals.

Curriculum—learning options. With assistance of faculty team, students prescribe their own academic program, which delineates the student's learning objectives, modus operandi, and offers breadth and depth deemed worthy of a degree. Options include seminars, classes, workshop, travel, and independent study. Students maintain an evaluative record of their development.

Degree requirements. Degree requirements are flexible and unique to each learner. Quality and integrity are paramount. One year's participation in program is required. A final project is prerequisite for the degree.

Supportive services—financial aid. Dialogues with advisers provide necessary support for the progress of the student. Financial aid programs of Howard University are available: BEOG, SEOG, NDSL, CWS, etc. Eligible students may apply for VA benefits.

WASHINGTON INTERNATIONAL COLLEGE
814-20th St. N.W.
Washington, D.C.   20006
(202) 466-7220

Philosophy and goals. In response to educational needs of students, WIC designed a learning process that begins with student's needs and goals and uses them as the guiding principle in development of individualized degree programs.

Degrees and certificates offered. A.A., B.A.

Accreditation. WIC was chartered by the District of Columbia in February 1970, licensed by Washington, D.C., Board of Higher Education in September 1973, and granted candidate status in January 1974 by the Middle States Association of Colleges and Secondary Schools.

Academic calendar. Open enrollment throughout the year.

Part-time enrollment—pace. Students are expected to have self-motivation and commitment; participate in design and development of their programs, evaluate and be responsible for their progress.

Residency—required contact with program. No information available.

Costs. Credit hour, $60.00. Application fee, $15.00. Nonrefundable tuition deposit, $180.00. Tuition calculated by credit hours registered for. The college has a deferred payment plan for <u>full-time</u> students.

Admission requirements. Open admissions policy in terms of traditional entrance criteria. A high school diploma or its equivalent required for degree program. Students with 30 or more credits with grades of C or better from other colleges or universities do not need to supply a high school transcript. Applications may be submitted at any time during the year. The college may accept applicants not having a high school diploma or General Education Development (GED) certificate as special student. After having successfully completed 12 credit hours of college work at WIC, student may become a candidate for a degree.

Assessment of prior learning. There are four categories of advanced standing credit recognized by WIC: credit transferred from other accredited institutions (grades of C or better); credit through recognized testing programs such as CLEP; possible credit for attending seminars, conferences or classes at nonaccredited institutions; possible credit for learning which can be documented as having occurred in a particular life experience. In the two last instances, documentation produced by student working in contract with a faculty adviser is assessed for credit by faculty members in the subject field.

There is an additional charge for the second, third and fourth methods of obtaining credit. Credits awarded then become a part of student's degree program.

Curriculum—learning options. All students must begin with the Career-Life Planning Seminar, in order to assess skills, abilities, interests and prior creditable learning, identify and articulate current career and life goals, and develop from them an individualized degree plan to be implemented at WIC.

Students are then assigned to planning advisers who help them implement their curriculum. In addition to the competencies necessary for the student's career-life goals, competency must be developed in each of the following: analysis, interpretation, humaneness, communication, creativity, implementation, and evaluation.

Each learning experience for which the student desires academic credit must be performed in a Learning Contract designed by student and a planning adviser with review and approval of the dean; may be designed in the form of independent study, a seminar or regular classes, a tutorial, an internship or studio.

The overall quality of a student's education is the responsibility of his/her degree program committee, which meets periodically and consists of the Dean of the College, two or three appropriat faculty members and another WIC student.

Degree requirements. Students must demonstrate competence in their career-life goals and in the seven areas identified by the college. A minimum of 127 credit hours needed for graduation.

Supportive services—financial aid. For graduating students, the college conducts a three-hour implementation seminar to help student make the transition to career field or other area of endeavor.

WIC is eligible for federal student aid funds and participates in BEOG, NDSL, SEOG, CWS or FISL. The college is approved for veteran's benefits for the A.A in sales and sales management and the B.A. in communications and performing arts.

FLORIDA

FLORIDA INTERNATIONAL UNIVERSITY
Tamiami Trail

Miami, Florida   33199
(305) 552-2376

Philosophy and goals. Authorized by Florida
Board of Regents to administer the State University
System external degree program (EDP), enabling
students to take advantage of all educational
resources throughout Florida, without requiring
residency on any campus. It is a self-directed
program for residents of the State of Florida.

Degrees and certificates offered. Operated
through the faculty of the regular departments
and divisions in Florida International's college
and schools. Degrees offered are the same as the
regular undergraduate degrees offered by the College
of Arts and Sciences, the School of Health and Social
Services, the School of Technology, the School of
Business and Organizational Sciences, and the School
of Hospitality Management but they are earned
through alternative means.

Accreditation. Fully accredited by the Southern
Association of Colleges and Schools.

Academic calendar. Quarters. Students may enroll
in the program and begin their course of study at
any time.

Residency—required contact with program. Most
external degree students take some formal classroom work, but classroom instruction is not required.

Part-time enrollment—pace. Possible. Student
works at own speed.

Costs. Tuition for fall, winter and spring terms:
$16.50 per class hour. For summer term: $10.50
per class hour.

Admission requirements. Admission limited to
Florida residents and to students qualified for
regular degree programs. Students with Associate
of Arts or Science degrees or with 90 quarter hours
(60 semester hours) from an accredited institution,
and who have completed general education requirements
of the University, are eligible for admission.
Students who have not completed these requirements
may do so either at the university or another
accredited institution, or by achieving a satisfactory score on the appropriate CLEP test.
Acceptance as EDP student by faculty adviser
necessary.

Assessment of prior learning. Credit transfer from
four-year colleges: up to 135 quarter (90 semester)
hours; from two-year colleges: up to 90 quarter
(60 semester) hours. Maximum credits earned under
CLEP (general and subject examinations combined):
45 semester (67.5 quarter) hours; not more than 6
semester (9 quarter) hours each in English,
humanities, mathematics, natural sciences, social
sciences, and history. Departmental credit by
examination available to regular, degree-seeking
students for certain courses. Credit from non-
accredited institutions, military schools and foreign
institutions will be considered on an individual
basis. Transfer of credit for D grades subject to
review and approval. Credit for life/work experience
available to degree-seeking student, who must
submit a portfolio describing and documenting
prior learning; experiences must be applicable to
the student's degree program.

Curriculum—learning options. Individual study
plans are designed for each student in the form of
an educational contract, which specifies the program
of study, outlining what remains to be done for
the completion of a baccalaureate degree.

Some formal classroom work possible, but not
required. Arrangements for independent study at
home or on the job can be worked out through
reading lists, research papers, and educational
projects.

Degree requirements. Bachelor's degree awarded
upon: successful completion of a minimum of 180
credit hours; completion of the last 45 credit
hours of coursework at Florida International
University; satisfactory completion of University's
general educational requirement; maintenance of at
least a 2.0 G.P.A. on all course work; recommendation
by the faculty of the college of school awarding
the degree; certification by the dean of the
college or school concerned that all requirements
of the degree being sought have been completed.

Supportive services—financial aid. The principal
source of support is the student's adviser.
Assistance is available to students through all
major state and federal programs including BEOG,
SEOG, NDSL, CWS.

NOVA UNIVERSITY
Center for Higher Education
3301 College Avenue
Fort Lauderdale, Florida   33314
(305) 587-6660, ext. 246

Philosophy and goals. Three-year programs designed
to provide in-service education for education
professionals. Primary objective is improvement
of higher education services; programs have been
designed to increase theoretical knowledge through
practical exploration and for practical use. The
emphasis is on practicability.

Degrees and certificates offered. Ed.D. for
community college faculty; Ed.D. in vocational,
technical and occupational education.

Accreditation. Chartered by the State of Florida,
accredited by the Southern Association of Colleges
and Schools, and affiliated with the New York
Institute of Technology.

Academic calendar. Program operates year-round
and is organized into semesters and summer seminars.

Residency—required contact with program. Students
in the Ed.D. programs must attend two eight-day
summer institutes at Nova University. Frequent
cluster group meetings are arranged.

Part-time enrollment—pace. Part-time enrollment
is not possible, but programs are flexible enough
to allow participants to work.

Costs. Tuition: $2,100.00 per year
Application fee: 25.00

53

A $200.00 deposit must be submitted with the application. Both full payment and partial payment plans are available, in which additional fees of $15.00 for registration are charged and, in the case of partial payments, $25.00 service fees. Students who do not complete the program in three years pay an additional $350.00 for each four-month term in which university services are used.

Admission requirements. Program is performance-oriented. Quality is monitored through examinations and evaluation reports. Enrollment in Ed.D. program is restricted to individuals who hold a master's degree granted by an accredited institution, a community college certificate (if this is a state requirement) and are employed by a community college or area of higher education that deals with community college transfers. Three letters of recommendation from leaders in community colleges are necessary, indicating performance of the applicant as a teacher or administrator. A personal interview with the central staff in the locale of the cluster is also required.

Students in the vocational, technical, and occupational education program can be accepted with only a bachelor's degree, but they must be certified, and employed and recommended by members of appropriate institutions. Applications include an essay concerned with immediate goals upon graduation together with long-range goals.

Assessment of prior learning. Prior learning is considered in the application process and is assessed by examinations, evaluation reports, and a personal interview.

Curriculum—learning options. Students are organized into cluster groups of twenty-five or more, and although education is pursued individually, group communication is important. In the first two years, students study six learning modules. There are lectures by national lecturers, readings detailed in prepared study guides, and the creation and completion of module-related practicums by the students in consultation with practicum evaluators. In the community colleges program, modules include curriculum development, college governance, applied research and evaluation, learning theory and applications, educational policy systems, and societal factors. In the vocational, technical, and occupational education program, modules include administration of programs, applied educational research and development, management information systems, curriculum and instruction, personnel, and trends, issues, and foundations.

In the third year of the program, students devise and complete MARPs (Major Applied Research Projects) in consultation with MARP advisers. Students also participate in two eight-day summer institutes in which they, cluster coordinators, practicum evaluators and nationally known educators express and share ideas.

Note: Candidates in the vocational, technical, and occupational education program holding bachelor's degrees spend the third year on a Major Institutional Implementation Project within the educational setting, and proceed to the MARP in the fourth year.

Degree requirements. Completion of seven core

modules, five practicums, MARP, detailed individualized evaluations of program and student's achievements, and attendance at two eight-day summer institutes.

Supportive services—financial aid. Each cluster is served by a cluster coordinator who acts as administrative leader, business manager, and liaison between the students and university.

Program approved for benefits by the Veterans Administration and participants are eligible for GSLs.

Additional information. There are thirty-one cluster groups located in various parts of the country.

SAINT LEO COLLEGE
External Degree Program
P.O. Box 2248
Saint Leo, Florida 33574
(904) 588-2800, ext. 260-1

Philosophy and goals. To provide quality educational programming to all qualified adults unable to participate in normal college education. The criminal justice program prepares for leadership in the law enforcement profession, and stresses knowledge of law, police science administration, public service, and society.

The Bachelor of Arts for Registered Nurses degree is not a degree in nursing, but a means of broadening an R.N.'s academic education in many areas of higher education.

Degrees and certificates offered. Associate of Arts and Bachelor of Arts in Criminal Justice; Associate of Arts and Bachelor of Arts for Registered Nurses.

Accreditation. Fully accredited by the Southern Association of Colleges and Schools.

Academic calendar. Semester.

Residency—required contact with program. Provides for the completion of the degree program without on-campus residence, but all courses are not available by independent study; however, program may be completed with a minimum of on-campus study.

Part-time enrollment—pace. Students may proceed at their own pace.

Costs. Part-time tuition rates:

Hours	Charge	Hours	Charge
1	$ 35.00	7	$ 550.00
2	70.00	8	700.00
3	105.00	9	850.00
4	200.00	10	1,000.00
5	300.00	11	1,100.00
6	400.00	12	1,200.00

Admission requirements. Mature, in-service law enforcement officers may apply for admission to program. Students not in service may apply for admission and be admitted into the criminal justice degree; they must attempt a 6-credit practicum during their senior year.

Registered nurses may present their certificates of graduation as evidence of academic achievement, apply for admission into the External Degree Program for Registered Nurses, and begin work leading to the B.A.

Assessment of prior learning. Saint Leo recognizes credit from regionally accredited institutions and military service courses. Work in which a grade of D or better was made will be transferred if student achieved an overall minimum grade point average of 2.0; otherwise only those grades of C or better will be transferrable. Transfer courses must be applicable to the student's program at Saint Leo.

Credit awarded for CLEP general examinations and subject examinations. Up to 30 credits may be earned through general examinations. credit may be granted for DANTES College Level Examination tests at discretion of registrar. College Board Advanced Placement Examinations will be evaluated with the possibility of offering both college credit and advanced placement.

Saint Leo College will accept students holding associate's degree from a junior college into its B.A. program.

Curriculum—learning options. Program combination of independent study and traditional class work. Required areas of Basic Studies for both programs: two courses in English; one each in fine arts, language and literature, philosophy and theology, social science, and natural science and mathematics; three other Basic Studies courses from any of the above divisions for a total of 30 credits.

The concentration in criminal justice is designed to develop in-depth knowledge in professional law enforcement.

Students entering the External Degree Program for Registered Nurses may elect the R.N. Certificate as their concentration. Course work taken in the SLC program, through cluster work, independent study, or on-campus work, will be applicable toward the 30-semester-hour in-program requirement, and will be applicable toward the B.A. degree. Students electing a specific concentration beyond the R.N. program may be required to attend certain on-campus courses, depending on the concentration chosen.

Degree requirements. To earn the Bachelor of Arts degree the student must complete the Basic Studies program; have a minimum of 120 semester hours, inclusive of transfer credit, a minimum of 40 semester hours at the 300-400 level; attain a cumulative grade point average of 2.0, and complete a minimum of 30 semester hours in the Saint Leo College program.

Supportive services—financial aid. The principal source of support is the student's adviser. Assistance is available through all major state and federal programs, including BEOG, SEOG, NDSL, and CWS.

UNIVERSITY OF SOUTH FLORIDA
Bachelor of Independent Studies External Degree
Tampa, Florida 33620
(813) 974-4058

Philosophy and goals. The BIS program is based on a curriculum of interdisciplinary or cross-disciplinary studies of an academic nature whose objective is an intellectual lifestyle characterized by the capacity to analyze, criticize, synthesize, and make independent, creative judgments.

Degrees and certificates offered. Bachelor of Independent Studies.

Accreditation. Fully accredited by the Southern Association of Colleges and Schools.

Academic calendar. Program operates year-round. Seminars are customarily offered in June, July, and August, but may be offered at other times if enough students are interested.

Residency—required contact with program. Each of three directed independent tutorials is followed by a three-week seminar on campus. In addition, degree candidate must appear on campus for one day at the conclusion of studies to defend final thesis in oral examination. Degree candidate is expected to contact adviser at least once a month.

Part-time enrollment—pace. Study is independent at student's pace. Each tutorial may take from six to twenty-four months, as may thesis.

Costs. Tutorials, $300.00 each $900.00
Thesis tutorial 650.00
Admission fee 15.00
Pre-enrollment fee 60.00
The total is $2,525.00, but may be substantially reduced through waiver of up to two of the independent study sequences. Such waivers are obtained, in part, through an examination for which fee is $75.00.

Admission requirements. Same general requirements for admission as other degree-seeking students. High school graduation or equivalency is required. Applicants also need to satisfy the BIS committee that they are likely to succeed in and profit from an external degree program. Application forms available from director.

Assessment of prior learning. Prior learning assessed through waiver and abbreviated reading program. Waiver of up to two independent study areas can be obtained by a letter to the director requesting such a waiver, an on-campus interview with a study area counselor, and successful completion of a comprehensive examination in the study area. In the abbreviated reading program, student, in consultation with the study area faculty adviser, is directed away from disciplines in which he or she is competent and toward those in which he or she needs work. Transfer credits as such are not accepted. Education represented by such credits is evaluated by foregoing methods.

Curriculum—learning options. The curriculum is divided into four study areas: social sciences, natural sciences, humanities, and interarea studies. Each area is pursued on the basis of a predetermined core of readings, until the adviser feels student is prepared for comprehensive examination in particular area, after which student may proceed to studies in another area. Upon successful completion of such an examination, or upon recommendation from an adviser, the student may participate in a three-week on-campus seminar to supplment readings and reinforce the learning process. Seminar participation is evaluated by the seminar faculty team on the basis of both oral and written contributions.

The fourth study area (thesis tutorial) is designed to integrate learning from the first three areas. The student works with a primary adviser to devise an appropriate thesis prospectus and the thesis then is completed under the direction of a thesis committee comprised of the three advisers who worked with student through the first three study areas.

Degree requirements. Three units of guided independent study, and successful completion of study area examinations, three seminars, and a thesis and its oral defense.

Supportive services—financial aid. The student's various advisers are the student's main source of guidance. Contact financial aid office for information on financial aid.

Additional information. Current enrollment is 100+.

WALDEN UNIVERSITY
Institute for Advanced Studies
801 Anchor Road Drive
Naples, Florida   33940
(813) 261-7277
Western Branch:
1000 Welch Road, Suite 208
Palo Alto, California   94304
(415) 326-8412

Philosophy and goals. The Walden University model of advanced education offers mature people of many ages a new and flexible, individualized way to earn their degree without sacrificing academic rigor.

As an institution, Walden has been concerned exclusively with doctoral level research, and its students, who have completed most of the course work for the doctorate before entering the university, start immediately on the research process.

Degrees and certificates offered. Doctor of Philosophy (Ph.D.), Doctor of Education (Ed.D.).

Accreditation. Walden has candidacy status of accreditation with the Southern Association of Colleges and Schools.

Academic calendar. Semesters: spring and fall. Summer residency session.

Residency—required contact with program. Students must attend initial four-week intensive summer program.

Part-time enrollment—pace. The program is self-paced.

Costs. Tuition rates and fees apply to the academic year and are guaranteed for that year as indicated in the Schedule of Tuition and Fees. These rates may change from year to year.
Tuition, 1978-1979

Summer residency session	$1595.00
Research semester	
Fall	1375.00
Spring	1375.00
Other fees:	
Application	$ 35.00
Course materials	50.00
Dissertation processing	135.00
Commencement	125.00
Transcript (after initial set)	2.00
Extension of semester fee	350.00
Optional research semester	
(summer)	1375.00

Admission requirements. To be eligible for admission students must have a master's degree plus at least 16 graduate semester hours of course work, or equivalent—46 graduate semester hours of course work.

Assessment of prior learning. Prior learning is assessed only in relation to admissions. Once admitted into the program, all students must complete the same amount of work.

Curriculum—learning options. All students attend an intensive summer session at which they participate in structured, competency-based learning experiences. Course work in the summer program is designed to help students develop competencies in effecting change in their professional areas, in basic research design and methodology, and in the development of research proposals. Proposal development is done on a one-to-one basis in consultation with a faculty member. During the summer session, each student also builds a three-person review committee with which they work throughout their enrollment.

Degree requirements. The degree is awarded once the student has fulfilled the academic requirements of the university, which include approval of dissertation by the review committee.

Supportive services—financial aid. The student's principal source of support is the review committee. Limited financial assistance is available.

HAWAII

CHAMINADE UNIVERSITY OF HONOLULU
Division of Continuing Education

3140 Waialae Avenue
Honolulu, Hawaii 96816
(808) 732-1471, ext. 106

Philosophy and goals. Program designed to
assist any qualified adult to obtain a college
degree through a combination of academic
experiences, military and/or civilian experiences,
and the College Level Examination Program.

Degrees and certificates offered. B.A.
(Bachelor of Arts), B.B.A. (Bachelor of Business
Administration), B.F.A. (Bachelor of Fine Arts),
B.G.S. (Bachelor of General Studies), B.S.
(Bachelor of Science--Criminal Justice), A.G.S.
(Associate of General Studies).

Accreditation. Accredited by the Western
Association of Schools and Colleges.

Academic calendar. Operates on a semester
system, including summer sessions. There
are four accelerated semesters per year.

Residency—required contact with program. At
least 30 semester hours of credit for all
degrees must be completed in residence at the
university.

Part-time enrollment—pace. Part-time study
possible.

Costs. Application fee: $20.00. The tuition
charge in the university's accelerated sessions
is $45.00 on-campus per credit hour, $37.00
off-campus per credit hour.

Admission requirements. Requirements for
unclassified students are a completed application form submitted with the fee, an acceptable
high school transcript and/or high school GED
certificate, and college transcripts if the
student has studied at other institutions.
Classified students who are officially candidates for a degree, file a formal application/
evaluation form and CLEP or GED examination
reports. An unclassified student who has earned
at least 65 semester hours of credit from all
courses is usually expected to become a degree
candidate. Military personnel, law enforcement
officers, and nurses enrolled in special programs
must file appropriate official reports of their
experiences.

Assessment of prior learning. CLEP, approved
educational and life experiences, and college
correspondence courses may not aggregate more than
65 hours. Not more than 25 hours may be earned
through combinations of college correspondence
and USAFI courses. For the A.G.S., aggregate
hours may not exceed 32 and no more than 12 hours
may be earned through USAFI courses.
   Professional and on-the-job training, work
experience, self-study, and other learning
experiences may be approved for credit hours as
described in the Life Experiences form available
from the Counseling Center. Transfer credits
from accredited institutions may be obtained
for courses in which student has received a

minimum grade of C. A lower grade, although it
cannot be applied toward the 124 credit hours
required for graduation, may be applied against
a specific course requirement in developing the
student's individualized learning contract.

Curriculum—learning options. Through a
combination of course work, military and/or
civilian experiences, and proficiency exams,
students can work in general studies, with
special programs for military personnel, criminal
justice personnel, R.N.s, radiologic technology
personnel and the general adult community.

Degree requirements. For all baccalaureate degrees,
124 credit hours are required, of which 30 hours
must be taken in residence; 60 credit hours are
required for the associate degrees, of which 30
hours must be taken in residence.

Supportive services—financial aid. Admissions
Office, Counseling Center. Approved for benefits
by the Veterans Administration; contact financial
aid office for information about other aid.

ILLINOIS

CENTRAL YMCA COMMUNITY COLLEGE
Life Experience Credentializing Program,
Division of Extended Learning
Chicago, Illinois 60606
(312) 222-8294

Philosophy and goals. The program assumes that
learning is, can, and should be a life-long process
and that a person may become educated as the result
of a variety of nonacademic experiences. The
program attempts to help students identify the
knowledge they have acquired in such areas as
work experience, community involvement, and
noncredit study and determines whether or not
some of this learning can be equated with academic
competencies.

Degrees and certificates offered. Associate in Arts,
Associate in Business Administration, Associate
in Science, and Associate in Applied Science degrees.

Accreditation. Fully accredited by the North
Central Association of Colleges and Secondary
Schools.

Academic calendar. Open calendar.

Residency—required contact with program. There
is no residency requirement; however, students
are expected to maintain regular contact with
adviser.

Part-time enrollment—pace. Students may proceed
at their own pace.

Costs. Admission fee $10.00
         Analysis and evaluation $50.00 to $100.00
         Credentialing $25.00 per course

credited by LEC (with adjustments for partial LEC credentialing

Degree granting	$15.00
Credit courses at CYCC	$50.00 per credit hour

Costs for proficiency tests, CLEP tests, independent study projects, correspondence study, additional course work and recording are not included in the above schedule. Costs for further counseling, evaluation, accreditation and transcript fees, and course or testing fees vary according to individual need and are reviewed individually with students by the program staff.

Admission requirements. No specific requirements but previous experience in concentrated area is considered.

Assessment of prior learning. With guidance from the LEC staff, students compile a portfolio that describes and documents activities for which college credit might be awarded: work experience, community involvement, noncredit study, apprentice-ships and job training, military training, or intensive/extensive independent projects. After materials in the portfolio have been assembled, evaluations for credits are made by appropriate faculty and divisional personnel. As part of the evaluative process, the candidate may be asked to assemble additional materials, take examinations, write papers, read from a selected bibliography, or participate in one or more interviews aimed at determining the candidate's level of knowledge.

Curriculum—learning options. A degree program is structured according to the candidate's previous experience and current needs; and may include (1) course work at this or other accredited insti-tutions; (2) credit earned through proficiency tests or other standardized tests such as CLEP; and (3) independent study projects that will demonstrate competence or integrate past experience with new skills. Occasionally, there are students who wish to have credit evaluation for work purposes, certification, or advanced study without incorporating those credits into a two-year degree program. Evaluations and transcript records can be arranged in such cases.

Supportive services—financial aid. A course in self-assessment and portfolio preparation is offered as an option for those individuals who feel they can benefit from an exploration of career and academic objectives in a group setting. Eligible students may receive financial aid. Interested applicants are interviewed and counseled on the applicability of this program to their needs before being admitted.

DEPAUL UNIVERSITY
School for New Learning
23 Jackson Boulevard
Chicago, Illinois   60604

(312) 321-7901

Philosophy and goals. The School for New Learning is an urban-oriented, competency-based program featuring contract learning and individualized curriculum. Adult learners have responsibility for designing their own educations and opportunity to get credit for life experience gained outside the traditional walls of a university.

Degrees and certificates offered. Bachelor of Arts from DePaul University

Accreditation. Fully accredited by the North Central Association of Colleges and Schools.

Academic calendar. Semester

Residency—required contact with program. A certain degree of contact is required with the school. In addition to a great number and variety of courses offered by the school (none of which are required), students must participate in an initial discovery workshop, portfolio preparation workshop, program design seminar, summit seminar, and a final evaluation.

Part-time enrollment—pace. Students may proceed at whatever pace they are interested in and capable of performing.

Costs. Tuition at SNL is computed at a quarter-hour equivalency rate of $48.00 per hour for night school; day school rate is higher and depends upon the total number of hours for which the student registers.

Discovery workshop	$105.00 (2 quarter-hours course)
Life experience evaluation	288.00 (6 quarter-hours course)
Learning pact negotiation and committee counseling	288.00 (6 quarter-hours course)
All courses: including classroom, independent studies, etc. for SNL only (based on 4 quarter-hours base)	48.00 per quarter hour (3 SNL courses of 4 quarter-hours each and one major seminar of 6 quarter-hours is the minimum. Cost: $864.00)
Internship	$288.00 (6 quarter-hours course)
Major piece of work	288.00 (6 quarter-hours course)
Final evaluation and summit seminar	288.00 (6 quarter-hours course)
Minimum cost of B.A. degree program at SNL	$2409.00
Estimate of full-time cost for one year (based on minimum 12 hours per quarter)	$1728.00
Cost per single learning course (4 quarter-hours credit)	$ 192.00

Admission requirements. Students must be 24 years or older. No other specific requirements.

Assessment of prior learning. Student develops a portfolio of evidence for crediting life experience competencies. This portfolio is evaluated to determine which competencies have already been fulfilled by the student.

Curriculum—learning options. SNL program is based on five areas of competence that cut across lines of traditional academic disciplines: the world of work, communications and interpersonal relations, the human community, quality of life, and life-long learning. Specific learning strategies are designed. This includes course work done at the seven traditional schools at DePaul, learning experiences at the SNL and at other schools or institutions anywhere in Chicago where the needed learning can best take place (independent study, field work, internships, seminars, group learning forums, etc.).

Degree requirements. Students must complete all the learning strategies contained in their learning pact and demonstrate competence in the five major areas.

Supportive services—financial aid. Full-time administrative staff is available for counseling and interviews, to help students become advocates for themselves.
   DePaul University is approved for participation in major state and federal financial aid programs.

CHICAGO STATE UNIVERSITY
BOG/B.A. Program
East 95th Street at King Drive
Chicago, Illinois   60628
(312) 995-2213

Philosophy and goals. Designed for mature adults, preferably 25 years of age or older, who wish to enter or reenter undergraduate school and generate credit for prior learning experiences; especially created for working adults who can benefit from its flexibility and life experience credit possibilities.

Degrees and certificates offered. Board of Governor's Bachelor of Arts.

Accreditation. Fully accredited by the North Central Association of Colleges and Secondary Schools.

Academic calendar. Trimesters. The academic calendar is divided into four sessions: winter (January), spring (May), summer (June), and fall (September). Academic year includes only three of these.

Residency—required contact with program. Students design their own degree programs, and may develop them to include a minimum of on-campus contact. Applicants must attend a prospective students' meeting in order to apply for the BOG program.

The program offers two mandatory portfolio preparation workshops each term for students who wish to have their life experiences assessed. Out-of-town applicants can still meet the requirement that students take 15 credits at any combination of BOG institutions by making arrangements with faculty members for correspondence courses or independent study projects.

Part-time enrollment—pace. Part-time study is possible and students proceed at their own pace.

Costs. Besides the $15.00 application fee, there is a $30.00 fee for assessment of learning experiences. Tuition and fees total $295.00 per term for full-time and $21.00 per semester hour for part-time students. Out-of-state students pay $800.00 per term for full-time and $64.00 per semester hour for part-time study.

Admission requirements. Graduation from a four-year high school recognized by the appropriate State Superintendent of Public Instruction or successful completion of the High School Equivalency Examination.

Assessment of prior learning. All previous credit from accredited institutions is transferable so long as a passing grade was granted for a course. Mandatory portfolio preparation workshops are given twice each term for students interested in having their life experience assessed. Documentation of such experience is required.

Curriculum—learning options. Independent study, correspondence study, internship agreements, and regular course work are available to the learner. Students have the option of developing their own program or following an area of concentration. There may be concurrent enrollment at any accredited school if the student so desires, in addition to participating in the programs of BOG schools.

Degree requirements. For BOG/B.A., 120 total semester credits or equivalent; 40 semester credits or equivalent at the junior-senior level; 15 semester credits actually taken in any order at any combination of Board of Governor's universities; 12 semester credits each from social science, natural science and humanities gained in any combination or under any approved method; selection of a particular Board of Governor's institution to sponsor the degree. Chicago State University requirements which must be met by BOG students are formal admission into Chicago State University; constitution examination or credit in at least one of the following courses: Political Science 101 or 303 and History 130, 131, 208, 209, or 215; 2.0 cumulative G.P.A. for graduation.

Supportive services—financial aid. BOG students may utilize all the services offered by Chicago State University. The university participates in all major federal financial aid programs: BEOG, SEOG, NDSL, CWS in addition to state grants and awards. Approved for veterans. The staff is available to provide assistance and counseling to students.

CHICAGO STATE UNIVERSITY
University Without Walls
East 95th Street at King Drive
Chicago, Illinois   60628
(213) 995-2221

Philosophy and goals. Designed for persons with an
unusually high level of self-direction and responsibility who wish freedom from the customary constraints
of a traditional school setting. High priority is
placed on ability to frame short-term as well as
long-term learning objectives.

Degrees and certificates offered. Bachelor of
Arts and Bachelor of Science.

Accreditation. Fully accredited by the North
Central Association of Colleges and Secondary
Schools.

Academic calendar. Trimester. Enrollment is
continuous; however, learning activities may be
completed before the end of any trimester or
extend into more than one term.

Residency—required contact with program. It is
possible to design a degree program that requires
minimum on-campus attendance. Students are expected
to maintain regular contact with their advisers.

Part-time enrollment—pace. Student proceeds at
own pace.

Costs. Tuition and activities fees are the same
as for other full-time students: $744.00 annually
or $295.00 per trimester for Illinois residents,
and $800.00 per trimester or $2,400.00 annually
for nonresidents. Full-time tuition is paid
regardless of the academic load carried.

Admission requirements. Admissions are relatively
open to those whose academic, professional, or
personal needs can be met through the program. A
high school diploma or its equivalent is required,
but an extensive portfolio of the student's learning
experiences may be accepted in its place. Prospective student meetings are held approximately
every month.

Assessment of prior learning. Prior learning
experiences are assessed by learning coordinator
in consultation with student's advisers on the
basis of prior educational history and evidence
of competencies acquired through relevant life and
work experiences. It is from this that students
are assigned levels of entry as beginning or
advanced freshmen, sophomores, or juniors.

Curriculum—learning options. Students can become
involved in educationally relevant community
activities, in independent research, or apprenticing
to individuals who have mastered particular skills
or arts. They may concentrate on specific questions,
issues, or problems within a given field or any
combination of fields.

     Each student works with any of several learning
coordinators from the UWW staff, largely on the
basis of his/her area of interest. The student
enters into trimester learning contracts with
two advisers: an academic adviser from university

faculty or that of some other university in the
area, and a field adviser, a practitioner in the
student's field of interest or employment. The
student's final learning contract is usually a
"culminating project" relevant to his/her field of
interest.

Degree requirements. There are two basic requirements for graduation: demonstrated competence in
the student's chosen field of specialization, and
his/her capacity to maintain critical perspectives
on his/her field. The degree is usually awarded
after successful completion of at least three
academic trimesters within the program.

Supportive services—financial aid. UWW students
may utilize all of the services provided by Chicago
State University. The university participates
in all major federal financial aid programs:
BEOG, SEOG, NDSL, CWS, in addition to state grants
and awards. The university is approved for veterans
and eligible students may apply for veterans'
benefits.

GOVERNORS STATE UNIVERSITY
Board of Governors Degree Program Office
Park Forest South, Illinois   60466
(312) 534-5000, ext. 2515, 2516, 2517

Philosophy and goals. For the intelligent adult
already in the world of work who has acquired an
amount of education through experience. The BOG
program was created as a response to the growing
geographic and career mobility of the American
people.

Degrees and certificates offered. Bachelor of
Arts from GSU.

Accreditation. Fully accredited by the North
Central Association of Colleges and Secondary
Schools.

Academic calendar. Trimester, starting in September,
January, May and July.

Residency—required contact with program. Students
may individually design their learning programs
for minimum contact with the program. At least
15 units (semester hours) must be completed at
one, or a combination of, Board of Governors
institutions.

Part-time enrollment. Students may attend the
program part-time.

Costs. The application fee is $15.00. The fee
for assessment of nonacademic learning experiences
is $30.00. Tuition is $21.25 per unit (semester
hour) for Illinois residents, $63.75 per unit for
non-Illinois residents. Full-time (12 units or more)
tuition is $255.00 for Illinois residents, $765.00 for
non-Illinois residents. Activity fees are $15.00 per
trimester.

Admission requirements. Primarily for mature

adults with previous college work and/or extensive nonacademic learning experiences. Thus, all students must have at least 60 semester credits or the equivalent prior to admission. Students with more than 54, but less than 60 credits, may petition for admission. Deadlines for submission of applications and transcripts are usually about one month prior to the start of a trimester.

Assessment of prior learning. Any passing credits from accredited institutions may be transferred but no more than 80 lower division credits. Credit for CLEP examinations may be earned or transferred. Six credits may be awarded for Military Service Basic Training, plus credit for other service educational experiences. A student with an R.N. certificate will be awarded 45 semester credits.

Other nonacademic learning experiences are evaluated by faculty on basis of a student-prepared portfolio demonstrating relevant prior learning experiences. Assistance is available for portfolio preparation. Credits granted may be applied toward admission and graduation requirements.

Curriculum—learning options. Individually-designed student programs may be built around a particular area of study or may be quite general. Students develop their programs with members of the BOG degree program or university faculty staffs. Evaluation is on pass/no credit basis. No failing evaluation will be recorded.

Degree requirements. The student must receive 120 total semester credits or the equivalent. Of these, 40 must be at the junior-senior level, 15 must actually be taken at BOG universities, and 12 semester credits must be earned in each of these groups: social sciences, natural science, and humanities. The overall average at graduation must be a C or better.

Supportive services—financial aid. BOG students are eligible for all state and federal programs, including BEOG, SEOG, NDSL, and CWS. The program is approved for eligible veterans.

GOVERNORS STATE UNIVERSITY
University Without Walls
Special Programs Office
Park Forest South, Illinois   60466
(312) 534-5000

Philosophy and goals. Program combines a competency-based major area of specialization with a liberal arts component and basic communication skills. No courses are offered. Instead, access to multi-learning opportunities are provided, facilitating learning wherever, whenever, however, it takes place. This is accomplished through intensive personalized advising, resource identification, assessment of prior and current learning, evaluation and record-keeping.

Degrees and certificates offered. Students may receive a Bachelor of Arts degree from Governors State University or a Bachelor of Arts from the Union of Experimenting Colleges and Universities.

The latter requires payment of a supplemental graduation fee.

Accreditation. Governors State University is fully accredited, and the Union of Experimenting Colleges and Universities has been awarded candidacy status, by North Central Association of Colleges and Secondary Schools.

Academic calendar. Trimester, with courses offered on a year-round basis. Enrollment at the beginning of each trimester; activities begun in one trimester may be extended to subsequent trimesters.

Residency—required contact with program. It is possible to design a degree program that requires minimum contact with the program. However, students are expected to maintain regular contact with their advising team, and are expected to appear in person before the graduation review team.

Part-time enrollment—pace. While the program is self-paced to some extent, students are encouraged to finish studies in a reasonable time.

Costs. Beyond the initial $15.00 application fee and additional assessment fee for those presenting a portfolio ($25.00), student pays full-time tuition each trimester, and must be enrolled on a continuous basis to maintain admission status; however, students may satisfy this requirement by enrolling in alternate trimesters for zero credit. Tuition covers administration and advisement, use of all university services and the opportunity to take courses at GSU. Tuition per semester is $270.00 plus $9.00 optional insurance for Illinois residents, $780.00 for out-of-state residents without insurance.

Admission requirements. GSU is an upper-division institution requiring 60 semester hours or the equivalent for admission. To supplement or replace all or part of these, a portfolio may be developed for assessing learning from prior nonacademic experiences. Student must possess certain characteristics that are viewed as basic criteria for admission: aptitude for self-directed, experiential learning; capacity to deal with nonstructure; organization; maturity; ability to identify educational goals, and to locate resources to attain those goals.

Assessment of prior learning. Previous college credits consonant with the student's approved learning agreement will be accepted for transfer. Credit for prior nonacademic learning experiences may be awarded by appropriate faculty or other experts on the basis of a portfolio.

Curriculum—learning options. Every student will have a three-person advising team, consisting of an academic adviser from GSU, an adjunct adviser from the community at large, and a process adviser from the UWW staff. These will help the student develop a degree plan and a terminal project. The degree plan is the agreement between the student and his/her advising team defining the competencies to be mastered, the learning activities to be engaged in, the assessment techniques to be utilized, the persons to do the assessment and the terminal project. The terminal project which provides the student with the opportunity to do an in-depth study of some aspect of his/her area of emphasis, and demonstrate to the university his/her competency in that area. The student, working with the advising team, will identify, develop, and agree on the assessment technique to be used in evaluating the project.

Degree requirements. Degrees are awarded when the student and adviser have agreed that the competencies defined in the degree plan have been gained.

Supportive services—financial aid. Instructions to assist in portfolio preparation are available on request. UWW students are eligible for all state and federal programs, including BEOG, SEOG, NDSL, and CWS. The program is approved for eligible veterans.

HARPER COLLEGE
Liberal Studies Program
Algonquin and Roselle Roads
Palatine, Illinois   60067
(312) 397-3000

Philosophy and goals. The program is designed for adults with significant learning experiences. The major emphasis is to allow the individual, with assistance of a faculty adviser, to develop a program of study that is unique for that student. This program is free from traditional degree requirements and may consist of any valid learning experience on or off campus that applies to the student's educational goals.

Degrees and certificates offered. Associate in Liberal Studies (ALS).

Accreditation. Fully accredited by the North Central Association of Colleges and Secondary Schools.

Academic calendar. Semester.

Residency—required contact with program. Students are required to complete 9 hours of liberal studies seminar credit. While independent study, directed study, work and travel are all available as learning options, some additional contact with the program and faculty adviser is expected.

Part-time enrollment—pace. Students determine the pace of their learning programs.

Costs. Tuition is $14.00 per credit hour for residents of the college district. Activity fees of $10.00 per semester for full-time students and $5.00 per semester for part-time students are also charged. Tuition and fees are subject to change without notice.

Admission requirements. A student who wishes to seek an ALS degree must first be admitted to Harper College according to the procedure outlined in the

college bulletin. The student is then required to have a personal interview with the program director. After the student has been admitted, a faculty adviser will be selected to assist him/her in developing the learning contract.

Assessment of prior learning. Advanced standing may be achieved on the basis of an evaluation of life and work experiences, proficiency examination, and previous college courses. To receive advanced standing in the ALS, documentation is required through official college transcripts or proficiency test scores. If advanced standing is sought on the basis of life/work experiences, student must develop a portfolio that documents and explains skills and knowledge. This portfolio is evaluated for college-level credit by college faculty. A maximum of 30 hours of credit may be attained through advanced placement.

Curriculum—learning options. The heart of the program is the learning contract developed between the student and faculty adviser. It is this agreement that provides the structure and identifies all of the learning activities that the student must accomplish. The learning contract can be revised and changed at any time pending approval of the student, faculty adviser, and director of the program.

With the assistance of the faculty adviser, student may submit a proposal to earn from 1 to 3 hours of independent study credit at any time during the semester. This project may be conducted on or off campus and may be in conjunction with travel, work, or directed study.

Degree requirements. To receive an ALS degree, a student must complete all of the requirements and learning experiences identified on his learning contract. This contract must contain 9 hours of liberal studies seminar credit to be taken from three different divisions of the college. In addition, the contract must contain the equivalent of 60 semester hours of work with a minimum 2.0 grade point average.

Supportive services—financial aid. The principal source of support is the student's adviser. Assistance is available to students through all major state and federal programs, including BEOG, SEOG, NDSL, and CWS.

LA SALLE EXTENSION UNIVERSITY
417 South Dearborn Street
Chicago, Illinois   60605
(312) 427-4181

Philosophy and goals. The program is designed to meet the needs of the working adult. First correspondence institution approved by state to offer college degree programs entirely through home study.

Degrees and certificates offered. Associate in Business and Bachelor of Science degrees.

Accreditation. Approved by the Illinois Office

of Education; recognized by the U.S. Civil Service Commission.

Academic calendar. Enrollment is on a continuing basis.

Residency—required contact with program. All contact with the school is by written correspondence.

Part-time enrollment—pace. Program designed to be completed on a part-time basis. The first 30 credits of a program must be completed within two years.

Costs. Tuition: $895.00 for each 30 credits. For students requiring more than 30 but less than 60 credits to complete a degree, $29.83 for each credit over 30.

Transcript evaluation fee: $10.00, which is deducted from tuition if student enrolls.

Admission requirements. A high school diploma or its equivalent is required for enrollment. Exceptions for certain individuals may be made by education director. Students complete a "retail installment contract" and enroll for 30 credits at a time.

Assessment of prior learning. Satisfactory CLEP scores are accepted for transfer credit insofar as they fit within each degree program. Up to 30 credits of approved college level courses, in areas related to the stated course objective, can be applied toward the Associate in Business degree and up to 90 credits towards the Bachelor of Science degree.

Curriculum—learning options. Associate degrees in business, with majors in accounting, hotel and restaurant administration, business management, and banking and finance, and Bachelor of Science degrees in commerce and social studies are offered. Lesson assignments are obtained by mail. When the student completes an assignment, he/she sends examination, project or problem to LaSalle for grading.

Degree requirements. Sixty credit hours are required for an associate's degree, 120 credit hours for a B.S. degree. These are completed in 30 credit units, with associate's degree a prerequisite for obtaining the B.S. The 30 credit units for each of the four associate's degrees consist of 20 prescribed courses within each of the fields ot study. The B.S. degree consists of 120 credit units made up of 40 prescribed courses. A minimum of 30 credits toward any degree must be completed with LaSalle.

Supportive services—financial aid. Consultation with instructors is available by written correspondence. Approved for benefits by Veterans Administration.

MORAINE VALLEY COMMUNITY COLLEGE
Subdivision for Non-Traditional Learning

Palos Hills, Illinois   60465
(312) 974-4300

Philosophy and goals. The programs are designed for working adults and other students who want to "free up" their schedules.

Degrees and certificates offered. Associate of Arts, Associate of Science, and Associate of Applied Science degrees.

Accreditation. Accredited by the North Central Association of Colleges and Secondary Schools.

Academic calendar. Semester.

Residency—required contact with program. Contact with the program varies considerably depending upon the learning modes a student selects. All learning modes require some degree of contact; however, the emphasis is on flexible and accessible education.

Part-time enrollment. Part-time study is possible.

Costs. Residents of the district pay $12.00 per semester hour. Nonresidents are charged $50.00 per hour. A $15.00 fee is charged for each course for which credit might be granted through the assessment of prior knowledge process.

Admission requirements. Admission is open to all those possessing a high school diploma or its equivalent.

Assessment of prior learning. All credits earned at other accredited colleges are transferable without restriction. Results of standardized testing procedures such as CLEP and USAFI programs are applicable toward meeting degree requirements.

Students may seek evaluation of prior knowledge, which may involve written tests, oral examinations, evaluation of portfolios, or demonstrations.

Curriculum—learning options. a. Autotorial: students work at their own pace, using programmed books, cassettes, videotapes, and films. At least six of ten scheduled evening or Saturday morning sessions are required. Individual conferences are held.
b. Flexible schedule: one evening or Saturday morning class must be attended each week, while other course requirements are completed on one's own. The courses involve frequent interaction with instructors and other students.
c. Individualized instruction: courses are suited to those with irregular schedules. Students work at their own pace and are required to attend two of four scheduled evening or Saturday seminars. Extra credit may be earned for outside projects.

Other options include newspaper courses; TV courses; travel, mostly to foreign countries and interdisciplinary in nature; weekend classes; self-paced tutorials in industrial engineering technology; and homebound courses designed for people who cannot easily leave their homes. Details can be obtained from the Associate Dean for Non-Traditional Learning.

Degree requirements. Credits earned in the courses apply toward a necessary 62 hours for the associate's degree.

Supportive services—financial aid. All students in the program have access to a staff of professional counselors. Approved for participation in the NDSL, SEOG, CWS, BEOG, GSL, and veterans benefits. Information on other possible sources of financial aid is also available at the financial aid office.

MUNDELEIN COLLEGE
Weekend College
6363 North Sheridan Road
Chicago, Illinois   60660
(312) 262-8100

Philosophy and goals. Open, flexible time-space framework, traditional and nontraditional studies. Designed primarily for men and women of all ages who, as full-time workers, are often hindered by traditional school patterns.

Degrees and certificates offered. Bachelor of Arts.

Accreditation. Fully accredited by the North Central Association of Colleges and Secondary Schools.

Academic calendar. Trimester.

Residency—required contact with program. Students ordinarily spend five weekends per term on campus.

Part-time enrollment—pace. Students may proceed at their own pace.

Costs. Costs and fees are $75.00 per semester hour, $5.00 student activity fee.

Admission requirements. Admission is based on a comprehensive review of the applicant's academic record, work and/or community related experiences. Applicants are required to submit an application form; submit a nonrefundable $15.00 application fee; be interviewed by an admissions adviser; submit high school transcripts, score reports of either the SAT or ACT aptitude test, official CLEP reports, and college transcripts, if appropriate.

Assessment of prior learning. Credits from accredited institutions are transferable. Further information is available from the director of Weekend College.

Curriculum—learning options. The program utilizes traditional course work, internship, independent study, work experience as learning modes. Curriculum divided into four broad, interdisciplinary areas of concentration: management; community studies (social sciences, natural sciences, education psychology, history, and home economics); English/communications; and personal universe (arts and humanities). In addition, already-established alternatives are available: topical major, liberal studies major, contractual college degree, and cooperative education/internships. Other majors may be offered upon sufficient

student demand.

Degree requirements. A minimum of 120 semester hours, including 30 hours at Mundelein, is necessary. Fifteen courses are required for a major in one of the four areas of concentration described above, plus ten other courses: strategies for learning (a special course designed for students returning to college) and three courses in each of the three other areas of concentration.

Supportive services—financial aid. The principal source of support is the student's adviser. Financial assistance is available to students through major state and federal programs, including BEOG, SEOG, NDSL, CWS, and GSL.

NORTHEASTERN ILLINOIS UNIVERSITY
University Without Walls
5500 N. Saint Louis Avenue
Chicago, Illinois   60625
(312) 583-4050

Philosophy and goals. A competency-based, alternative method of learning requiring strong motivation, self-direction, maturity, self-sufficiency, and clear academic goals on the part of the student. UNI-UWW allows geographical flexibility, curricular individuality, and chronological latitude. Graduation is based upon demonstrated competence, not credit hours.

Degrees and certificates offered. Bachelor of Arts or Bachelor of Science degree.

Accreditation. Fully accredited by the North Central Association of Schools and Colleges.

Academic calendar. Trimesters of sixteen weeks, beginning in May, September, and January.

Residency—required contact with program. A limited amount of contact is required with the program. Contact is required through the admissions and orientation/introductory process.

Part-time enrollment—pace. Study is self-paced, but students are encouraged to register for consecutive trimesters because this facilitates advisement, encourages interrelated learning, combines academic and experiential resources, and provides for documentation of learning.

Costs. Current tuition and fees are $289.00 per trimester for Illinois residents; and $801.00 per trimester for out-of-state residents.

Admission requirements. Selection of students for the program rests with the UNI-UWW Advisory Committee and UNI professional staff. Although applications are accepted continuously, deadlines are: last Friday in February (May trimester); last Friday in June (September trimester); last Friday in October (January trimester).
    Criteria for admission depend heavily upon the Committee's and staff's assessment of the student's potential. Some major criteria for

admission are evidence of the applicant's need for a self-directed, nontraditional program; indication of motivation, perseverance, and maturity; identification of proposed area of concentration; previous applicable learning experiences; proposed competencies to be acquired during UWW; resources available off-campus; and UNI's ability to provide other resources.

Assessment of prior learning. No information available.

Curriculum—learning options. Students may study for the Bachelor of Arts or Bachelor of Science degree through individually designed programs employing a variety of learning options. Evaluation of learning is on the basis of a final written document.

Degree requirements. The degree is awarded upon successful completion of learning goals and objectives as mutually defined by student and adviser.

Supportive services—financial aid. Principal source of support is student's adviser. Contact financial aid office for information on financial aid.

ROOSEVELT UNIVERSITY
External Degree Program, College of Continuing Education
430 S. Michigan Avenue
Chicago, Illinois   60605
(312) 341-3500

Philosophy and goals. Designed especially for adults with job or family responsibilities that conflict with the regular schedules of classroom study, and for adults who cannot travel to the university, or who simply prefer independent study over classroom study.

Degrees and certificates offered. Bachelor of General Studies (B.G.S.).

Accreditation. Fully accredited by the North Central Association of Colleges and Secondary Schools.

Academic calendar. Semester.

Residency—required contact with program. The program is designed to minimize campus contact. The pro-seminar and the senior seminars are available externally for all students.

Part-time enrollment—pace. Students proceed at their own pace.

Costs.		
Undergraduate tuition per semester hour		$ 82.00
Pro-seminar (6 semester hours)		492.00
Integrating seminar (6 semester hours)		492.00
Internship		246.00

Application fee	15.00
Admission fee	30.00
Proficiency examination fee/credit hour	10.00

Admission requirements. High school diploma or GED certificate, and passing of Roosevelt University entrance examination. Students with at least 12 semester hours of satisfactory (C-level) work at another accredited college or university usually need not take the entrance examination. Applicants must be 25 years or older.

Assessment of prior learning. The university accepts transfer credits for courses with grades of D for general education course requirements in all programs, except in the Bachelor of General Studies Alternate Program, for which grades of C or better are required in the major.

Credit toward graduation may be granted for the completion, with grades 3, 4, or 5, of the College Entrance Examination Board Advanced Placement Examinations, and for successful completion of one or more CLEP examinations. However, credit will be awarded only after the student completes 12 semester hours with a cumulative grade point average of 2.0 at Roosevelt University. Transfer CLEP credit from an accredited college or university will be honored. Proficiency examinations are also available.

Curriculum—learning options. Students may register for courses at any time, and at their own pace, taking up to a year to complete a course or finishing within weeks through concentrated work. Courses are the same as those offered in the classroom but with study guides prepared by the instructor to replace the class work. External courses are divided into learning units or modules.

The pro-seminar is the introductory course in the B.G.S. sequence which is required of all students entering the program. It carries 6 semester hours of credit and has as its objectives reorientation to the academic world, reestablishment of academic skills, and evaluation of prior academic achievement. The interdisciplinary senior seminars in the social sciences, natural sciences, and humanities are meant to be more broadly educative, and each carries 6 semester hours of credit. The internship in urban experience (BGS 399), a 3-semester-hour course, stresses the notion of self-confrontation.

Degree requirements. Requirements for the Bachelor of General Studies degree are 120 credit hours from the pro-seminar; further introductory work in the disciplines and academic skills; a concentration; the senior seminars or advanced seminars in the social sciences, natural sciences, and humanities; the internship in urban experience.

Candidates for the B.G.S. must also meet the university's writing requirement.

Supportive services—financial aid. The principal source of support is the student's adviser. Assistance is available to students through all major state and federal programs, including BEOG, SEOG, NDSL, and CWS.

INDIANA

ST. MARY-OF-THE-WOODS COLLEGE
Women's External Degree, Guerin Hall
St. Mary-of-the-Woods, Indiana   47876
(802) 535-4141

Philosophy and goals. Designed for adult women who have been unable to participate in traditional on-campus study because of family or professional obligations. The intention of the program is to enable the student to complete the bulk of her study at home and in her community.

Degrees and certificates offered. A.A., A.S., B.A., and B.S. Secretarial certificates are also available.

Accreditation. Fully accredited by the North Central Association of Colleges and Secondary Schools.

Academic calendar. Semester.

Residency—required contact with program. The WED student begins with a four-day residency for counseling and program design, and returns every six months, until the program is completed, for four days of evaluation of past work and planning for the coming semester. During independent study, the student contacts her faculty adviser every two weeks.

Part-time enrollment. Possible.

Costs. Tuition $47.00/credit hour
         Application fee   15.00

Admission requirements. Open to women 25 years of age and older with some college credit completed. However, women not meeting these requirements will be considered on an individual basis. In most cases admission is based primarily on college transcripts. Application forms should be requested from the Admissions Office.

Assessment of prior learning. Credits may be transferred from any accredited institution for courses in which the student has earned a minimum grade of C. Credits are also granted for CLEP general and subject exams, as well as advanced placement tests, and for correspondence courses. Credit may also be awarded for skills or knowledge attained through one's job, vocation, hobby, or other life experience.
   The college also will consider the award of the following credits: for secretaries certified (CPS) by the Institute for Certifying Secretaries, 28 semester hours; for registered nurses, 60 semester hours for the academic content of the R.N. diploma, in addition to transfer credits from other institutions; for licensed practical nurses, 25 semester hours; and for medical record personnel, 13 semester hours upon completion of the American Medical Record Association's correspondence course, or 36-40 semester hours upon completion of a hospital-based study program leading toward the RRA designation; for courses offered by the American Institute of Banking, the Institute of Financial Education, the Life Office Management Association, and the Insurance Institute of America. Veterans may receive credit for courses taken under the sponsorship of the military and/or business, industry, and government agencies according to the guidelines published by the American Council on Education.

Curriculum—learning options. First objective of program is to insure a liberal arts education, with a basic foundation in theory, criticism, and expression of ideas through humanistic, scientific, and artistic approaches. In addition to these areas, student may choose to complete degree requirements through a departmental major of a planned sequence of courses approved by the department; through a concentration consisting of a minimum of 20 hours in a given area, planned to give foundation and scope to the study; and through a specially designed plan of study. Studies are offered in art, business, creative writing, drama, English, French, geography, history, home economics, humanities, journalism, philosophy, political science, psychology, religion, religious education, social science, social work, sociology, and Spanish.

Degree requirements. Students must complete 60 semester hours of credits for the A.A. and A.S. degrees, and 120 semester hours of credits for the B.A. and B.S. through a combination of credits earned outside of the WED program and credits earned in association with the program. Fifteen semester hours of credit for the associate's degrees, and 30 semester hours of credit for the bachelor's degrees, must be earned from courses sponsored by the college.

Supportive services—financial aid. The student's advisers from the advisory committee and the faculty are the student's primary source of support from the college. The WED program is approved for benefits by the Veterans Administration. Contact financial aid office for information on other aid available.

SYSTEMWIDE OFFICE FOR THE SCHOOL OF CONTINUING STUDIES
External Degree Programs
1125 East 38th Street, Room 060
Bloomington, Indiana   47401
(812) 332-0211

Philosophy and goals. The External Degree Programs bring the resources of the Indiana University system to individuals who want to earn a college degree but who have been unable to begin or to complete their college education because of work schedules or domestic responsibilities.

Degrees and certificates offered. Associate of General Studies (A.G.S.), Bachelor of General Studies (B.G.S.). Special concentrations in labor studies are also available for both these degrees.

Accreditation. Fully accredited by the North Central Association of Colleges and Secondary Schools and the State Board of Higher Education.

Academic calendar. Semester—fall, spring, summer.

Residency—required contact with program. While most students attend some class sessions at one of the Indiana University campuses, it is entirely possible to obtain a degree through minimal contact with the program.

Part-time enrollment—pace. Courses are available to those individuals who are <u>unable</u> to be at a specific place at a specific time, to complete a course in a specific length of time, or to finish a degree in residence or on a full-time basis.

Costs. On-campus course fees are the prevailing fees at the campus on which the student enrolls, $23.00 per credit hour at most branches. Independent study course fees are similar.

Admission requirements. Open to all qualified high school graduates or individuals with the General Educational Development (GED) certificate. In the absence of these, adults over 21 years of age may be given provisional admission. After they have demonstrated their ability to pursue college-level course work by successfully completing 12 semester hours of credit, they may apply for admission as regular students.

Assessment of prior learning. A maximum of 50 hours of credit previously earned at Indiana University or other accredited institutions can be applied to the A.G.S. degree; a maximum of 100 hours of credit from Indiana University or 96 hours from other institutions with at least a C grade can be applied to the B.G.S. degree. In addition, credits may be awarded for correspondence courses; for self-acquired competencies; for military training and experience; and through departmental and non-departmental examinations.

Curriculum—learning options. Each degree program requires completion of course work in three major areas of learning: arts and humanities; science and mathematics; and social and behavioral sciences. These courses may be completed through a combination of independent study by correspondence, credit by examination through guided instruction, television courses, or on-campus classes. The number of hours in a single subject area is limited to 21 for the B.G.S. degree, except for the concentration in labor studies, which is 30 hours, and except for 27 hours toward any major or concentration in the School of Buisness. The number of hours in a single subject area is limited to 15 for the A.G.S. degree.

Degree requirements. For the associate's degree: 60 credit hours with a minimum of 12 semester hours taken within the Indiana University system; and a minimum of 10 semester hours taken after the student has been admitted to the School of Continuing Studies.

For the bachelor's degree: 120 credit hours with a minimum of 24 semester hours taken within the Indiana University system; a minimum of 20 semester hours taken after the student has been admitted to the School of Continuing Studies; and a minimum of 30 semester hours at the upper-division level.

Supportive services—financial aid. Counseling, a faculty adviser, and the directors of continuing studies on all Indiana University campuses are available to all students, as well as vocational counseling, reading and study skills programs, and special counseling programs.

Financial assistance may be available. Its availability will depend upon the student's needs and circumstances. Questions should be directed to the financial aid office on the campus on which the student is or will be enrolled.

Indiana University Campuses and Centers

Indiana University at Bloomington
James Hertling, Director of Continuing Studies
Owen Hall
Bloomington   47401
(812) 337-8995

Indiana University East
Howard C. Gongwer, Director of Continuing Studies
2325 North Chester Boulevard
Richmond   47375
(317) 966-8261

Indiana University-Purdue University at Fort Wayne
Clinton Butler, Director of External Degree Programs
2101 Coliseum Boulevard East
Fort Wayne   46805
(219) 482-5811

Indiana University-Purdue University at Indianapolis
Marjorie P. Leamnson, Director of Continuing Studies
1201 East 38th Street
Indianapolis   46205
(317) 264-4501

Indiana University at Kokomo
Larry G. McDougle, Director of Continuing Studies
2300 South Washington Street
Kokomo   46901
(317) 453-2271

Indiana University Northwest
Frank M. Parrish, Director of Continuing Studies
3400 Broadway
Gary   46408
(219) 980-6828

Indiana University at South Bend
James Ryan, Director of Continuing Studies
1825 Northside Boulevard
South Bend   46615
(219) 237-4261

Indiana University Southeast
John P. Briscoe, Director of Continuing Studies
4201 Grantline Road, Box 679
New Albany   47150
(812) 945-2306

Columbus Center of IUPUI
Dan Ebling, Coordinator
2080 Bakalar Drive
Columbus   47201
(812) 373-8266

IU Northwest Center
Division of Labor Studies
Building F, Room 122
3400 Broadway
Gary   46408
(219) 980-6825

IUSB Center

Division of Labor Studies
1825 Northside Boulevard
South Bend   46615
(219) 237-4469

IUPUI Center
Division of Labor Studies
114 Ball Residence
1232 West Michigan Street
Indianapolis   46202
(317) 264-3471

IFPW Center
Division of Labor Studies
TROM 5, Room 53
2101 Coliseum Boulevard East
Fort Wayne   46805

Indiana University at Bloomington
Division of Labor Studies
312 North Park
Bloomington   47401
(812) 337-9082

UNIVERSITY OF EVANSVILLE
College of Alternative Programs
P.O. Box 329
Evansville, Indiana   47702
(812) 479-2472

Philosophy and goals. The external studies program
is an alternative bachelor's program allowing the
student to work independently at an individually
designed degree program.

Degrees and certificates offered. Bachelor of Arts
and Bachelor of Science.

Accreditation. Accredited by North Central Association of Colleges and Schools.

Academic calendar. Students working independently
are not required to follow a quarter-system calendar
unless they choose to take a classroom course.

Residency—required contact with program. Students
are required to complete the Educational Planning
Workshop after acceptance. Students working
independently are working under the direction of
a faculty monitor and must earn a minimum of 36
hours of UE-sponsored learning credits, not
necessarily on campus.

Part-time enrollment—pace. The program allows
for self-paced learning.

Costs.	Admission fee	$15.00
	Intensive advising fee	60.00/quarter
	Evaluation of life learning	8.00/credit
	Departmental challenge exam fee	15.00
	Tuition (all courses/ projects)	39.00

Admission requirements. Applications for admission
are evaluated on the basis of demonstrated academic
ability and demonstrated ability to work independently.

Assessment of prior learning. Credit may be earned
through the assessment of life learning on the
job, in the community, at home. These assessments
are made after acceptance into the program and
after completion of the educational planning
workshop. Credits are based on the learning
demonstrated.

Also considered are transfer credits from
accredited institutions, military training, correspondence courses from other accredited institutions,
CLEP exams, and departmental challenge exams.

Curriculum—learning options. Credits are granted
upon satisfactory completion of external study
projects. These are sponsored learning experiences
designed by the student under the direction of a
member of the faculty. They may be designed,
where practical, to earn credit for a catalogued
course. Projects may also be designed to meet
student's individual needs. The University of
Evansville does not offer predesigned correspondence
courses.

Degree requirements. Students must earn a minimum
of 182 quarter hours of credit with an overall
grade point average of at least 2.00 (C). The
grade point average in the major must also be at
least 2.00. A minimum of 60 of the required 182
hours must consist of upper-division (junior/senior
level) credits and at least 36 of the 182 hours
must be for learning sponsored by the University
of Evansville.

The external studies program requires that 10
credit hours be earned in each of the following
divisions: written and spoken English; human
relations; a communications system other than
English (computer science, mathematics, Braille,
shorthand, foreign language, etc.); social science;
natural science; humanities; behavioral science.

For completion of a major 60 hours of credit
are required. The student must also complete 16
quarters in an area study chosen from one of the
general education areas that is not part of his
major. At least 4 of the 16 credits must be earned
through an external study project.

Supportive services—financial aid. Students are
assisted by a learning resource counselor, an
academic counselor, faculty, and community resource
people as needed. Contact financial aid office
for information on financial aid.

IOWA

UPPER IOWA UNIVERSITY
Coordinated Off-Campus Degree Program
Fayette, Iowa   52142
(319) 425-3311

Philosophy and goals. Designed to meet the educationa
needs of adults in professional or semi-professional
careers by offering them the opportunity to earn
a degree principally by studying at home and without
giving up their jobs.

Degrees and certificates offered. B.A. in public

administration or business administration.

Accreditation. Approved by the Department of Public Instruction in the State of Iowa and fully accredited by the North Central Association of Colleges and Secondary Schools.

Academic calendar. Semester.

Residency—required contact with program. Students entering the program with 60 or more semester hours of credit at grade C or better from accredited institutions are required to spend one two-week session on campus and complete 4 semester hours in their major field.

Students entering the program with less than 60 semester hours of credit at grade C or better from accredited institutions are required to attend one of the following: one four-week session (June or July); one three-week session (January); or two two-week sessions (June or July). Students must complete 4 semester hours in their major field and 3 semester hours of an elective during one of the above. Applicants residing in foreign countries should write for additional information regarding residence requirements.

Part-time enrollment. Possible. Most of the students are working adults attending on part-time basis.

Costs. Each course is offered as one complete block of instruction valued at 8 semester hours and called a module.

Application	$ 50.00
Module tuitions (8 semester hours	
at $55.00 per hour)	440.00
Book charge (per module)	40.00
Conversion fee (per module)	50.00
Reactivation fee	25.00
On-campus residency (per semester hour)	85.00
Graduation fee	20.00

Admission requirements. High school diploma or equivalent required. To apply students must submit the following: official transcripts from each secondary and postsecondary school attended; certificates from any workshops, seminars, in-service training or other formal training received outside of schools; scores on any examinations taken; and a complete résumé of life experiences.

Assessment of prior learning. Transfer credit from accredited college and university will be accepted at full value if grade is C or better. In cases where pass/fail grading is used, only the P grades transfer. All credits in quarter or semester-hour values will be converted into modules if they are curriculum-related.

Up to 32 semester hours (four modules) of CLEP examinations will be accepted.

Credit for curriculum-related daily work will be based upon time in service, supervisor's evaluation, job description, and relationship to curriculum.

Curriculum—learning options. Students in the public administration program study government, management, personnel administration, political

science and other topics related to public administration. Students in the business program study accounting, economics, management, finance, marketing, money and banking, labor relations, and decision-making.

Degree requirements. The following requirements must be completed in order to qualify for the bachelor's degree:
  a. Sufficient credit to amount to fifteen modules (120 semester hours), plus the residence requirement (4 or 7 semester hours).
  b. Completion of a minimum of four modules (32 semester hours) by directed off-campus study.
  c. An accumulated grade point average of no less than 2.0 and no less than 2.0 in one's major.
There are six required modules for each major area.

Supportive services—financial aid. Each student is assigned a professor who is the major source of support. The off-campus degree program is approved for BEOG and GSL, as well as veterans' benefits.

KANSAS

KANSAS STATE UNIVERSITY
Office of Non-Traditional Study
Umberger Hall
Manhattan, Kansas   66506
(913) 532-5686

Philosophy and goals. Oriented toward self-directed students who have clear educational objectives but have encountered obstacles—distance from educational resources, time losses in college attendance, institutionalization, the inflexibility of the regular academic schedule, job and family responsibilities—in meeting these goals.
At the same time, they require access to a broadened learning environment, a new kind of relationship with academic faculty and community resource persons from nonacademic settings.

Degrees and certificates offered. B.A. or B.S. in most KSU majors, and B.G.S. from Kansas State University.

Accreditation. Accredited by the North Central Association of Colleges and Schools, Commission on Institutions of Higher Education.

Academic calendar. Program operates year-round.

Residency—required contact with program. B.A. or B.S. candidates are required to take 30 credit hours of course work at KSU, although this requirement may be waived in individual cases. B.G.S. students have no residency requirements, but frequent contacts with the student's adviser are considered important.

Part-time enrollment—pace. Possible. Students

proceed at own pace.

Costs. Tuition: $18.00 per credit hour or credit hour equivalent. B.A. and B.S. programs generally require 120-126 credit hours; B.G.S. programs are more flexible.

Admission requirements. High school diplomas are not required. NTS candidates submit an application which includes biographical data, career objectives, and learning background, together with any previous college transcripts and military DD214 forms, if applicable. In addition, the application requires an explanation of reasons for the student not being able to pursue an education by conventional means. An independent study project proposal must also be submitted; this proposal should include a title, a discussion of the student's background in the field of study, reasons for interest, objectives of the project, resources for learning, methods of learning, goal of the project, a proposed study schedule, a listing of faculty and nonfaculty advisers or monitors the student will need for the study, criteria for evaluation of the project, and a proposed bibliography.

Decisions on admissions are made by the Committee of Overseers for Non-Traditional Study.

Assessment of prior learning. Credit is granted for previous college work, informal or nonsponsored learning, and by examination. KSU accepts credits from most accredited colleges and universities. For informal or nonsponsored learning, student develops documentation in consultation with the student adviser. Testing for credit includes CLEP, DANTES, and KSU examinations. KSU examinations are offered in business administration, chemistry, physical education, modern languages, speech, and English.

Curriculum—learning options. All NTS students work with an adviser and with faculty monitors. Programs are devised, "learning contracts" are drawn up in consultation with the adviser, and submitted to the Program Advisory Committee, which makes final determination on the advisability of individual programs. Students may pursue their studies by a variety of methods, including conventional course work, off-campus course work, the special "Telenet" program offered by a coalition of Kansas colleges and universities, television courses, correspondence courses, workshops, seminars, internships, job-related experiences, and independent study. In addition to traditional day courses, KSU offers classes at night, two- to three-week intersession courses, and three-week summer workshops.

Degree requirements. B.A./B.S. candidates fulfill regular KSU departmental degree requirements by a combination of traditional and nontraditional means worked out with the student adviser and the departmental adviser. A B.G.S. candidate must develop a program which involves both depth and breadth in an area of focus, three projects in two study categories not directly related to the area of focus (arts and letters; social sciences; or science and mathematics, technology, and agriculture), communication skills, both written

and oral, an ability to design and carry out independent study projects, and an original contribution to the area of focus. Readiness for graduation is judged by the Committee of Overseers, which generally requires that students submit a prospectus for graduation, which briefly outlines evidence of the above-mentioned requirements, six months in advance of application for graduation. The final determination is made on the basis of the student's portfolio, which contains transcripts, scores on standardized examinations, logs documenting learning from life experiences for academic credit, and copies of such products as position papers, tapes, films, research papers, and works of art, together with narrative transcripts summarizing studies and adviser and faculty monitor evaluations.

Supportive services—financial aid. The student adviser is the primary source of guidance. Kansas State University is approved for participation in major government financial aid programs.

LOUISIANA

UNION FOR EXPERIMENTING COLLEGES AND UNIVERSITIES
New Orleans Human Services Institute
2929 Tulane Avenue
New Orleans, Louisiana   70119
(504) 827-1595 or 1998

Philosophy and goals. To serve the educational goals of resourceful, imaginative and intellectually lively people who cannot, otherwise, have access to higher education; and to provide options for individualized, flexible degree programs.

Degrees and certificates offered. Bachelor of Arts or Bachelor of Science degree.

Accreditation. This institution is a formal candidate for accreditation by the North Central Association of Colleges and Secondary Schools.

Academic calendar. Students may enroll in the program at any time.

Residency—required contact with program. The program is designed to allow minimal contact. Students are expected to maintain a contracted amount of contact with their faculty advisers.

Part-time enrollment—pace. Students may proceed at their own pace.

Costs. Effective July 1, 1978:
      Tuition $2,600.00
      Activity fee, books, etc.   175.00

Admission requirements. A high school diploma or its equivalent is generally required although people of any age who feel they can benefit academically from the program are encouraged to apply.

Assessment of prior learning. Assessment of prior

learning is awarded in the form of advanced standing. Assessment is made with faculty assistance, through learning contracts, transcripts from collegiate and noncollegiate educational programs, letters of evaluation from professionals with whom student has worked, CLEP and CPE test results, artistic and scholarly products, publications and other evidences of prior learning.

Curriculum—learning options. Normally, students work on learning contracts with individual faculty or outside professionals. Where possible, these contracts incorporate use of the student's ongoing daily activities. A learning contract may include course attendance; however, learning contracts were designed to replace the course as the basic unit of student work. Tutor and student agree about what products must be submitted to enable the tutor to assess student achievement of educational objectives. Products can and have included written reports, short papers, annotated bibliographies, research papers, journals, art works, test results.

When the contract is completed, student/tutor prepares a summary of what was learned. The tutor reviews the summary and writes an evaluation, noting strengths, weaknesses, and especially the level of competence attained or demonstrated.

Degree requirements. Satisfactory contract work must be completed and prior learning documented. Specifically, UECU/NOHSI students are expected to develop competence in one field of endeavor, and have an informed sense of three general areas of human thought: the humanities, the social sciences and the natural sciences. The student's individualized degree program evolves within this framework. Student will be recommended for graduation after satisfactory completion of a final project.

Supportive services—financial aid. The program participates in all major federal financial aid programs, including BEOG, SEOG, NDSL, CWS and GSL.

MARYLAND

COLUMBIA UNION COLLEGE
External Degree Department
Flower Avenue
Takoma Park, Maryland   20012
(301) 270-9200

Philosophy and goals. This program is designed to serve the adult high school graduate who finds on-campus college attendance impossible or unsuited to his/her needs, but is able to work on a home study basis.

Degrees and certificates offered. A.A., B.A. in liberal arts.

Accreditation. Fully accredited by Middle States Association of Schools and Colleges.

Academic calendar. Program operates year-round on a standard semester system: fall, spring and

summer. Students may, however, apply and initiate studies at any time.

Residency—required contact with program. Students are not required to participate in classroom work at CUC.

Part-time enrollment—pace. The program is geared for the part-time student. There are no time constraints placed on the work.

Costs.   Tuition $ 50.00 per semester hour
Program entrance fee   200.00
Continuance fee   50.00 per year
Application fee   20.00
Credit by examination
   program   10.00 per exam
Tuition per credit hour
   gained by examination   10.00
     Tuition rates do not include the cost of study materials and shipping costs.

Admission requirements. A high school diploma or equivalent certificate required. Applicant must assemble all transcripts of high school work, showing total units, grades, test scores and date of graduation.

Assessment of prior learning. Standardized proficiency exams such as CLEP and APP are available to students. CUC-prepared challenge examinations may be taken for course credit. Waiver examination may be accepted in lieu of a requirement; however, it does not give course credit. A validation examination may be required for some transfer students.

Curriculum—learning options. The external B.A. degree does not require a major or minor field of concentration. The emphasis is on a liberal studies program that is both integrated and suited to the student's need. The plan of study is decided upon by the student and a faculty adviser from the course offerings of the college. Courses are graded on the letter grade system.

Degree requirements. For the B.A. degree, 128 semester hours are required; 64 hours are required for the A.A. degree. For the B.A. degree, course requirements are: English, 12 hours; speech, 3 hours; language, 6 hours; math and science, 12 hours; religion, 12 hours; fine arts, 3 hours; and health principles, 2 hours. Course requirements for the A.A. degree are as above with semester-hour requirements proportionately distributed. The remaining elective credits are chosen from the schools basic curriculum.

The last 45 hours before graduation with the B.A. degree and 30 hours for the A.A. degree must be taken under the direction of the college.

Each candidate for a degree is required, during the six months prior to expected day of graduation, to write a major paper on a specific topic; to produce a creative work in literature, science, or the arts, in consultation with the director of the External Degree Department; or to write a comprehensive examination.

Supportive services—financial aid. The director of the External Degree Department and an external degree counsellor are available to help students plan and carry out their study palns.

Columbia Union College is approved for participation in major government financial aid programs.

COMMUNITY COLLEGE OF BALTIMORE
Division of Continuing Education and Community Services
Independent Home Study Program
2901 Liberty Heights Avenue
Baltimore, Maryland 21215
(301) 396-0437

Philosophy and goals. Designed for students who are unable to attend classes for various reasons.

Degrees and certificates offered. Associate of Arts in General Education.

Accreditation. The college is fully accredited by the Middle States Association of Colleges and Secondary Schools.

Academic calendar. Semester.

Residency—required contact with program. No residency or on-campus attendance required.

Part-time enrollment—pace. Part-time enrollment is entirely possible and students may proceed at their own pace.

Costs. Per semester:

	Baltimore city residents	Maryland residents	Out-of-state & foreign residents
Full-time students tuition	$193.25	$373.25	$553.25
Part-time students tuition (per cr/hr)	18.00	36.00	54.00

Admission requirements. Admission to the college is open to all high school graduates or holders of high school equivalency certificates and other mature adults who desire post-high school education. Admission into a specific program is dependent upon meeting program's special requirements and availability of space. The college reserves the right to determine whether to admit persons having more than three semesters of college work.

Assessment of prior learning. No special provisions made for the assessment of prior learning. Standard policy regarding transfer credits. CLEP and other standardized tests accepted.

Curriculum—learning options. Student does necessary course work for a currently offered subject, under the direction of a faculty member, but does not use class attendance as one of the ways to implement learning. Program involves a project evolved by the student with a faculty member, presented to a committee for approval of the idea and implementation and the credits to be assigned. This project must be in a current subject area such as English, political science, drafting, etc., and is equivalent to one course.

Degree requirements. To qualify for the degree of Associate in Arts, the student must:
a. Complete at least 60 semester credits of work in addition to the requirement in physical education. less than 15 of these, including those of the last full semester prior to graduation, must have been earned at the Community College of Baltimore.
b. Earn a quality point average of 2.0 or more (C or better).
c. Every curriculum leading to the Associate in Arts degree must contain at least 24 credits in the area of general education and must be distributed among three education groups.

Supportive services—financial aid. Students have full access to all support services of the college. The institution maintains a full-time financial aid office and participates in most federal and state programs. The school is approved for veterans' benefits. Orientation programs for new students are held each semester.

URBAN REGIONAL LEARNING CENTER
University Without Walls
Harbor Campus, Room 501
Lombard at Market Place
Baltimore, Maryland 21202
(301) 752-0176

Philosophy and goals. Designed to provide flexible, off-campus education individually structured to the learning needs of the student, with special emphasis on the concerns of the minority community.

Degrees and certificates offered. Bachelor of Arts and Bachelor of Science of the Union for Experimenting Colleges and Universities (UECU).

Accreditation. The UECU is a candidate for accreditation with the Middle States Association of Colleges and Secondary schools.

Academic calendar. Quarter system.

Residency—required contact with program. Some degree of contact with the program is expected. Students are required to appear before the admissions committee, to attend an admissions workshop and an introductory colloquium.

Part-time enrollment—pace. Part-time study is generally not possible.

Costs. Tuition is $500.00 per quarter ($2,000.00 per year).

Admission requirements. Evidence of capacity for self-directed work; willingness to serve as adviser/resource person to other students in the program; interest in a minority group community as evidenced by proposed project outline; learning goals can be obtained best through an alternative educational model.

Prospective students can apply by mail, attend admissions workshop, core faculty interview, admissions committee interview.

Assessment of prior learning. Up to 60 percent of a student's degree can be earned through various types of learning done prior to enrollment.

Curriculum—learning options. The first formal activity for new students is the colloquium. Its purpose is to build a sense of community; to provide time together to share and exchange ideas, information, resources, etc., to evaluate proposed learning plan from committee of faculty, peers, and adjunct advisers.

From the colloquium, the student has identified other students and faculty as committee members. The other two members of his/her committee (adjunct advisers) may be community or college persons who can make a contribution to the student's learning.

Students design degree plans, the basic outline for which includes: goal, plan to reach goal, area of study, study plan, internship, major project (tentative outline).

Once the student and his/her committee agree on the degree plan and sign it, the student begins to implement it.

Each UWW student, as a degree requirement, is expected to develop a major project which addresses the programmatic focus of ameliorating societal ills as they are manifested in minority group communities. The project may take the form of a written report, proposal, film, book, mediated presentation, services, change strategies, or the traditional thesis.

Degree requirements. A degree will be awarded on the basis of the following criteria:
a. Significant contribution to a field of study with focus on ameliorating societal ills as they are manifested in minority communities.
b. Evidence of broad general knowledge.
c. Competence in communication skills.
d. Employment in field of study or acceptance into graduate school.
e. Recommendation by the Graduation Review Committee.

Supportive services—financial aid. The program adviser is the major source of guidance available from the program. Eligible veterans may receive benefits under the G.I. Bill. Students may apply for federal financial aid through the program.

MASSACHUSETTS

FRAMINGHAM STATE COLLEGE
Division of Continuing Education and Special Programs
Framingham, Massachusetts   01701
(617) 872-3501

Philosophy and goals. Nontraditional approach to education, designed to provide higher education for various segments of population who for one reason or other cannot enter a traditional program. Flexible in terms of admissions requirements, curriculum, delivery systems, ways of earning credit, and scheduling.

Degrees and certificates offered. B.A. in liberal studies from Framingham State College.

Accreditation. Accredited by the New England Association of Schools and Colleges, Commission on Institutions of Higher Education; the American Dietetic Association; and the National Council for Accreditation of Teacher Education.

Academic calendar. Program operates year-round.

Residency—required contact with program. Twenty-four semester hours of course work on campus; a two-week seminar during each of three summer sessions; six weekend seminars during each of two years; or by alternate arrangements approved by the student's advisory committee. In addition, students must appear for a one-hour interview prior to admission, and for a half-day session with the advisory committee once admitted. No frequency of contact with the advisory committee is specified.

Part-time enrollment. Possible.

Costs. Application fee	$ 10.00
Processing and advising fee	250.00
College equivalency credit fee	to be determined
Tuition fee	25.00/semester hour
Registration fee	10.00/semester
Library fee	5.00/semester
Core area competency fee	to be determined
Graduation fee	5.00

Admission requirements. Applicants must furnish evidence of either a high school diploma or equivalency certificate and will be scrutinized for maturity, a high degree of motivation, an ability to study independently, and wide-ranging interests. They must submit application forms and fees, a high school transcript and be interviewed by Assistant Dean of Continuing Education or one of his assistants.

Once accepted, a student submits complete transcripts of all formal education or training after high school, résumé forms concerning types of experience that may be assessed for credit, together with any supportive letters and documents requested, as well as assessment and advising fees.

Assessment of prior learning. Students may earn credit through employment experience, community service, military service, travel, college courses, independent study, correspondence courses, instruction by technology, noncredit educational experiences, and CLEP or other proficiency examinations. Up to 96 semester hours or college equivalency credits may be granted, with the following maximums: life experiences such as employment and community services—16; independent study—20; correspondence courses—20; instruction by technology—24; military service—8; noncredit educational experiences—16; and travel—16.

Curriculum—learning options. Individual study programs are devised by student in consultation with advisory committee. Required semester hours or college equivalency credits are 128 of which 76 must be distributed as follows: humanities, including at least 6 semester hours of communication skills—24; social sciences—24; natural sciences—20; and mathematics—8. The additional 52 credits may be earned either in liberal studies areas or in electives determined in consultation with advisory committee.

Degree requirements. Students must complete 128 semester hours or college equivalency credits with the distribution requirements described above; no more than 96 may be earned by examination only. In addition, the student must successfully complete a Core Area Competence demonstration in each of the four liberal studies areas: humanities, social sciences, natural sciences and mathematics.

Supportive services—financial aid. The student's advisory committee is the main source of advisement and consultation. Framingham State College is approved for participation in major government financial aid programs including BEOG, SEOG, NDSL, CWS, GSL and VA benefits.

UNIVERSITY OF MASSACHUSETTS
The University Without Walls
Wysocki House
Amherst, Massachusetts   01002
(413) 545-0844

Philosophy and goals. UWW students are adults with a broad range of life experiences whose job and/or family responsibilities or other life circumstances make full-time classroom attendance impossible. They seek the advantage of combining practical experience in their chosen field with exposure to theoretical knowledge through independent study and classroom work.

Degrees and certificates offered. Bachelor of Arts and Bachelor of Sciences from the university through the UWW with individual concentration (major area of concentration) noted.

Accreditation. Fully accredited by the New England Association of Schools and Colleges.

Academic calendar. Standard semester system. Entrance is based on fall and spring semesters.

Residency—required contact with program. Most students find it necessary to be on campus at least three to four times per semester. Frequency of contact between program adviser and student individually negotiated.

Part-time enrollment—pace. No minimum or maximum length of time given. Students are expected to take full-time loads each semester (12 or more credits) but may take a reduced load or become inactive for one or more semesters.

Costs. UWW students pay regular University of Massachusetts tuition, which, for spring semester 1977, was $184.00 for Massachusetts residents (minimum one year's residence) and $775.00 for nonresidents. In addition, UWW students living forty or more miles from Amherst or those who take two or fewer regular classroom courses during any semester need only pay off-campus fees, currently $36.00 per semester. Those not eligible pay approximately $190.00 in fees per semester. In either case, these fees are in addition to tuitio

Admission requirements. Application to the program consists of: attendance at information session, where application forms will be available; UMass/UWW application; at least one letter of recommendation; transcripts from high school if fewer than 9 previous college credits, or from all colleges attended if 9 or more previous college credits.
   Completed applications due October 15 for spring entrance and April 1 for fall entrance.

Assessment of prior learning. Credits may be granted for such learning. Students prepare portfolios which identify and analyze learning derived from experience, rather than simply describi the experience itself. Portfolios are evaluated by appropriate faculty and outside experts, who recommend an award of academic credits.

Curriculum—learning options. Learning options available to UWW students include: regular classroom courses at UMass/Amherst, UMass/Boston, any of the five colleges and universities in the Amherst area, and/or any other accredited college or university; UWW classroom courses, independent studies, practica, internships, CLEP, challenge, equivalency exams, prior learning.

Degree requirements. Degree requirements include 120 credits, with a 2.0 cumulative grade point average (C) and university core requirements. These 120 credits must include 45 residency credits (credits earned through UMass, including prior learning), and 15 graded credits.
   Core requirements: are designed to provide students with an introduction to major areas of lear ing and consist of two courses in rhetoric (English) composition), three courses in the humanities, three courses in the social sciences and three courses in either the natural sciences or mathematic for a total of eleven courses.
   UWW program requirements: Student needs to draw up a statement of overall educational goals, called the degree plan, which defines the area of concentration and outlines the learning experiences which will allow the student to fulfill these goals. Each semester, student files a semester study program, which lists the learning experiences planned for that semester and explains how these fit into overall objectives. A finalized version of the degree plan, along with a semester study program, completes the student's UWW program requirements.
   Area of concentration: may be broader in scope than a traditional major (e.g., movement

therapy) or more narrow (e.g., adolescent psychology). Developed by the student and faculty sponsor.

Supportive services—financial aid. UWW students have the same eligibility for financial aid from the university as any other students: BEOG, SEOG, NDSL, CWS, GSL and VA benefits.

MICHIGAN

CENTRAL MICHIGAN UNIVERSITY
Institute for Personal and Career Development
Mount Pleasant, Michigan 48859
(517) 774-3865

Philosophy and goals. To provide higher educational opportunities for a new clientele—mature adults who are prohibited from pursuing traditional educational opportunities because of personal or professional barriers. A comprehensive national education system, it maintains program centers located throughout the country, where instruction and advising services may be obtained.

Degrees and certificates offered. At the under-graduate level, bachelor's degrees are offered in management and supervision, community development, liberal studies, and individualized studies. At the graduate level, master's degrees are offered in management and supervision, community leadership, and education.

Accreditation. Central Michigan University is accredited at the doctoral-degree level by the North Central Association of Colleges and Schools. This accreditation includes baccalaureate, master's and specialist degree programs and the Doctor of Psychology degree offered on the Mt. Pleasant campus as well as bachelor's and master's degrees offered through the Institute for Personal and Career Development.

Academic calendar. Semester.

Residency—required contact with program. All pro-grams are individualized and may be completed at the student's own rate of speed.

Part-time enrollment. No minimum campus time.

Costs. Tuition for undergraduate instruction through the institute is $60.00 per credit hour, for graduate instruction $76.00 per credit hour.

Admission requirements. Undergraduate: evidence of a high school diploma or successful completion of the GED examination.
   Graduate: evidence of a baccalaureate degree or its equivalent from an approved institution.
   Both: submit to the regional program center the completed Application form, $15.00 application fee, and two copies of transcripts of all high school (undergraduate applicants only) and college work.

Assessment of prior learning. Experiential learning: after appropriate evaluation, academic credit may be given for acquired skills or knowledge—up to 60 semester hours of undergraduate credit and up to 10 semester hours of graduate credit. Experiential learning credit is entered on the student's record after successful completion of 5 semester hours of residence credit with CMU. Experiential learning credits will not fulfill CMU residency requirements.
   Credit by examination: available to any student who has no transferable credit or advanced course work in the area to be examined. (CLEP is for undergraduates only.)
   Undergraduate transfer credit: up to 94 semester hours from approved schools may be applied toward a degree. Credit for military educational experience is available when documented. Evaluation will take place only after all transcripts and documentation have been received.
   Graduate transfer credit: student must submit a graduate transfer credit request form signed by adviser. Up to 15 semester hours of credit from accredited schools may be applied (6 semester hours from a previously earned master's degree may be applied when appropriate). Transfer credit must have been earned with a grade of **B** or better and within seven years or less of date of application. No credits used to satisfy requirements for an undergraduate degree are eligible.

Curriculum—learning options. Classes and seminars: courses are offered on campus, through the institute and through the School of Continuing Education and Community Services. All courses taken through CMU, whether on or off campus, meet CMU residency requirements.
   Independent study: courses available for undergraduates and graduates wishing to pursue a special area of interest. Options include directed readings, research, work-study programs, and intern-ships.
   Learning packages: self-paced, individualized instruction employing a variety of print and nonprint media may be used to supplement traditional study.
   Correspondence study: available through the CMU School of Continuing Education and Community Services at the undergraduate level only.
   Planned experience: undergraduates enrolled in individualized degree programs may earn up to 30 semester hours of self-directed learning credit. No more than 15 hours of credit may be earned for one planned experience. Student and adviser determine objectives, method, and evaluation of the experience. Self-directed learning resources include in-service training, professional workshops, and community resources.

Degree requirements. Undergraduate: a minimum of 124 semester hours of credit (of which 40 hours must be at the 300-level or above) earned with a cumulative grade point average of 2.00 (C). A minimum of 30 semester hours of credit earned from CMU and the completion of all courses required by the program plan.
   Graduate: a minimum of 30 semester hours of credit earned with a cumulative grade point average of 3.00 (B). A minimum of 15 semester hours of credit earned from CMU. Completion of all courses

required by the program plan.

Supportive services—financial aid. Students may register for and attend classes and may obtain most student support services on site.

Library resources available to students. A WATS line provides free direct access to the CMU library for institute students in the continental United States except Michigan, on-site libraries of core materials serve students in selected areas, and cooperative arrangements with local libraries have been established. Institute also provides an extensive program of academic advising.

Institute programs have been approved for VA benefits. Contact financial aid office for information on other available aid.

NORTHWOOD INSTITUTE
3225 Cook Road
Midland, Michigan   48640
(517) 631-1600

Philosophy and goals. External degree program is an off-campus program aimed at highly motivated individuals with specific career goals who cannot attend classes on campus. Permits student to bypass course work for which there is equivalency in one's background.

Degrees and certificates offered. Associate's degree programs available include accounting, advertising, automotive marketing, automotive replacement management, business management, executive secretarial fashion merchandising, hotel and restaurant management, interior marketing and merchandising, liberal arts, and retail merchandising. The Bachelor of Business Administration degree is the four-year degree, with majors in management or accounting.

Accreditation. Fully accredited by the North Central Association of Colleges and Schools.

Academic calendar. Trimester enrollment at any time during the academic year.

Residency—required contact with program. Attendance at two three-day seminars is required of B.B.A. graduates. B.B.A. graduates also take an oral comprehensive examination at the end of the program with an examining panel at a prearranged time and location.

Part-time enrollment—pace. Students may enroll for part-time courses even if they do not intend to pursue degrees.

Costs. Application for admissions fee $ 15.00
Work-life evaluation and counseling fee   200.00
Project course fee   45.00
  Project courses are in the nature   (per course)
  of projects directly tied to a
  person's on-the-job goal. Final
  form is a 15- to 30-page written
  report.
Comprehensive exam fee   45.00
  Comprehensive examinations are   (per course)

of several types.
On-campus seminars   50.00
                            (per credit hour)
Thesis project   100.00
Oral comprehensive examination fee   200.00
Graduation fee   25.00

Admission requirements. Application form and non-refundable $15.00 application fee. Applicants must have high school diploma or its equivalent.

Assessment of prior learning. A person's work-life experiences are evaluated in terms of required and elective courses for a specific degree program. Students must develop a statement on how the North-wood degree fits into their overall plan. Documenta-tion of work-life experience is then sent to Northwood for advanced standing evaluation: record of all post-high school work; statement of informal education and training such as company seminars or trade association groups; certification by employer of all work experience; an autobiography; etc. CLEP examinations also accepted, in addition to credits for special examinations designed by instit (see below).

Curriculum—learning options. Comprehensive examinations: special open-book comprehensive examinations are available for many courses. Students research answers to highly structured topics, questions, exercises, which guarantee comprehension of the subject matter if satisfactori executed. Suggested references are provided, and students submit completed material, with a payment of $45.00 for entire course, for evaluation by a professor. There is no time limit in this method and payment is not due until course is completed.

For Accounting 101, 102, 103: Northwood provides guidance in preparing for its comprehensiv accounting examinations held under supervision. Before examination date and supervision are arrange a fee of $45.00 is paid for each course.

Individual colleges have special programs, these are recognized when students get approval from Northwood in advance of testing date.

Project courses: may be arranged between students and their advisers for completion of courses. Project courses often relate to a person's employment and tie in with specific work-related areas. Final form is a 15- to 30-page written report.

Correspondence courses: consist of a series of lessons evaluated by a professor on a lesson-by-lesson basis. There is a 90-day time limit for these courses, and fees are reimbursable under the VA benefits program.

Guest student status: A student may enroll at another college and complete course work. A guest student form and prior approval by Northwood Institute are required. The only fee is that charged by the college at which the student is a guest.

Degree requirements. Seminars: attendance at two three-day seminars required. Dates, times, and locations are announced well in advance for proper planning. A project is completed after attendance at each seminar. Each seminar carries

4 hours of credit. Fees for the seminars are $50.00 per credit hour, payable upon enrollment for the seminar.

Thesis: people working toward the four-year B.B.A. degree are required to complete a thesis project of 6-quarter hours of credit on a topic arranged by the advising professor before taking the comprehensive oral examination.

Comprehensive oral examination: required to be taken on-campus before a panel as a last step in the program. The examination will last for several hours and be based on questions provided to the student in advance.

Quarter-hour degree requirements: A minimum of 90 quarter-hours is required for an associate's degree. Each curriculum has a prescribed number of required courses and electives. A minimum of 180 quarter-hours is required for the Bachelor of Business Administration degree. A management or accounting major (36-quarter hours) is required for the B.B.A. To be awarded both the associate's and bachelor's degrees, an individual must have a grade point average of 2.0.

Supportive services—financial aid. VA benefits: the on-campus seminars are approved for VA benefits. The comprehensive examinations and project courses do not fall within VA guidelines for reimbursement. Traditional correspondence courses of a lesson-by-lesson approach are available at $50.00 per credit hour and are VA reimbursable at 90 percent of cost.

Additional information. NI has campuses at Midland, Michigan; West Baden, Indiana; and Cedar Hill, Texas.

SIENA HEIGHTS COLLEGE
External Degree Program
21700 Northwestern Highway, Suite 1190
Southfield, Michigan 48075
(313) 569-6490

Philosophy and goals. Aimed primarily at the working adult student. Typically, provisions may be made for accepting transfer credits, gaining credit by competency testing and evaluating prior learning experience.

Degrees and certificates offered. A.A., B.A., and B.S., Siena Heights College.

Accreditation. The college is fully accredited by the North Central Association.

Academic calendar. Applications may be made at any time during the school year and course work may be initiated upon admission to the program.

Residency—required contact with program. A minimum of 18 semester hour credits of course work must be completed at the college. Provisions are made for students to attend weekend meetings if necessary.

Part-time enrollment—pace. Depending upon the awarding of credits based upon prior learning experience or competency testing, the program should be completed by most students in twelve to eighteen months.

Costs. Tuition, per semester hour $40.00
for credit granted for prior learning,
   per semester hour   25.00
Application fee, nonrefundable   15.00
Books, per course   25.00
Correspondence fee, one-time,
   nonrefundable   25.00
Assessment fee   50.00
Graduation fee   30.00

Admission requirements. Students may be accepted on a probationary basis if their previous college grade point average is below 2.0. If admitted on this basis, students may be required by the college to take more than 18 semester hours at the Southfield campus. The applicant is responsible for arranging to have all transcripts and test scores sent to the college.

Assessment of prior learning. Students may receive academic credit for prior learning through past work, military service, volunteer activity, or other experiences. CLEP general examinations also accepted.

Curriculum—learning options. Traditional classroom teaching, credit by examination, independent study, or correspondence. The pro-seminar is an interdisciplinary course for all external degree students at the outset of the program. Course includes academic planning, competency testing, and exploration of learning alternatives. Students who cannot attend classes at the external degree center can elect the independent study option, working with faculty members to design course guidelines and assignments.

Degree requirements. Credit of 120 semester hours needed, including a minimum of 18 semester hours at the SHC campus. Students must pass competency examinations in reading, writing and math at college level, and must successfully complete a senior project and maintain a 2.0 grade point average.

Supportive services—financial aid. A full staff to help students with questions concerning admission, course plan, financial aid, and accomodations is available. Michigan residents may qualify for State of Michigan educational benefits. Family reduction rates are extended to families having two or more full-time students at SHC.

WAYNE STATE UNIVERSITY
Bachelor of General Studies Degree Program
University Studies/Weekend College Program
Criminal Justice Building
Detroit, Michigan 48202
(313) 577-0832

Philosophy and goals. Committed to meeting the intellectual interests and academic needs of adults in nontraditional ways, with a curriculum that is relevant and instructional methods that are flexible. Program is designed to accommodate educational backgrounds of adults which may differ from typical recent high school graduates.

Degrees and certificates offered. Bachelor of General Studies degree.

Accreditation. Fully accredited by the North Central Association of Colleges and Secondary Schools.

Academic calendar. Quarters.

Residency—required contact with program. Designed to minimize traditional contact with the program; however, a degree of flexibly scheduled contact is required. While some of the prescribed curriculum can be obtained through TV courses, students must participate in once-a-week workshops, held at seventy locations throughout southeast Michigan, and weekend conferences, held on the main campus twice a quarter.

Part-time enrollment—pace. Most students take a full course load of three courses (twelve credits) during each quarter, but those unable to do so may take fewer courses per quarter, depending on their individual time requirements.

Costs.

Credit Hours	Freshman/Sophomore	Junior/Senior
4	$130.00	$143.00
8	228.00	249.00
12	326.00	355.00

Admission requirements. High school diploma or GED certificate. Credits are transferable from other institutions. Holders of associate's degrees from community colleges may earn their bachelor's degree in two years.

Assessment of prior learning. Credit for courses taken at community colleges and other institutions of higher education may be transferred to the program provided the student has been accepted as a matriculated student in the college; and the grades for these courses have been satisfactory. A maximum of 96 quarter credits (64 semester credits) may be transferred from a community college. A maximum of 120 credit hours may be transferred from a four-year college. In addition, elective credit will be granted for successful completion of CLEP tests and police academy training or military base training.
    Special examination: upon recommendation of department chairman and with written approval of appropriate college or school office, student may earn credit in a course offered by a department without enrolling in course but by passing a special examination; not more than 24 credits in any one subject may be earned in this way; not more than 48 credits may be included in the minimum credits required for graduation; credit will be recorded with grade but will not be considered in computing honor point average; will not be considered residence credit. To be eligible to earn credit by examination, a student must have been regularly admitted or have attended with guest status, have enrolled for one quarter, and have completed at least one course.

Curriculum—learning options. The Weekend College Program employs a combination of techniques to carry "classroom" instruction to students:

television courses, once-a-week workshops, and weekend conferences. Television courses are broadcast over local TV stations during early morning hours, early evening hours, and repeated on weekends. Workshops (small discussion groups of approximately twenty students) meet once a week with an instructor. Weekend conferences are scheduled for two weekends per quarter. Most are held on campus, but occasionally some are held at other locations as needed. For a full load of 12 credits a quarter, the student takes simultaneously one 4-credit course in each of the three delivery techniques listed above. The basic curriculum is divided into three areas:
Lower Division   108 quarter credit hours
    Science and technology, social studies, urban humanities.
Electives   36 quarter credit hours
Upper Division   36 quarter credit hours
    Theory and method, senior seminar, project or major essay.

Degree requirements. Candidates for the BGS degree must complete 180 quarter credit hours with a 2.0 cumulative honor point average, including 24 credits in theory and method courses and 12 credits in the senior seminar, during which each student must prepare an essay or project to fulfill the degree requirement. In addition, students must complete one team-taught workshop in one of the lower-division sequences, during which members of the program's language arts teach with other faculty in designated workshops to improve student writing.

Supportive services—financial aid. Special tutoring in reading, writing, and math skills is available to all students and can be arranged during the day or evenings.
    Financial assistance is available on a limited basis if a student and his family are unable to meet their educational expenses. Basic types of aid include scholarships, grants, loans, work-study employment, and a newly funded scholarship for adult women who demonstrate financial need. The program is approved for VA benefits.

MINNESOTA

BEMIDJI STATE UNIVERSITY
External Studies Program
Bemidji, Minnesota   56601
(218) 755-2000

Philosophy and goals. To serve adults unable to participate in traditional on-campus programs; to provide a flexible program to meet individual needs, time, manner and place of study; to incorporate previously attained skills and training into the academic program; and to provide opportunity to achieve a college degree.

Degrees and certificates offered. Associate's degree in criminal justice and community service; B.S. degrees in criminal justice, community service, history, geography, English, vocational education, and industrial technology; B.A. degree in history, political science, geography, sociology, English and humanities.

Accreditation. Accredited by the North Central Association of Schools and Colleges.

Academic calendar. Program operates year-round, with continuous registration throughout the year.

Residency—required contact with program. There is no required amount of campus contact.

Part-time enrollment—pace. Part-time study is possible.

Costs. Application fee $10.00
Tuition 21.15 per quarter-hour (out of state)
10.65 per quarter-hour (in state)
Transfer fee 1.00 per quarter-hour for all work transfered from professional schools
2.00 per quarter-hour for transfer of work experience credit

All fees are subject to change.

Admission requirements. A high school diploma or its equivalent is required for admission. Programs in vocational education and industrial technology are generally restricted to Minnesota residents.

Assessment of prior learning. Credit for prior learning is awarded on the basis of a conference with program faculty who assess documented evidence of learning. Such documentation includes evaluations from work supervisors, job descriptions, content outlines of courses taken, reports written, etc.

Students must complete a minimum of 45 quarter-hours while enrolled in the external studies program.

Curriculum—learning options. There are three basic learning options. These are: regular courses offered through Bemidji University, extension courses offered throughout the state, and off-campus independent study. Off-campus independent study which is done in field work situations is assessed as it equates with learning done in regular Bemidji courses.

Courses are available in subjects listed under "Degrees and certificates offered," as well as in general education and general elective areas.

Degree requirements. One hundred and eighty quarter-hours of credit are required for the B.A. degree; 196 for the B.S.; and 96 for the A.A. All degree programs include a major concentration, a general education concentration and general electives.

Supportive services—financial aid. Faculty advisers from each major are the main source of support for students. Additional counseling is available as needed.

Students in the external studies program are eligible for financial aid programs administered by the Bemidji financial aid office: BEOG, SEOG, NDSL, CWS, GSL, Law Enforcement Education grants, state-sponsored financial aid programs, financial aid offered by the school itself. The school is also approved for VA benefits.

METROPOLITAN STATE UNIVERSITY
Seventh and Robert Streets
Saint Paul, Minnesota 55101
(612) 296-3875

Philosophy and goals. An upper division institution designed expressly to serve adults in the Minneapolis-St. Paul metropolitan area whose needs were not being met by other postsecondary institutions. Experimental in its approach, it has avoided replicating existing educational opportunities, and has focused on alternative approaches to educating adults. Program is student-centered, highly individualized and competence-based.
Degrees and certificates offered. Bachelor of Arts degree.

Accreditation. MSU was fully accredited in 1975 by the North Central Association of Schools and Colleges.

Academic calendar. The academic calendar at MSU is divided into four three-month quarters, beginning July 1, October 1, January 1, and April 1.

Residency—required contact with program. Students must maintain close communication with university as well as sustain a very high level of motivation and self-direction. Students far from the Twin Cities often find it difficult to complete a program without the stimulus of resident faculty and group activities.

Part-time enrollment—pace. Part-time enrollment is possible and students proceed at their own pace.

Costs. Application fee $10.00
Basic quarterly tuition (BQT) 30.00
MSU-sponsored learning activities:
Fees for the following types of learning activities include the cost of instruction and the cost of assessment.
  a. Individualized educational planning course (IEPC) 46.00
  b. Group learning opportunity (GLO) 46.00
  c. Independent study 46.00
  d. Internship 46.00
Non-MSU sponsored learning activities:
Fees for the following activities include the cost of MSU assessment only. The student pays cost of instruction directly to the sponsoring institution or individual.
  e. Assessment of prior learning 35.00/competence
  f. Assessment of other learning 35.00/competence
  g. Recording of other institution learning 7.00/competence
Late fee (GLO registration only) 10.00
Fees listed here are for Minnesota residents who have been officially admitted to the university.

Fees for nonresidents and for special enrollment students are available by calling the Office of Admissions at (612) 296-4465.

Admission requirements. Students must have either an Associate of Arts degree, 88 quarter credit hours or 60 semester hours in an undergraduate program at a college or university, with a minimum grade point average of 2.0 or the equivalent of 80 quarter credit hours in postsecondary programs in an institution authorized to offer such training.

For those unable to fulfill the above requirements but who believe they have the equivalent of two years of college study gained through life experience, there are ongoing admissions workshops. Successful completion of the workshop process qualifies students for admission to MSU as a junior.

Assessment of prior learning. MSU assesses life experience through the admissions workshops and by accepting current competencies toward the degree completion requirements.

Curriculum—learning options. Following admission, students must enroll in an Individualized Educational Planning Course (IEPC) which is designed to assist them to (a) understand university policies, including assessment policies and practices; (b) learn the principles of self-directed, independent study; (c) identify their current competencies and their learning needs; and (d) design their upper-division degree plans.

The degree plan specifies the competencies the student wants included in upper-division program, past and future. Plan also specifies the learning strategies used to attain prior and future competencies; the techniques that will be employed to assess the competencies; and the names and qualifications of the expert judges who will evaluate the competencies.

Once IEPC is successfully completed, student is accepted as a candidate for the B.A. degree. Then student receives a faculty adviser and begins to implement the degree plan. Students are encouraged to use community-based learning activities as well as those sponsored by the university. Student must provide documentation in support of each of the competencies in the degree plan which must meet the university's standards.

Degree requirements. When the student has successfully demonstrated attainment of each of the competencies listed in the degree plan, he or she is ready for graduation.

Supportive services—financial aid. Students receive faculty advisers with whom they maintain frequent contact.

Metropolitan State University makes use of federal, state and private funds to assist students. BEOG, SEOG, NDSL, CWS, as well as federally insured student loans, Minnesota state student loans, and the Law Enforcement Program. Federal veterans' benefits also are available for eligible students. Financial aid is extended only to students who have been accepted for admission to MSU and have paid the basic quarterly tuition.

UNIVERSITY OF MINNESOTA
Continuing Education and Extension Services
319 15th Avenue, Southeast, Room 120
Minneapolis, Minnesota   55455
(612) 373-3905

Philosophy and goals. Designed to allow adults to continue their education and receive credit for knowledge and skills gained in and outside the classroom.

Degrees and certificates offered. General College: Associate of Arts, Bachelor of Applied Studies, Bachelor of General Studies.

College of Liberal Arts: B.A. in Liberal Arts, B.S. in Liberal Arts.

Bachelor of Science in Business Administration (B.S.B.).

M.A. in English and speech communication.

Accreditation. The University of Minnesota is fully accredited by the North Central Association of Colleges and Secondary Schools.

Academic calendar. Quarters—summer, fall, winter, spring.

Residency—required contact with program. While most students have considerable on-campus contact, it is possible to put together a program which would minimize necessary contact. Registration can be completed by phone or mail.

Part-time enrollment—pace. Students may proceed at whatever pace they wish.

Costs. Undergraduate tuition ranges between $16.50 and $18.50 a credit and graduate tuition is $28.50 per credit.

Admission requirements. No specific admission requirements, just desire for growth.

Assessment of prior learning. CLEP is accepted; however, the various colleges use different criteria in accepting results. Transfer credits from other accredited institutions and, in some cases, technical courses completed at approved institutions are also accepted. In addition, credit may be earned through independent study, experience, or study at a noncollegiate institution, if subject is covered by a particular university course, by passing a special examination in that course. Students must be enrolled in extension program at time of examination and must obtain approval from the department offering the course. There is a $20.00 fee.

Curriculum—learning options. In addition to extension courses offered both at the main campus and several out-of-area locations, a great number of extension as well as degree credit courses are available as extension independent study. Extension students can also earn college credit for individuall designed study or research projects, which may be organized around job activities, involvement in the community or special interests. TV and radio courses are also available to students.

Degree requirements. Vary with individual degree being sought. In general, 180 credits are needed for bachelor level programs, 90 for associate. Most degree programs maintain some type of distribution requirements.

Supportive services—financial aid. The principal source of support is the student's adviser. Assistance is available through major state and federal programs including BEOG, SEOG, NDSL, CWS, and GSL. The extension division also maintains a full-time counseling office for prospective and current students.

UNIVERSITY OF MINNESOTA
University Without Walls, University College
201 Wesbrook Hall
Minneapolis, Minnesota   55455
(612) 373-3919

Philosophy and goals. Originated in 1971 as part of the effort to provide an alternative route to a baccalaureate degree, and seeks to combine university with other resources in order to build highly individualized and flexible student programs.

Degrees and certificates offered. UWW offers B.A. and B.S. degrees of University College.

Accreditation. The University of Minnesota is fully accredited by the North Central Association of Schools and Colleges. The UWW experiment (1971-78) was comprehensively evaluated by a University of Minnesota faculty committee and has been granted permanent program status as of 1978-79.

Academic calendar. Quarter system.

Residency—required contact with program. Periodic contact with the administrative offices is helpful. Students negotiate contact with program and faculty advisers. On-campus residency not required.

Part-time enrollment—pace. Part-time is not possible.

Costs. (In-state) tuition is $262.50 per quarter (subject to annual increases).

Admission requirements. The UWW staff provides preadmissions counseling for those applying to the program. Applications are reviewed by the UWW Admissions Committee to determine whether applicant has ability to conceptualize short-term learning goals, workable long-term learning goals, and whether UWW is able to help achieve applicant's learning objectives.
    Deadlines for applications are July 15 for fall quarter admission; October 15 for winter quarter admission; January 15 for spring quarter admission; April 15 for summer quarter admission.

Assessment of prior learning. Students must document and evaluate the learning derived from prior experience, which, if approved, becomes part of the baccalaureate degree program. Students are encouraged to combine prior and present learning

experiences and formal education into a coherent, thoughtful educational program.

Curriculum—learning options. UWW students must be able to design and carry out their own study projects. Study project proposals include: a. a statement of learning objectives; b. methods of study; c. learning resources; d. rationales for studies pursued; e. study time-tables; f. a statement of anticipated outcomes; g. criteria for the evaluation of learning. Students, with the assistance of their program advisers, develop a long-term degree plan at the beginning of their academic program. In addition, students take advantage of the course offerings of the University of Minnesota, including extension and independent study courses, and are encouraged to use prior experience as a mode of learning.

Degree requirements. Credits are not the basis for determining eligibility for a degree. Instead, students are required to develop evidence of learning in self-directed study skills; communication skills; academic achievement; variety of learning activities; scientific inquiry; artistic expression; major project.
    Students prepare graduation dossier and they initiate graduation process by requesting that a preliminary review committee be convened. After approval by the preliminary committee, a full graduation committee is formed. If full committee decides to approve student for graduation, it also recommends whether the B.S. or B.A. degree shall be awarded.
    Student must present at least 45 credits awarded by the University of Minnesota. Of the last 45 credits earned prior to the award of a degree, 30 credits must be awarded by the university.

Supportive services—financial aid. UWW students are eligible for financial aid programs on the same basis as other regular University of Minnesota students (BEOG, SEOG, NDSL, CWS, GSL). Qualified students are eligible for VA benefits and other tuition assistance programs.

Enrollment in program. 250 students.

MISSOURI

THE INTERNATIONAL UNIVERSITY
501 East Armour Boulevard
Kansas City, Missouri   64109
(816) 931-6374

Philosophy and goals. The purpose of TIU is to promote and facilitate higher education as fully as possible by overcoming the barriers of time, distance, national borders, and all other impediments to developing and enhancing the human mind.

Degrees and certificates offered. A.A., A.A.S., B.A., B.S., B.F.A., B.M., B.S.B.A., M.A., M.S., M.B.A., M.F.A., Ed.S., D.A., Ph.D.

Accreditation. Accredited by Association of International Colleges and Universities. Associate member, European Council of International Schools.

Academic calendar. Enrollment is continuous. Students may begin studies at any time.

Residency—required contact with program. Students must maintain some contact with their faculty tutor; however, TIU is committed to providing flexible programming to meet individual circumstances of learners.

Part-time enrollment—pace. TIU encourages part-time study as a viable way for working persons and others with responsibilities making full-time resident study unsuitable to earn academic credits.

Costs. TIU's total cost for a year of tutorial instruction at the university level is $900 for undergraduate and $1500 for graduate students.

Admission requirements. The university is totally committed to an open admissions policy without regard to any socioeconomic factors. All applicants are admitted provisionally, but high school equivalency is normally expected.

Assessment of prior learning. Life and work experiences are evaluated by faculty-advisory team and awarded in the form of advanced standing. Students may earn up to 30 percent of their degree requirements by this method.

Curriculum—learning options. Study is conducted primarily by the tutorial method. A faculty member is assigned as a tutor to a student, on the basis of academic interests and geographical proximity. Tutor and student work together to set up a course of study, to successfully complete that course, and to evaluate final results. Based on evidence of work completed and the tutor's evaluation, a university faculty board determines the credit and/or degrees to be granted by TIU. Learning is augmented by travel and contact with new, different cultures. Most study will be conducted in the academic discipline chosen by the student, but student is allowed to study where and when opportunities are best.

Degree requirements. Any student enrolling in a degree program must satisfy the academic demands of tutor, the faculty requirements within the chosen field of study, and the university's faculty review committee, which oversees the student's program and academic progress. In addition, the following minimal credits must be successfully completed to earn the respective degrees:

Associate's degree: 60 credit hours.
Bachelor's degree: 120 credit hours.
Master's degree: 150 credit hours.
Specialist degree: 180 total credit hours.
Doctorate degree: 210 total credit hours.

Supportive services—financial aid. Large number of substantial financial aids and scholarships available, disbursed on the basis of financial need and academic ability. In cases of proven financial need, substantial reductions in tuition are available.

Enrollment. 375.

ST. LOUIS UNIVERSITY
Metropolitan College
221 North Grand Boulevard
St. Louis, Missouri   63103
(314) 658-2330

Philosophy and goals. Developed especially for adults, the college offers flexible programs.

Degrees and certificates offered. Associate's degrees in liberal studies, urban affairs, and community service, materials management. Bachelor's degrees in liberal studies and urban affairs and community service. There are also certificate programs.

Accreditation. St. Louis University is fully accredited by the North Central Association of Colleges and Secondary Schools.

Residency—required contact with program. Evening and weekend classes are the principal form of learning. At least 30 credits must be taken at St. Louis University. This usually amounts to about 120 hours of campus contact for the entire degree program.

Part-time enrollment—pace. Nearly all students are enrolled part-time.

Costs. Tuition at Metropolitan College is $50.00 per credit hour. Admission, graduation, and certificate fees are assessed on a one-time basis.

Admission requirements. Any person 22 years of age or older who has a high school diploma or a GED certificate is automatically eligible for admission.

Assessment of prior learning. Through the Prior Learning Outcomes (PLO) or CLEP programs, credit can be earned for work-related or other experiences in which learning has occurred.

Persons who have taken classes in the armed force can receive college credit for courses which have been evaluated through the USAFI/DANTES program. A similar program sponsored by the American Council on Education (ACE) enables persons who have taken classes in specified, company-sponsored programs to receive college credit.

Curriculum—learning options. Curriculum depends on area of emphasis. Classes are held at six locations throughout the metropolitan area. Students may also contract for independent study, enroll at other institutions, or do extensive self-directed study.

Degree requirements. Associate's degree requires completion of 60 credits; bachelor's degree, completion of 120 credits, of which at least 30 must be taken at the college.

Supportive services—financial aid. Extensive advisory staff available for personal, academic or financial planning assistance. The school is approved for BEOG, GLS, veterans' benefits, and operates a number of financial aid programs of its own. Students in criminal justice or black church leaders programs can apply for special funds.

Additional information. A weekend college program was begun in the fall of 1978.

OTTAWA UNIVERSITY
College Without Campus
605 W. 47th, Suite 317
Kansas City, Missouri   64112
(816) 753-1431

Philosophy and goals. Established to meet the educational needs of adults whose jobs or family responsibilities make traditional degree programs impractical.

Degrees and certificates offered. CWC graduates receive the same B.A. degree awarded residential students of Ottawa.

Accreditation. Fully accredited by the North Central Association of Colleges and Secondary Schools.

Academic calendar. Work may be begun at any time; there are no semesters or other CWC terms, excepting special group packages of intensive courses, which last a few days or a few weeks.

Residency—required contact with program. The student must attend a seminar held in Kansas City, every month, except July and December. The course meets one night a week for eight consecutive weeks. The student also needs to be in Kansas City on occasion for advising. If you live outside the Kansas City area, these course meetings and advising sessions may be a problem for you, and it may be difficult for us to meet your needs at this time. Thereafter, all work is completed through independent study.

Part-time enrollment—pace. Students may progress at their own speed, especially through independent studies.

Costs.

Semester hour cost	$ 50.00	
Per four-hour course	190.00	
Application fee	10.00	
Pro-seminar	190.00	
First learning contract		
	760.00	
Graduation review	190.00	
Minimum degree completion fees	$1150.00	

The usual learning contract consists of 16 hours.

Admission requirements. Once students' applications and $10.00 fees are on file, they are considered formally accepted.

Assessment of prior learning. Work done at accredited institutions may be transferred to CWC at face value. Work at unaccredited colleges may also be eligible for credit, if certain standards are met. Credit for on-the-job training is evaluated and assigned credit-hour equivalents according to the American Council on Education's Guide to Non-Collegiate Training. CLEP is accepted. Credit for life experience, if it can be related to equivalent academic courses, is also acceptable in some instances.

Curriculum—learning options. A learning contract is negotiated by student and adviser and ratified by the CWC dean. It sets forth what each will do and what goals will be reached. There are also scheduled classes—the general education courses being most notable. In addition, small groups of students interested in taking the same subject arrange meeting times/places with their instructor and study together.

Degree requirements. All graduates must demonstrate breadth in four basic competency areas: communica-tion/self-education—using communication skills (oral, written and behavioral) for life-long learning and productive interaction with others; social/civic—exploring relationships, organization patterns, processes of change and the value systems of societies; work/leisure—acquiring a sense of meaning and direction related to career and non-career activities on an individual and societal basis; value/meaning—reflecting on the world view that provides a framework for life activities.

Competency requirements are defined as demonstrations and may take the form of a listing of previous academic work (minimum requirement is 8 credit hours in each breadth area) along with interpretive statements; work or life experiences with interpretive statements, and/or examinations, either written or oral.

Assembling these demonstrations and defining areas in need of further study is a process that continues throughout a student's association with CWC. In addition, 3 courses are required: the pro-seminar; educational planning and resource development; and graduation review.

Supportive services—financial aid. The student's adviser is the main source of support, although, through special cooperative arrangements, students may have access to the support services of nearby universities. In addition, a special counseling service is operated for women who are considering college. This service is not restricted to students in the program.

College Without Campus is approved for BEOG, GSL, and Kansas State Tuition grants. Information is maintained on other, privately sponsored programs that may exist.

PARK COLLEGE SCHOOL FOR COMMUNITY EDUCATION
Scarritt Building
818 Grand Avenue
Kansas City, Missouri   64106
(816) 842-6182.

Philosophy and goals. The program is designed for adults wishing to pursue the bachelor's degree without leaving full-time positions in business, industry or government.

Degrees and certificates offered. A.A., A.S., B.A., and B.S.

Accreditation. Park College is fully accredited by the North Central Association of Colleges and Schools.

Academic calendar. The program does not operate exclusively on a standard fall, spring, and summer semester system. Eight-week terms and tailor-made calendars are also possible.

Residency—required contact with program. Students must complete a minimum of 24 semester hours at the school toward a bachelor's degree or 15 hours toward an associate's degree. Students must also meet with the faculty adviser to plan the matriculation proposal which is the basis for being accepted into the portfolio plan. For students who do not reside or cannot matriculate at the campus, resident centers have been set up at several locations in the Kansas City metropolitan area, as well as at 24 military installations in Texas, Arkansas, Louisiana, Colorado, Kansas, Virginia, New Mexico, Idaho, Missouri, Illinois, South Carolina, Arizona, and Michigan.

Part-time enrollment—pace. Although the program should be completed in one year after matriculation, under special conditions a two-year program may be approved.

Costs. Tuition: $2000.00
Evaluation fee: 30.00
Advising fee: 100.00
Academic board fee: 100.00

If a program of more than twelve months is set up, the tuition charge will increase proportionately. If the student is required to attend classes at another school, the tuition will be paid by Park College.

Admission requirements. Priority is given to those applicants who have completed a significant number of college level courses. However, applicants who do not meet these criteria may be considered on an individual basis. The applicant is responsible for the receipt by the college of all transcripts and test scores.

Assessment of prior learning. The program accepts transfer credit for degree candidates only. Block credits are awarded for A.A. degrees (60 hours) and registered nurses' training (60 hours). Additional credits may be awarded to students upon evaluation of documentation from the following sources: service school credits; military service (8 credit hours; additional credit based on occupational skill level, to maximum of 24 credit hours); validated learning equivalence by petition on approval; CLEP general examinations; USAFI/DANTES/CLEP subject examinations.

Curriculum—learning options. The interim objective of the program is a matriculation agreement proposal which, if accepted by an academic board of experts, becomes a learning agreement between the student and the college. The learning experiences to satisfy this agreement may include individual study, tutorials, and traditional classroom work. There are thirteen major fields of study.

Degree requirements. B.A., B.S.: 120 semester hours; A.A., A.S.: 60 semester hours. Grade point average of 2.0 for all credits earned at the college. The student must satisfy all requirements for a major and complete a minimum of 30 hours of upper-division work. The student must also complete the undergraduate program examinations and have not less than 6 hours in English composition and 30 hours distributed among the humanities, social sciences, and natural sciences/mathematics, but outside the student's major field of study.

Supportive services—financial aid. The program administers two sources of financial aid: BEOG and FISL. The program is also approved for veterans' benefits and financial counseling is available.

A faculty adviser is available to students to determine their educational goals, previous learning experiences, the competencies which are missing and how the student may best work toward gaining these competencies.

UNIVERSITY OF MISSOURI-COLUMBIA
College of Agriculture
Nontraditional Study Program
103 Whitten Hall
Columbia, Missouri 65201
(314) 822-6287

Philosophy and goals. Provides opportunity for interested and qualified individuals to satisfy the requirements for the B.S. degree in agriculture even though they cannot return to campus as full-time students.

Degrees and certificates offered. B.S. in Agriculture.

Accreditation. Fully accredited by the North Central Association of Schools and Colleges.

Academic calendar. There are no calendar constraints placed on the nontraditional study program. Application and enrollment can take place at any time during the year.

Residency—required contact with program. The program attempts to make educational opportunity available in as many ways and in as convenient locations as is economically feasible, with no residency requirements.

Part-time enrollment—pace. UMC has removed time constraints on course completion and on degree completion.

Costs. Tuition: $38.50 per semester hour. Application fee: there is a registration and supplemental fee of $50.00 every six months.

Admission requirements. Presently priority is given to those students who have completed most of the general education requirements for the B.S. degree. This usually means 50-60 college hours. However, interested students should file an application even if they did no previous college work, and NSP staff will advise them on how to obtain the necessary credits for admission. To be eligible, an applicant must not have been enrolled as a full-time student in an educational institution during the five years immediately preceding admission to NSP.

Assessment of prior learning. UMC accepts credits by transfer from colleges previously attended, as well as by examination (CLEP). Credit may be awarded for documented, relevant, life-learning experiences, for various military course work, and for some training programs of the U.S. Soil Conservation Service and the ASCS.

Curriculum—learning options. Students may enroll in regularly scheduled courses on campus or at other accredited colleges and universities, both public and private; in correspondence study courses through UMC's own Independent Study Department or through other accredited correspondence study departments of recognized colleges and universities; in evening division courses or extension courses for credit offered by this or other accredited colleges or universities; in specially designed courses offered by UMC directly to NSP students. UMC has also developed a traveling seminar for credit.

Degree requirements. A total of 128 semester hours, including 12 hours in communications skills, 16 hours in natural sciences and math, 14 hours in humanities and social sciences, 8 hours in business and economics, 48 hours in agricultural and supporting area courses, and up to 30 hours of electives. A grade point average of 2.0.

Supportive services—financial aid. Each student will be assigned a faculty adviser from the appropriate department within the College of Agriculture. Financial aid available through major government programs and the school has been approved for VA benefits.

Additional information. UMC is in the process of redesigning about 30 additional agricultural courses for use by the Nontraditional Study Program students.

NEBRASKA

McCOOK COMMUNITY COLLEGE
Associate of General Studies Degree
McCook, Nebraska   69001
(308) 345-6303

Philosophy and goals. Designed to meet the needs of those whose educational goals are not satisfied through the traditional college transfer or vocational-technical programs, whose responsibilities limit their on-campus attendance, and whose post-secondary careers may include employment or other experiences with educational value. Offers selected adults considerable latitude in designing a program of study around their individual experiences, competencies, and goals.

Degrees and certificates offered. Associate of General Studies (AGS).

Accreditation. Accredited by the Nebraska State Department of Education. The credits received at McCook Community College are transferable to other colleges. The college has completed the first phase of accreditation by the North Central Association of Colleges and Secondary Schools, having earned "candidacy" status.

Academic calendar. Semester.

Residency—required contact with program. A student with 60 credits of transfer work and credit-by-exam can conceivably complete the AGS degree with only 15 credits of resident classroom instruction. Courses are offered in the evenings and at satellite centers throughout the state.

Part-time enrollment—pace. Students may proceed at their own pace.

Costs. Tuition per semester
a. Residents of Nebraska
    Each semester hour, 1-13 $ 12.00
    Maximum charge, 14 or more   168.00
b. Residents of other states
    Each semester hour, 1-13   16.50
    Maximum charge, 14 or more   231.00

Admission requirements. Admissions is on a rolling basis, so that applicant is promptly informed of acceptance. Graduation from an accredited high school or satisfactory completion of the General Educational Development test is required. Admission involves submission of an application for candidacy and an interview with the dean of instructional services.

Assessment of prior learning. Credit awarded for understanding acquired through experience or continuing education courses. When examinations are not available to demonstrate proficiency in academic subject areas, degree candidates may submit other forms of evidence to the Curriculum Council for evaluation. The council may award academic credit, up to a maximum of 20 semester hours. Credit may also be awarded for advanced placement, CLEP and Challenge Examinations, as well as for military service schooling.

Curriculum—learning options. On-campus and satellite center course work are the primary learning options. Up to 12 hours of directed study may be applied toward the degree. Directed study courses are designed to supplement rather than replace regular course offerings within a subject area or at a subject level not otherwise available.

Degree requirements. Completion of 60 semester hours with a C average. The final 15 hours of course instruction must be earned in residence for an arts or applied science degree. The requirement for the general studies degree is also 15 hours, but these need not be the final hours of instruction. Credit by examination may not apply toward residency.

Supportive services—financial aid. The principal source of support is the student's adviser. Assistance is available to students through all major state and federal programs including BEOG, SEOG, NDSL, CWS, and GSL.

NEW HAMPSHIRE

NEW ENGLAND COLLEGE
School of Continuing Education
Henniker, New Hampshire   03242
(603) 428-2252

Philosophy and goals. The Diploma Nurse Program (DNP) is designed for R.N.s who possess a diploma from a three-year hospital school of nursing or an associate's degree in nursing, and leads to a Bachelor of Arts degree.

Degrees and certificates offered. Bachelor of Arts in Psychology-Sociology and Liberal Studies.

Accreditation. Fully accredited by the New England Association of Colleges and Secondary Schools.

Academic calendar. Semester (fall, winter, spring).

Residency—required contact with program. The primary mode of learning is classroom attendance. The minimized campus contact comes primarily through the great amount of transfer credits awarded to students accepted into the program.

Part-time enrollment—pace. Students may proceed at their own pace.

Costs. Tuition is $165.00 for each course. The other fees connected with the program are an application ($25.00), matriculation ($25.00), and graduation fee ($100.00).

Admission requirements. Open to R.N.s who possess a diploma from a three-year hospital school of nursing or an associate's degree in nursing.

Assessment of prior learning.
For diploma school education
88 credits (equivalent to 22 New England College courses)

Nursing practice academic equivalent	Non-nursing courses taken at other institutions
Assumption of work experience included in credit allowance for Diploma School Education. No additional credit.	Courses from universities, colleges, junior colleges may be transferred.

For associate's degree in nursing
56-64 credits (equivalent to 14-16 NEC courses)

Maximum 24 credits (equivalent to 6 NEC courses). Work experience is evaluated as follows: 1st 6 months=8 semester hours 2nd 6 months=8 semester hours 3rd 6 months=4 semester hours 4th 6 months=4 semester hours	Courses from universities, colleges, junior colleges may be transferred.

Students who submit professional work experience to be evaluated for credit may be asked to submit appropriate supporting evidence.

Curriculum—learning options. Students seeking either degree program follow specified degree requirements for each major. The specific requirement for the liberal studies major is a distribution requirement. This requirement is met by completing 5 courses from among 12 discipline areas, with the restriction that not more than 2 courses be from the same area.

Students may also elect a concentration, which requires 4 courses in a single discipline or subject matter.

Degree requirements. Completion of 34 courses, including credit allowed for course work in nursing and other previous studies. Completion of at least 8 courses under the auspices of New England College. Students must also meet the general requirements of their major program.

Supportive services—financial aid. The principal source of support is the student's adviser. Assistance is available to students through major state and federal programs including BEOG, SEOG, NDSL, and CWS.

UNIVERSITY OF NEW HAMPSHIRE
School of Continuing Education
Lee Center, East
Durham, New Hampshire   03824
(603) 862-1715

Philosophy and goals. An alternative route for adults to continue their undergraduate studies. It is geared specifically to New Hampshire adults who cannot return to full-time, on-campus study, yet who want earnestly to complete their baccalaureate degrees. The core of the program is that of assessment of prior skills and accumulated knowledge while still embracing the basic educational philosophies and standards of the university system itself.

Degrees and certificates offered. Bachelor of General Studies.

Accreditation. Fully accredited by the New England Association of Colleges and Secondary Schools.

Academic calendar.   Quarters.

Residency—required contact with program.   The
program was created to minimize the amount of
contact needed to complete the degree.   Students
may design study programs which require no on-
campus learning.

Part-time enrollment—pace.   Time element is
flexible and not based on regular college semester
timetables.   The speed is set by learner.

Costs.	In-state	Out-of-state
Tuition	$1,150.00	$3,500.00
Room & board	1,480.00	1,480.00
Student activity	23.00	23.00
Memorial union	35.00	35.00
Rec. & phys. ed.	30.00	30.00
Student services	10.00	10.00
Books & supplies	175.00	175.00

Admission requirements.   A minimum of two years
of academic work beyond the secondary level, or
its equivalence; varied and significant career
background or a spectrum of valid life experiences;
ability to study independently and to initiate self-
designed study; life goal that is specialized in
a particular area of learning.

Assessment of prior learning.   The recognition of
nonformal learning and the assessment process
are central to the program.   Learner and a
sponsor describe, analyze, and categorize specific
learning experiences.   A report which describes
these experiences and knowledge gained through
them is presented to an assessment team, consisting
of the learner, the sponsor, and university system
faculty.   Based on an analysis of the assessment
report and the learner's ability to demonstrate
achieved competence, appropriate credits are
assigned.

Curriculum—learning options.   Students have a full
range of academic options to choose from and
can design virtually any type of academic program.
Together with an adviser, students draw up learning
contracts which generally define and describe a
particular amount of work to be conducted by the
learner for a negotiated amount of credit.   Contracts
can cover various lengths of time, any amount of
work, and all disciplines or areas of knowledge.

Degree requirements.   The completion of a minimum
of 124 credits, including preadmission credits,
60 of which must be academic credits from
accredited colleges and/or universities (30 of
these 60 may be completed through approved
college-level examination programs, i.e., CLEP,
USAFI, etc.) with a minimum grade point average
of 2.0 on a 4.0 scale.
     The completion of distribution requirements
as follows:
a.   A minimum of 15 credits in the sciences and/or
     mathematics;
b.   A minimum of 15 credits in the humanities;
c.   A minimum of 15 credits in the social sciences.

The completion of at least 30 credits of the last
60 credits within the university system (by

learners who have not previously attended a UNH
system college) under the supervision of a UNH
system faculty adviser or an adviser approved by
the appropriate academic unit.   The completion of
at least 30 credits in an approved area of
specialized study leading to a specific educational
goal, but not necessarily within any one department,
division, school or college.   At least one half
of these credits must be completed at the upper-
division level.   The number of these credits
which must be completed within the UNH system will
be determined by the candidate's faculty adviser.

Supportive services—financial aid.   The principal
source of support is the student's adviser.
Assistance is available to students through all
major stated and federal programs including
BEOG, SEOG, NDSL, and CWS.

NEW JERSEY

THOMAS A. EDISON COLLEGE
Forrestal Center
Forrestal Road
Princeton, New Jersey   08540
(609) 292-8096

Philosophy and goals.   The college was established
in recognition of the fact that many individuals
who have not had the opportunity to complete their
formal education have acquired the equivalent
knowledge and deserve the opportunity to demonstrate
their accomplishment and receive college credit and
degrees.

Degrees and certificates offered.   Associate of
Arts; Bachelor of Arts; Bachelor of Science in
Business Administration; Associate of Science
in Management; Associate of Science in Radiologic
Technology.

Accreditation.   Degree granting authority from
the New Jersey Board of Higher Education.   In
the "candidate" stage of accreditation with the
Commission on Higher Education of the Middle
States Association of Colleges and Secondary
Schools.

Academic calendar.   Students may enroll in the
program at any time.   Subject area examinations
are offered on fixed dates throughout the year.

Residency—required contact with program.   Since
the college has no instructional facilities of
its own, the only direct program contact required
is appearnace at a designated testing center on
prescribed dates.

Part-time enrollment—pace.   Students may proceed
at their own pace.   Examination scores and other
credits are recorded on the transcript as they
are completed.

Costs.
Examination fees

3 credits	$25.00
4-6 credits	40.00
7-9 credits	50.00
Business environment and strategy	50.00
Languages Battery A	25.00
Battery B	15.00
Application fee	25.00
Enrollment fee	50.00
Graduation fee Associate's degree	25.00
Bachelor's degree	40.00

NOTE: Although it is possible to earn a degree entirely through examinations offered by the college, most students also use courses and tests from other colleges and testing agencies. This factor should be taken into account when figuring costs.

Admission requirements. Anyone may enroll regardless of age, residence, or previous educational experience. To enroll, the applicant must submit the enrollment form and fee and all existing documentation of past academic work. In order to enroll in the radiologic technology program, however, applicant must already have radiologic (X-ray) technology certification from a recognized agency.

Assessment of prior learning/Curriculum—learning options. The college offers no instruction of its own, and learning done prior to enrollment is assessed in exactly the same ways as learning done after enrollment. Edison employs a number of different methods of assessment. The first is applied to work that can be easily documented and verified: transcripts from accredited colleges; results from college equivalency examinations such as CLEP and USAFI; and, for military personnel, results of formal service schools. This type of evaluation is done primarily by the registrar, who sends the results of the evaluation to the student and records them on a transcript. It is possible for a student to qualify for a degree solely through this type of assessment.

Assessment of unsponsored learning is done through special assessment that involves the individual assessment of experientially based college-level knowledge and/or skills that aren't covered by the first evaluation: skills and knowledge acquired through experience, on-the-job training, independent study, course work completed at unaccredited institutions of learning, etc. Examinations are also offered for assessment purposes in business administration and in five foreign languages: French, German, Italian, Russian, and Spanish. Edison also offers examinations in connection with the new Associate in Applied Science in Radiologic Technology degree and the Associate in Applied Science in Management degree. The college makes available at no cost study guides, examination descriptions, and other information about the Thomas Edison College Examination Program. These exams are offered three times a year, in October, January and May.

All of a student's learning occurs outside of the college. The college staff estimates that nearly two thirds of all work done toward the B.A. degree is done within classroom situations at other institutions. The other one-third is done through Edison's individual assessment and proficiency examinations.

Degree requirements. Associate in Arts: the candidate must complete 60 semester hours of credits, of which 48 must be earned in the liberal arts according to a prescribed plan. The remaining 12 credits are allotted to free electives.

Bachelor of Arts: 33 credits distributed as required for the Associate in Arts degree in addition to 27 credits of required courses in liberal arts, 27 credits of liberal arts electives and 33 credits of free electives. Students have the option of specializing in a specific liberal arts discipline.

All degree candidates must pass a test administered by the college to measure writing proficiency. Students must achieve a 2.0 (C) grade point average for all courses used to meet degree requirements. Only those courses or examinations that the student wishes to apply toward a degree are recorded on his or her transcript.

Bachelor of Science in Business Administration: the program is comprised of a general education (liberal arts) component and a specialized business component. The general education component requires 48 credits in liberal arts, including 6 credits of economics and 12 credits of free electives. It can be completed through a combination of college courses, college proficiency examinations (such as CLEP tests), and/or individual assessment equal to 30 semester hours of liberal arts. The business component requires 33 credits in a business core, plus 18 credits of specialization in one of the following areas or 9 credits in each of two of the following areas: accounting, finance, management of human resources, marketing management, operations management, and general business administration. An additional 9 credits of business electives are required to complete the business component. Requirements can be met by passing the tests offered by the college, special assessment, or through college courses and/or proficiency exams taken currently or within the ten years prior to enrollment.

Associate in Applied Science in Radiologic Technology: 60 credits are required for the AART, 20 of which are earned automatically through possession of the radiologic technology certificate which is required for admission; 14 credits could be earned by special examination in the field; and the 26 remaining credits must be completed in the following liberal arts areas: communications (6 credits); natural sciences and mathematics (12 credits); humanities and social sciences electives (8 credits).

Associate in Applied Science in Management: 60 credits are required for the ASM, 39 of which must be in business-related subjects, while 21 must be in liberal arts subjects. The professional component includes 15 credits of required subjects in business-related areas such as economics and accounting; 12 credits in basic management; and 12 credits of professional electives. The liberal arts credits must include 6 credits of mathematics, 6 credits of social science, 6 credits of communications and 6 credits of liberal arts electives.

Supportive services. The college maintains a preadmission and postadmission counseling service. Counselors are stationed throughout the state and can be located by contacting the central office. Out-of-state students can receive counseling directly from the central office, either by phone or by correspondence.

The counseling service and a recently created clearinghouse for educational information are open to the general public without charge.

NEW YORK

THE COLLEGE OF SAINT ROSE
Degree Program for Experienced Adults
Albany, New York   12203
(518) 471-5276/5125

Philosophy and goals. A nontraditional under-graduate program which meets the needs of adult students with a variety of educational backgrounds and life experiences.

Degrees and certificates offered. Bachelor of Arts or Bachelor of Science.

Accreditation. Fully accredited by the Middle States Association of Colleges and Secondary Schools.

Academic calendar. Semesters (spring, fall and summer).

Residency—required contact with program. Provides for some independent work, but also includes seminars and work on campus. A program of study which can be pursued independently may be developed and submitted for consideration.

Part-time enrollment—pace. Students may elect to study full-time or part-time, in the day and/or evening sessions.

Costs.

Tuition for 12 to 17 credit hours (per semester)	$1,155.00

a minimum of 12 credits and a maximum of 17 credits is considered full-time. Additional credits will be charged at $75.00 per credit hour.

Tuition per credit hour, part-time	75.00	(day)
	57.50	(evening)
Tuition per credit hour, regular audit	35.00	
Tuition per course, alumni audit	25.00	
Student activity fee (per semester)	42.50	(full-time)
	5.00	(part-time)
Orientation fee	25.00	
Degree fee	35.00	

DPEA students pay a special fee for the evaluation of their previous learning/work experience. This one-time fee varies with the amount of credit granted:

For credits granted up to 32 credit hours	$150.00
For credits granted beyond 33 credit hours	200.00

Independent study is billed at the day session rate of $75.00/hour.

Admission requirements. Students are admitted to the program by director following an interview and submission of the following materials:
a. The completed application accompanied by the $15.00 application fee.
b. Three copies of a portfolio, which includes résumé; statement of career goals; and description of employment, informal education, achievements, interests and hobbies, and any other relevant information, together with supporting documentation.
c. Official educational transcripts and letters of validation attesting to career, professional and/or community experience.

Assessment of prior learning. Candidates may qualify for advanced academic standing in specific areas if they demonstrate a degree of knowledge and competence comparable to that which is usually acquired through college study; credit awarded becomes effective only when all degree requirements are met. An unlimited number of credits which may also be earned through the New York State Proficiency Examinations and the CLEP subject examinations. Students are required to pay only the examination fee. Examinations passed prior to entrance into the degree program are acceptable.

Curriculum—learning options. A special studies major is designed to meet the needs and interests of a student who wishes to combine areas and aptitudes, to study relationships in a particular way, or to work in a field not completely covered by CSR offerings. All DPEA students have a special studies major, whether they choose formal CSR concentrations in areas of business, education, fine arts, humanities, natural sciences, or social sciences, or design individualized, interdisciplinary programs. A program of independent study is available to students who have demonstrated the requisite abilities and motivation. The independent study may take the form of research, tutorials, reading programs, or special off-campus projects.

Degree requirements Completion of a minimum of 122 credits with a cumulative index of 2.0 and an index of 2.0 in the area of concentration. At least 60 of these credits must be completed at CSR or at one of the institutions of the Hudson-Mohawk Association of Colleges and Universities and a minimum of 16 credit hours at CSR.

Completion of a liberal arts core: three required courses in writing, speech, and values (9 credits); a minimum of 27 credits in four area distribution courses.

Supportive services—financial aid. Students have full access to all support services of the college. The institution maintains a full-time financial aid office and participates in most federal and state programs. The school is approved for veterans' benefits. Orientation programs for new students are held each semester.

EMPIRE STATE COLLEGE
2 Union Avenue
Saratoga Springs, New York   12866
(518) 587-2100

Philosophy and goals. Empire State College was created to devise new patterns of independent study and flexible approaches to learning, providing learning for young people and adults for whom an off-campus individualized instruction pattern will be more effective.

Degrees and certificates offered. B.A., B.S., Bachelor of Professional Studies (arts, technology, community and human services, business, management, and economics), A.A., A.S,, from the Empire State College, State University of New York.

Accreditation. Full regional accreditation from the Middle States Association of Colleges and Secondary Schools. State accreditation by the Board of Regents of the University of the State of New York.

Academic calendar. The program operates year-round. Formal enrollment occurs on a monthly basis.

Residency—required contact with program. There is no traditional residency requirement, although minimum periods of contact with adviser are required. Students enroll and study through the college's regional centers, which are located throughout New York State.

Part-time enrollment—pace. Students may enroll part- or full-time.

Costs.

Lower Division

	In-state	Out-of-state
Full-time:	$375.00	$600.00
3/4 time:	300.00	480.00
1/2 time:	200.00	320.00
1/4 time:	100.00	160.00

Upper Division

	In-state	Out-of-state
Full-time:	$450.00	$750.00
3/4 time:	360.00	600.00
1/2 time:	240.00	400.00
1/4 time:	120.00	200.00

Admission requirements. The principal requirements are a high school diploma, its equivalent, or the ability to do college-level work as demonstrated by the applicant's presentation of work or life experiences and responsibilities; the ability of the learning location to meet the applicant's explicit and educational needs and objectives.

Assessment of prior learning. Empire grants advanced standing for prior college-level learning based on previous college study, evaluated work and life learning, and/or standardized examinations. This prior learning must fulfill some part of the student's degree program and must be well documented and evaluated by the college. Candidate must prepare a portfolio with the help of a mentor, an assessment counselor, and, if necessary, other faculty and experts. The portfolio consists of an initial summary, a general essay, and an appendix of supporting evidence: transcripts, certificates of completion, other evidence from colleges, proprietary institutions, and other organizations; standardized examinations such as CLEP and USAFI; professional licenses; membership in some professional or trade associations; products completed (e.g., books published, paintings); demonstrations of performance; letters of support from colleagues or supervisors; and interviews or oral examinations.

Curriculum—learning options. A broad variety of learning options are available: formal courses scheduled on a traditional campus (Empire students have access to all the resources of the State University of New York system); programs of study designed by faculty and visiting fellows; correspondence or media courses designed for self-study; internships in a government or social agency; cooperative projects with fellow students; tutorials in a specialized area of knowledge; travel in this country or abroad with a specific study plan; independent research; and other possibilities. The student's work is planned, recorded and evaluated through learning contracts. Subject areas include: the arts; business, management, and economics; labor studies; community and human services; cultural studies; educational studies; historical studies; human development; science, mathematics, and technology; social theory, social structure, and change.

Degree requirements. Empire State College now measures progress toward the degree in terms of contract months (one contract month equals four weeks of full-time study or eight weeks of half-time study and is equivalent to four semester hours). A baccalaureate degree requires 32 months or 128 credits, of which 8 months must be completed at the college. An associate's (two-year) degree requires 16 contract months or 64 credits, of which 6 months must be done at the college.

Supportive services—financial aid. The student's mentor is the main college source of academic, personal, and vocational advisement.

The college participates in a broad range of federal (SEOG, NDSL, CWS, BEOG), state, and State University financial aid programs. There are special scholarships for students who wish to pursue education in the field of labor or law enforcement.

Additional information. Through the extended program, the college makes its program available to people who find it difficult to relate to a center of the college because of distance or other circumstances. The college is organized as a network with six regional centers, including a coordinating center, a center for labor studies, an urban studies center, and a center for state-wide programs.

FRIENDS WORLD COLLEGE
Lloyd Harbor
Huntington, New York   11743
(516) 549-1102

Philosophy and goals. Committed to world education through the process of experiential learning. The aims of the community's education program are to encourage men and women of all nations to learn through active involvement in the diverse societies of the world, to relate their learning aims to the urgent issues faced by the world and to develop a critical perspective on these, to gain the knowledge and skills appropriate to their aims and aptitudes and to learn how to use them for effective participation in work toward a more human society, and to accept the whole of humanity as their ultimate loyalty.

Degrees and certificates offered. B.A.

Accreditation. Accredited by the State Education Department of New York.

Academic calendar. The program operates year-round on a semester basis. Freshmen enter in the fall only. Transfer, "visiting" or adult UWW (University Without Walls) students enter in the fall or in the spring.

Residency—required contact with program. All entering United States students participate in an orientation and planning program at the North American Center on Long Island prior to engaging in field study. Freshmen entering directly from high school have a two-month residency beginning in September. Transfer, "visiting" and adult UWW students have a one-month program beginning in September of February (for North American field study programs) or in August or February (for those going overseas for initial study).
   The overseas centers of the college have four- to five-week orientation programs for students beginning initial work in those regions during September or March of each year. These are for the purpose of cultural orientation, language study and program planning.
   Students remain in close contact with faculty advisors at the center from which they are carrying out field studies. In addition, they often return to the centers during and at the end of their semester or year-long programs of field work for sharing, support, advisement and evaluation.

Part-time enrollment—pace. Students are generally accepted on a full time basis only. In certain cases, adult "University Without Walls" students may be admitted on a one-half time (8 semester hours credit) basis.

Costs. Tuition $2,750.00 per year
Application fee   20.00
   Fee for evaluation of experiential credit is

20 percent of current semester rate for each 15 credits assessed.
   In addition to tuition, students are responsible for their own room, board, travel and outside resource fees as well as for such personal expenses as clothing, medical care, immunization and passport fees. These variable costs depend greatly on the location and nature of each student's study program and may range from $1,300.00 to $1,800.00 per semester. Thus, the total costs for all expenses, including tuition, and travel for a full twelve-month year will average between $5,300.00 and $6,300.00.

Admission requirements. Applications are judged on their own merits. Students are expected to have finished a college preparatory high school course or its equivalent, with the exception of high school juniors entering the Early Admissions Program (see Curriculum—learning options). While primary emphasis is not placed on standardized tests and high school grades, clear evidence of the ability and the readiness to do sound college work is expected. A visit to the campus in Lloyd Harbor, New York, or at one of the regional centers and an interview is requested whenever possible.

Assessment of prior learning. A maximum of 60 semester hours of credit may be granted on the basis of prior learning (an additional 15 hours in exceptional cases of students with extensive work or study experience in a culture other than his or her own). This may include transfer credits from other recognized colleges or universities; for courses completed in the armed services or through the CLEP; and credit for experiential learning, such as work or independent study, if it embodies aspects of experiential world education and social concern. Students requesting experiential credit must prepare a brief résumé of the experience, a portfolio of support materials in consultation with a faculty adviser, and submit them with the adviser's evaluation. (Note: there is a fee of 20 percent of the current semester's tuition for each 15 semester hours' credit granted.)

Curriculum—learning options. The curriculum is basically a four-year, liberal arts program which combines academic study with field work and internships through centers in Latin America, Europe, Africa and Asia as well as from a 100-acre campus in Huntington, Long Island, New York. Projects or studies grow out of a student's own interests, and may cover almost every area of traditional college study outside of the formal laboratory sciences. If scientific training is required (for a pre-medical program, for example), students may take courses as visiting students in a conventional college or university along with their field work.
   The first year is spent working in North America. When this project has been completed, the student may go on to other parts of the world.
   Students keep extensive journals of their experiences, which are the basis for learning evaluation by the student and his or her adviser. A different project is undertaken each semester. In addition, a senior project or senior thesis is designed by the student in consultation with faculty advisers and the Coordinator of Senior

Studies. The project or thesis may take one or two semesters to complete.

In a special program developed for transfer and visiting students, a one-month intensive orientation on the Livingston Campus is directly followed by field work in any of the regional programs.

The UWW component has been inaugurated for adults who, due to family, employment, or financial limitations, are unable to study and work at the overseas centers of the college. Following a period of introduction and orientation at the Livingston Campus, such students combine periods of field study and work in North America with campus programs to complete the B.A. degree.

Degree requirements. 120 semester hours of credit, including the senior project or thesis, are required for graduation, of which 60 hours (75 in exceptional cases) may be earned via previous learning or experiential education. Each semester project is worth 15 credit hours. Without credit for previous learning, the program takes four years to complete.

Supportive services—financial aid. Students remain in close contact with faculty advisers in the regional centers throughout the world. Students are assisted in making travel and living arrangements, and each college center makes arrangements for student medical care, but the responsibility for costs incurred are the students' own.

The college operates an extensive financial aid program. Every effort is made to enable all admitted students to attend the college. Scholarships and aid are granted on the basis of need as determined through evaluation by the College Scholarship Service or the American College Testing Program. Approximately three quarters of the students attending the college receive financial aid.

Additional information. The Study Travel Department sponsors short international experiences (3 to 8 weeks) for high school students, college students, and adults.

HOFSTRA UNIVERSITY
University Without Walls
New College
Hempstead, New York   11550
(516) 560-3651

Philosophy and goals. A competence-based, liberal arts degree program for persons whose responsibilities, educational goals or preferred learning styles preclude enrollment in a conventional undergraduate program. It is designed especially for those who can spend only limited time on campus but whose life situations provide opportunities for full- or part-time learning.

Degrees and certificates offered. Bachelor of Arts.

Accreditation. Fully accredited by the Middle States Association of Colleges and Secondary Schools.

Academic calendar. Semester.

Residency—required contact with program. Designed to minimize the amount of campus contact required for a degree. However, there are six Saturday collegial seminars and two residence periods per year. While active in the program, a student must attend one residence period and five other collegial events per year to qualify for graduation from the program.

The student and adviser come to agreement on the amount of contact they will have and a schedule of student/faculty conferences is included in each learning contract.

Part-time enrollment—pace. Provisions have been made for half-time study.

Costs. Application fee	$ 25.00
Full-time learning contract	690.00
Half-time learning contract	345.00
Informal prior learning assessment for full graduation requirement	200.00
Informal prior learning assessment for half graduation requirement	100.00
Credit by examination (full graduation requirement)	200.00
Credit by examination (half graduation requirement)	100.00
Full graduation requirement fee	25.00
Half graduation requirement fee	15.00
Graduation fee (payable upon award of candidacy for degree status)	40.00

Admission requirements. Applicants for admission to UWW must demonstrate previous, above average performance in a liberal arts area or areas, strong aptitude for full utilization of the liberal arts resources at New College, serious motivation for academic work within the liberal arts, and particular need for the external and individualized opportunities offered by the program. All applications require an application form, official transcripts of all prior collegiate work, a biographical essay, a statement of reasons for seeking entry into UWW and an admissions interview.

Assessment of prior learning. Assessment of prior formal learning, such as undergraduate work at another college or university, is evaluated immediately after student enters the program and may satisfy appropriate graduation requirements. Students must register for assessment of prior informal or life-experience learning. The assessment process includes documentation of learning experiences and accomplishments. To be acceptable, all prior learning must clearly relate to specific graduation requirements. UWW also accepts satisfactory performance on CLEP or the New York State Board of Regents' College Proficiency Examination Program, as well as individually designed examinations.

Curriculum—learning options. In addition to courses, seminars and workshops at UWW, New College and other units at Hofstra, students may make use of individual learning contracts. These are negotiated by the student and an approved faculty supervisor and confirmed by the UWW Core faculty. Learning contracts specify immediate educational objectives, the ways those objectives will be pursued, the bases for evaluation of the student's accomplishment of those objectives, a schedule of student-faculty conferences and the duration of the contract.

A learning contract to satisfy a full graduation requirement may last 1, 16, 24 or 32 weeks. Learning contracts to satisfy half of a graduation requirement may also be undertaken for varying periods of time.

When admitted to UWW, students meet with a faculty adviser to begin developing a graduation plan, which specifies how the student's prior and proposed learning satisfy each UWW graduation requirement. As soon as feasible, the graduation plan is submitted to the UWW Core faculty for action.

Degree requirements. UWW students must satisfy fifteen graduation requirements which fall into four categories. Each requirement represents a competence which is normally gained through 8 semester hours of conventional college work.
a. Studies in breadth: knowledge of a culture other than student's own; ability to respond to works of the human imagination; knowledge of the behavioral sciences; knowledge of the natural sciences; competence in expository writing and one other form of communication.
b. Studies in depth: five requirements which allow students to develop competence and knowledge in their chosen field or area of concentration. That concentration may be of a traditional nature, e.g., psychology, literature, biology or it may be interdisciplinary, e.g., women's studies, problems of the aging, man and the environment, arts management.
c. Electives: four requirements which allow the student an informed choice of subjects within the liberal arts and of modes of learning.
d. Final project: to satisfy this last requirement, student must demonstrate the skills, knowledge, and intellectual abilities gained through participation in UWW. The final project is substantial. Frequently, it is of a research or experimental character. Normally, it is in an area related to the student's depth concentration.

With the exception of the final project, UWW does not prescribe the order in which graduation requirements are satisfied. At least 25 percent of the student's degree program must be completed under the auspices of UWW in order for the student to receive the B.A. degree through UWW.

Supportive services—financial aid. UWW students have access to all the services offered by Hofstra. The university is approved for veterans and participates in all major federal and state financial aid programs: BEOG, SEOG, NDSL, CWS, etc.

NEW YORK INSTITUTE OF TECHNOLOGY
Division of Continuing Education
External Degree Program

Box 170
Old Westbury, New York   11568
(516) 686-7610

Philosophy and goals. Designed to permit off-campus study of a caliber satisfactory to earn a standard college degree through independent study, while permitting student to maintain a normal schedule of activities around family and occupational requirements.

Degrees and certificates offered. Associate in Applied Science in electrical technology, mechanical technology, business administration; Bachelor of Science in community mental health, psychology, management, marketing, economics, political science; Bachelor of Technology: cross-disciplinary degree combining elements of electrical engineering, mechanical engineering, industrial engineering, and computer science. This is not an engineering degree.

Accreditation. Fully accredited by the Middle States Association of Colleges and Secondary Schools.

Academic calendar. Independent study courses are offered on a rotating basis and correspond to terms lasting 16 weeks in duration.

Residency—required contact with program. With the exception of possible seminar and laboratory requirements, all course components of these degree programs are available by independent study through correspondence instruction. Attendance at one regularly scheduled 2-week seminar a year is required, except by special waiver.

Part-time enrollment—pace. A student may enroll in one or two courses each term and is expected to complete the work required for each course by the end of the 16-week period.

Costs.

Transcript evaluation fee	$15.00
Tuition per semester hour of credit	60.00
Additional lab fees where applicable	30.00
Seminars, per semester hour of credit	60.00

Admission requirements. High school diploma or GED certificate. Matriculation without a high school diploma is possible under certain conditions. If students have completed 24 credit hours through the institute with grades of C or better, they may be able to obtain a GED certificate through the State of New York. Although the Scholastic Aptitude Test (SAT) is requested, it does not constitute a requirement for entrance into the program.

Assessment of prior learning. Transfer credit may be given for courses completed at an accredited college or other qualified institution. Courses used in transfer should be appropriate to the degree program selected by student. Courses which are not specified in the curricula, but are relevant to the ultimate educational objective of the student, may be accepted as electives. Institutional course challenge, CLEP and other examinations are available, as well as special assessments (evaluations of life experience credit); the maximum amount of credit from these which can be used in fulfilling baccalaureate degree requirements is 60 semester hours. In-person contact is sometimes required to properly assess an individual's independently acquired knowledge. It should be noted that life experience credits will not be recorded on the student's transcript until 24 semester hours of residence credit have been acquired through the program.

Military service school course credit is granted on the basis of college level course recommendations which are listed in the Guide to the Evaluation of Educational Experiences in the Armed Services, if these courses are appropriate to the degree program selected.

A minimum of 24 credit hours must be earned with NYIT, in order to satisfy degree requirements.

Curriculum—learning options. Most courses required in the degree programs are available through independent study and are offered in 16-week terms. A student may enroll in one or two courses each term and is expected to complete the work required for each course by the end of the term. Courses involve intensive independent study at home and are supplemented by direct contact with instructor.

Degree requirements. Associate level: satisfactory completion of 66 semester hours of credit in the applied technology program, or 67 hours in the business administration program is required to graduate. In addition, a grade point average of 2.0 on a maximum scale of 4.0 is required.

Baccalaureate level: satisfactory completion of the appropriate number of credit hours in the degree program selected and an overall grade point average of 2.0 on a maximum scale of 4.0 is required. Credit hours required for these degree programs are as follows: 120 semester hours in the business administration, economics and political science programs; 128 in the behavioral science programs; and 134 in the technology program.

Supportive services—financial aid. Academic advisers are available to assist in structuring each student program, and for help and guidance, but the student assumes full responsibility for conforming to all the regulations and curriculum requirements. Limited financial aid may be available, for information, contact the NYIT financial aid office. The program is approved for veterans' benefits (tuition and fees only).

NEW YORK UNIVERSITY
University Without Walls
25 Waverly Place
New York, New York   10012
(212) 598-7077

Philosophy and goals. For students, young and old, who could best pursue a true liberal education if they were allowed to move along their own individual track. Essential to every UWW program are individual advisement, independent study and field work.

Degrees and certificates offered. Bachelor of

Arts degree from New York University.

Accreditation. Fully accredited by the Middle States Association of Colleges and Secondary Schools.

Academic calendar. Semester system. Admissions continuous.

Residency—required contact with program. One of the requirements for the degree is that a minimum of 40 credits must be completed in classroom work, adhering to regular course standards. Admissions interview, graduation, exam, negotiated amount of contact with faculty adviser.

Part-time enrollment—pace. Part-time enrollment is possible; however, the fee schedule is designed to encourage full-time status.

Costs. Full-time tuition, per semester is $1,925.00 (includes a nonrefundable registration and services fee of $75.00).

Admission requirements. Admission to UWW is selective, with candidates accepted on the basis of predicted success in the program. Evidence of maturity and ability to work independently are essential. Among the items given careful consideration are secondary school records and other college records if applicable, letters of recommendation, scores on standard tests, and a personal interview with a UWW faculty member. Usually an applicant must have a high school diploma or equivalency.

Transfer candidates who have not been in good standing at another institution may be considered for admission if secondary school and other admissions credentials are satisfactory, and evidence is presented of likelihood to do well at NYU. Such evidence should usually be a transcript of good academic work completed, either as a matriculated or a nonmatriculated student, in another accredited college.

Assessment of prior learning. Life experience: a maximum of 30 life or work experience credits may be granted after 12 UWW credits have been completed at NYU. Life experience credits may be substituted for either independent study or internship credits. Past experiences are documented by a portfolio of photographs, tapes, copies of work done, etc. Life experience credits are offered without fee.

Curriculum—learning options. While the major emphasis of the program is on individually designed independent study programs, the undergraduate courses in any school at NYU are open to UWW students. Aside from required classroom work, students can complete as many credits as deemed desirable in independent study projects.

Degree requirements. A minimum of 40 credits must be completed in classroom work, adhering to regular course standards. In addition to work directly related to the granting of credit, there are several related noncredit requirements: evidence of reading depth must be demonstrated; mastery is required of those books listed as essential on the UWW humanities and social science reading list, which includes classics, philosophy, social thought, fiction, economics, and history. A two-hour oral examination is required for graduation. Students are expected to show substantive knowledge of their course work, independent study projects or internships, and a familiarity with the UWW reading list.

Supportive services—financial aid. Students have available the facilities and services of NYU. The program adviser is the main source of counseling.

Students may apply for such financial aid as the National Direct Student Loan Program, the College Work Study Program, the Basic Educational Opportunity Grant Supplemental Educational Opportunity Grant, and the New York State Tuition Assistance Program, as well as for guaranteed and federally insured student loans. Veterans' benefits available.

Additional information. In 1977, the division launched a graduate program, offering an M.A. degree, based on the UWW model. The emphasis in the program is independent study, including a thesis or project. Ten points of advanced standing in this 40-point program can be earned for proficiency credit.

PACE UNIVERSITY
School of Continuing Education
Bachelor of Professional Studies (BPS)
Bedford Road
Pleasantville, New York   10570
(914) 769-3200, ext. 427
Pace Plaza
New York, New York   10038
(212) 285-3355
Bachelor of Liberal Studies (BLS)
78 North Broadway
White Plains, NY   10603
(914) 949-9494

Philosophy and goals. Created to provide for the increasing demand for a college degree by mature adults, many of whom have been out of school for some years. The concept of translating "life learning" into college credit is fundamental.

Degrees and certificates offered. Bachelor of Professional Studies in teaching, business, performing arts, health sciences, community development, and early childhood education. Bachelor of Professional Studies in liberal arts areas.

Accreditation. Accredited by the Middle States Association of Colleges and Universities.

Academic calendar. Semester.

Residency—required contact with program. Up to 96 transfer and/or life learning credits may be granted, but the remaining credits required for the degree must be earned through classroom learning. Courses are offered during the day, evening, early morning, and on the weekend. Schedules are tailored to individual needs.

Part-time enrollment—pace. Students proceed at their own pace.

Costs. Tuition is $80.00 per credit. Evaluation of life experience is $80.00. Application fee is $75.00.

Admission requirements. Applicants to degree programs must have high school and previous college transcripts sent to admissions office. Those without a high school diploma may enroll in courses, but not in degree program. Pace will guide students in obtaining a high school diploma.

Assessment of prior learning. Up to 96 credits can be earned through assessment of prior learning and transfer credits. Through an extensive interview with the BPS administrator or a portfolio preparation workshop, students identify possible areas of life experience equivalency and construct a portfolio supporting their claim for equivalency. Transfer credit (where applicable) must be evaluated by the Office of Admissions beforehand. Once application is accepted, materials are reviewed by appropriate evaluator(s), who then recommend credit awards. Transfer credit, previous college attendance, professional objectives, the level and nature of professional experience, and personal strengths and weaknesses will all be considered in granting equivalency credit.

Curriculum—learning options. On-campus classroom attendance is the primary mode of learning after enrollment. Independent study is restricted to students who through the first half of their junior year have completed work toward a degree with an average of B or better.

Degree requirements. BPS requires completion of 128 credits, distributed as follows: general education core, 50 credits; professional concentration, 36 credits; and professionally-related electives, 42 credits. BLS also requires 128 credits, 66 of which must be divided among the following four areas with a maximum of 24 and a minimum of 6 in each area: literature and communication; philosophy and the arts; social science; mathematics and science.

Supportive services—financial aid. The principal source of support is the student's adviser. Assistance is available through major state and federal programs, including BEOG, SEOG, NDSL, and CWS.

SKIDMORE COLLEGE
University Without Walls
Saratoga Springs, New York   12866
(518) 584-5000

Philosophy and goals. Designed to provide self-paced off-campus higher education to all age groups, not just the 18- to 22-year-olds. The program demands that students play a major role in shaping their own education.

Degrees and certificates offered. B.A. or B.S. from Skidmore College.

Accreditation. Fully accredited by Middle States Association of Colleges and Secondary Schools.

Academic calendar. Continuous. Applications are

accepted at any time during the year, and a student may begin work immediately after admission.

Residency—required contact with program. Students are required to appear in person three times: first for an admission interview, second to have a pre-advisement meeting with a staff member and for an initial meeting with an adviser, and third to present a degree plan to the UWW faculty committee. Contact may be maintained with the adviser by mail and phone.

Part-time enrollment—pace. Most students are employed full-time and progress to the degree as fast as possible.

Costs. The application fee is $15.00. Each student will pay an annual enrollment fee of $700.00 upon acceptance into the program, and every year thereafter. This fee pays for the services of the student's adviser and the UWW staff. All other educational expenses are paid by the student directly. Other fees which the student incurs include the honoraria of $50.00 paid to each of the three evaluators of the final project.

Admission requirements. UWW is looking for mature students who can work independently, are highly motivated and self-directed. High school diploma or equivalent required.

Assessment of prior learning. UWW provides assessment of prior learning from nonclassroom experience in the form of advance standing toward completion of the degree plan which lists all completed learning experiences, including those in the distant past, if relevant. Learning is assessed primarily on the basis of its relevance to the student's degree and the extent to which it represents college-level learning.

Curriculum—learning options. Students may learn in a variety of ways: standard college courses; independent study, normally under the guidance of a tutor; internships, or other work experiences; and self-directed study. Most students use a combination of learning techniques, designing a curriculum suited to their individual needs and abilities.

There is no standard length for learning experiences; neither is there a fixed number of experiences which the student must undertake at any given time. A given learning experience may range in time from a few weeks to a year.

When learning experience has been completed, its evaluation is the student's responsibility. The evaluation form is used instead of grades, and is the student's transcript. On one form the student describes the learning experience in detail. The second form gives the student an opportunity to evaluate the instructor's contribution. The third form is completed by the instructor who evaluates the student's performance with regard to the student's learning objectives.

Degree requirements. Since there are no set requirements, each student's degree plan will be individual. The degree plan must, however, be directed toward the development of competency in

a specified area of concentration as well as the attainment of a broad, liberal education.

After having completed the educational program specified in the degree plan, each student will also complete a final project which has been approved by the faculty committee, and which allows the student to demonstrate competency in some tangible way. The project should also be of some use to the wider community.

The final project is evaluated by a committee of three, two of whom are nominated by the student. Once the final project has been completed and evaluated as acceptable and satisfactory evaluations of all experiences in the approved degree plan are received, the student graduates.

Supportive services—financial aid. The student's adviser and staff members will assist in designing a degree program which best suits the financial and professional needs of the student. The Skidmore UWW is approved for BEOG, GSL, VA, New York State Scholarships and the New York Tuition Assistance Program.

STATE UNIVERSITY OF NEW YORK AT BROCKPORT
Brockport, New York   14420
(716) 395-2211

Philosophy and goals. Specifically designed for people who have life commitments and responsibilities, who must deal with demands on their time and energies as they participate in college study.

Degrees and certificates offered. Bachelor of Arts degree by the State University of New York.

Accreditation. Fully accredited by the Middle States Association of Schools and Colleges.

Academic calendar. There are no specific dates for application or admission to the program; it is a continuous operation.

Residency—required contact with program. A certain degree of contact is required with the program: admissions interview, series of examinations, enrollment seminars, in addition to 6 of every 30 credits which must be received by attending the required seminar classes and submitting a project after the seminar is over. However, there are several courses from which to choose that do not require any on-campus attendance nor do all contacts have to be on campus.

Part-time enrollment—pace. Each student must enroll for at least the one-credit hour BALS tutorial course. For full-time students, a maximum of 15 credit hours of study per semester is usually advised.

Costs. Students entering the BALS program may be charged the following:
S.U.N.Y. application fee	$10.00
Comprehensive examinations fee	60.00
Enrollment seminar fee	30.00

The following tuition and fees will be charged,

depending upon the student's choice of course work and standing in class:

	Freshman/ sophomore level	Junior/ senior Level
Residents of New York		
Tuition (per credit hour)	$25.00	$30.00
State fee (required)	.85	.85
Student government fee (required)	2.50	2.50
Nonresidents of New York		
Tuition (per credit hour)	$40.00	$50.00
State fee (required)	.85	.85
Student Government fee (required)	2.50	2.50

The following fees will be charged for those students choosing to pursue independent reading and testing programs:

Discipline and area reading lists	$10.00
Integrating area study programs	30.00
Testing fees (per test)	20.00

Admission requirements. Admission is open to anyone 22 or more years of age who holds either a high school or general equivalency diploma.

To apply, it is necessary to complete two applications: one for the State University of New York at Brockport and one for the specific degree program. The processing and evaluation of applications usually takes from four to eight weeks.

Assessment of prior learning. The student registers for a series of examinations which will be used to award credit, if applicable, toward the BALS degree, and for diagnosing the student's academic strengths and weaknesses. The Area Comprehensive Examinations allow prospective students to demonstrate academic competency in areas of study in which they did not attend formal college courses. The following tests are also available: College Level Examination Program (CLEP) in English composition, natural sciences, humanities, social sciences, and mathematics (up to 30 credit hours may be earned); Comprehensive examinations in the humanities in literature, philosophy, speech, art, music, dance, theater (up to 24 credit hours); comprehensive examinations in the natural sciences in biology, chemistry, geography, geology, earth science, and mathematics (up to 24 credit hours); comprehensive examinations in the social sciences in anthropology, economics, history, political science, psychology, and sociology (up to 24 credit hours); reading and study skills inventory is used to advise additional help, if necessary, with reading styles and comprehension for the returning college student. A portfolio for documenting prior knowledge may be accepted. Given the student's standing, interests, and needs, a program of study leading to completion of the degree is then planned.

Curriculum—learning options. The Bachelor of Arts in Liberal Studies degree is composed of four areas of study: the social sciences, natural sciences, humanities, and integrating areas. Each of the four areas is comprised of 30 credit hours of study, for a total of 120 credit hours, the minimum for a baccalaureate degree.

Within the first three areas 24 credit hours of study for each area may be completed by

transferring courses from other colleges, receiving credit by examinations, evaluation of prior knowledge gained from noncollegiate educational experiences, correspondence study, or course work taken at Brockport. The remaining 6 credit hours for each of those areas are received by attending the required seminar classes or completing an appropriate learning contract and submitting a project at the completion of the seminar.

The integrating area of study is undertaken last. This segment may include independent study or courses at Brockport. The integrating 6 credit-hour seminar and project are administered in the same way as those mentioned above.

Supportive services—financial aid. The advisers in the Office of Continuing Education provide academic and career counseling during the advisement interviews. Additional career counseling programs are available through the Campus Counseling Center.

Various state and federal financial assistance programs are available for qualified applicants, including BEOG, NDSL, New York Higher Education Assistance, State University Scholarships, and others.

UNIVERSITY COLLEGE OF SYRACUSE UNIVERSITY
Independent Study Degree Programs
610 East Fayette Street
Syracuse, New York 13202
(315) 423-3269 or 423-3284

Philosophy and goals. Provides degree opportunities to those mature men and women who seek to advance their careers and broaden their horizons in an academic atmosphere that respects their backgrounds and individuality.

Degrees and certificates offered. B.A. in liberal studies, B.S. in business administration, M.F.A. in advertising design, M.F.A. in illustration, M.B.A., and M.S.Sc. from Syracuse University.

Accreditation. Fully accredited by Middle States Association of Colleges and Secondary Schools.

Academic calendar. Program operates year-round. B.A., B.S., and M.B.A. are on a trimester format.

Residency—required contact with program. An eight-day on-campus residency period is required of each bachelor's and M.B.A. candidate at the beginning of each trimester of registered course work in May, August, and January. M.F.A. and M.S.Sc. students are required to attend two-week sessions each year in July. Outside of the residency, faculty contact is maintained through correspondence, cassettes, phone and personal visits.

Part-time enrollment. Possible in all programs except M.F.A. A student may drop in and out without having to be readmitted.

Costs. Tuition: $ 25.00 application fee
80.00 per semester hour under-

graduate
140.00 per semester hour
graduate

Deferred payment option as follows: B.A./B.S./M.B.A.:
20 percent down, balance due in three subsequent
monthly installments; M.F.A. and M.S.Sc.: 20 percent
down, balance due in ten subsequent monthly
installments.

Admission requirements. Applications consist of an
autobiography and a transcript of past work and
are accepted at any time. The autobiography should
include an analysis of previous academic work, any
reprints or summaries of professional writings
and/or accomplishments, a description of community
activities as well as current readings and the
applicant's response to them, and an appraisal of
time available for studies. Admissions are
relatively open. Students who have not earned a
high school diploma may be awarded one upon
successful completion of 24 credit hours of college
courses.

For the graduate programs, the admissions
requirements differ in that a baccalaureate degree
from an institution of recognized standing is
required, plus the submission of three letters of
recommendation with the graduate application.
Additionally, M.B.A. applicants are required to
take the Graduate Management Admission Test and
to achieve a score acceptable to the program.
M.F.A. applicants must present a portfolio of
their work for faculty review.

Assessment of prior learning. The ISDP awards
credit only for prior learning that is judged
by its faculty to meet ISDP degree requirements.
Work previously earned through other accredited
institutions is recognized on the basis of a
transcript submitted by the student. Such work
must be at the level of C or above. Credit for
independent learning in related academic areas is
granted on the basis of College Board Advanced
Placement examinations, College Board College-Level
Subject examinations, New York State College
Proficiency exams, CLEP subject examinations (not
for CLEP general exams), and/or written examinations
prepared by the ISDP faculty. Credit for relevant
professional experience may be granted on the
basis of interviews with faculty.

Curriculum—learning options. Undergraduate programs
are offered in liberal studies, which requires study
in the humanities, mathematics, social sciences
and natural sciences; and in business administration,
which combines a liberal studies program with
concentration in such areas as accounting, finance,
management, and marketing.

Three graduate programs are offered at present.
One is in fine arts, with majors in illustration
or advertising design; the social sciences master
program places emphasis upon comparative cultural
analysis; the master in business administration
program is structured around the areas of
quantitative methods, managerial control and
managerial dynamics with selected elected areas
available.

Degree requirements. B.A. in Liberal Studies:
core requirements include 18 credits in the
humanities, 12 credits in mathematics, 12 credits

in the sciences, 12 credits in the social sciences,
and an additional 18 credits distributed among
three of the four areas. To complete the degree,
a student must also have 48 credits of specialized
studies, with no more than 30 credits earned in
one area alone. There is no major in any of
the areas, but some latitude is allowed in the
upper levels for students to pursue specific
areas of concern. A 2.0 cumulative grade average
must be maintained.

B.S. in Business Administration: the basic
requirements include 49 credits of liberal arts
and sciences; and 36 credits of business administration core requirements, including 9 credits in
financial information systems, 9 credits in environmental studies, 9 credits in logistics, and 9
credits in quantitative analysis. In addition, a
student must take 12 credits in one of the four
following areas of concentration: accounting,
finance, marketing, or management. A student
also has 9 credits of work to distribute among the
remaining three areas, and 14 credits of free
electives. A 2.0 cumulative grade average must
be maintained.

M.F.A. in Advertising Design/Illustration:
30 credit hours are required for the degree; 3
hours in art history; 3 hours of television
studio or animation lab; 12 hours with
a visiting professional and 12 hours of faculty-
monitored independent study course work. Requirements for the degree will vary according to the
faculty each student works with. All students,
however, are subject to the residency requirements.

M.S.Sc.: 30 credit hours are required
for the degree: 3 hours of introductory
seminar; 18 hours of core courses (European culture,
early and modern America, nonwestern, and international relations); and 0 to 9 hours of the final
project (depends on award, if any, of transfer
credit). Two summer seminars are required for
graduation.

M.B.A.: The maximum number of credits
needed for the degree is 52, the minimum is 36;
15 credits are required in managerial control
and 7 in quantitative methods, both of which
may be waived by examination or on the
basis of transfer credit award. Additionally,
15 hours are required in managerial dynamics and
between 15 and 21 hours in elective areas.

Supportive services—financial aid. Students
have access to the services of Syracuse University,
including counseling, job placement, and financial
aid, but the major support comes from a close
relationship between Syracuse University staff
and faculty and the students enrolled in the
programs.

Approved for benefits by the Veterans
Administration. State and federal educational
loans may be applied to the Independent Study
Degrees Program. New York State residents who
are full-time students may qualify for the
Tuition Assistance Program.

UNIVERSITY OF THE STATE OF NEW YORK
Regents External Degree Program
99 Washington Avenue

Albany, New York   12210
(518) 474-3703

Philosophy and goals. The purpose is to enable independent students with college-level knowledge to earn a degree without attending college, and to stimulate individuals to seek further learning in all institutions of higher education by recognizing a variety of valid traditional and nontraditional learning experiences.

Degrees and certificates offered. A.S., A.A., B.S., B.A., B.S.B.A. (business administration), A.A.S.N. (nursing), A.S.N. (nursing), B.S.N. (nursing), all from the University of the State of New York.

Accreditation. State accreditation from the New York State Board of Regents. Also, full accreditation with the Middle States Association of Colleges and Secondary Schools. Associate level nursing degrees are accredited by the National League for Nursing.

Academic calendar. Students can enroll in the program at any time.

Residency—required contact with program Examinations are offered at various testing centers across the country. The nursing degrees, however, each require one exam which must be taken in New York State. Most students interact with the program by mail, but a network of advisers exists in New York State.

Part-time enrollment—pace. Students may proceed at their own pace.

Costs. Examination fees: most examinations cost between $25.00 and $35.00, although certain examinations cost up to $150.00. Additional costs include:

Enrollment and evaluations of previous transcripts	$ 75.00
Annual records maintenance	25.00 or $50.00
Special assessment of prior learning	200.00 or $250.00
Graduation	25.00

Admission requirements. Anyone may enroll in the program regardless of age, residence, or previous education. An enrollment form (obtained from the program) is submitted along with the nonrefundable application fee. Once enrolled, the student is required to have transcripts of past college work forwarded to the program.

Assessment of prior learning. Since the program offers no instruction of its own, learning done prior to and during enrollment is assessed in the same way. Work done under the sponsorship of a regionally accredited college or recognized testing agency (i.e., CLEP or USAIF) is counted toward the degree, provided the work meets Regents degree requirements.

Two types of examinations are offered by the program itself and are used to assess independent learning: College Proficiency Exams (CPE), which test learning of at least one semester's work in twenty college-level subjects in liberal arts and sciences, education, and nursing; and Regents External Degree examinations, which test specific levels of competency in nursing, business, and foreign languages.

If a student requests assessment of knowledge that can't be adequately assessed by existing tests, or is not well documented, special assessment is arranged.

Curriculum—learning options. A.A.: humanities, social sciences, and natural sciences/mathematics; A.S.: similar to A.A., except more elective credits for courses of a technical nature.

B.A.: same as A.A. degree; A.A. degree may be credited toward a B.A.; B.S.: requirements are same as for the B.A., except more courses of a technical nature; B.S.B.A.: to fulfill requirements of the business component, one must progressively achieve three levels of expertise in the business field (accounting, management in human resources, finance, marketing, and operations management). The degree candidate must achieve general competency in all of the areas (Achievement Level I).

A.A.S.N.: general education and a nursing component. General education requirements include humanities, social sciences, natural sciences/ mathematics and electives and can be met in a variety of ways (college courses, proficiency examinations, special assessment, and military education courses). Nursing component involves demonstration of competence in areas of health, commonalities in nursing care, differences in nursing care, and occupational strategy; A.S.N.: nursing component is identical to that of A.A.S.N. However, the general education component requires more work in the liberal arts and sciences than the A.A.S.N.; B.S.N.: requires work in both general education and nursing. General education requirements can be met by same methods as in the AASN. Nursing component involves demonstration of knowledge and competence in written examinations covering content in health restoration, health support and professional strategies. Three performance examinations test knowledge and skills in clinical performance, health assessment (history taking and physical examination) and professional performance (including leadership, management of client care, research, collaboration, clinical decision-making, relating with others).

Degree requirements. For the associate's degrees, a total of 60 credits is required; for the bachelor's degrees, a total of 120 credits is needed. Requirements can be met by passing College Proficiency, Regents External Degree exams, or other nationally recognized tests, or by presenting transcripts of equivalent baccalaureate level college courses. All candidates must take the Regents exams in clinical and professional performance.

Supportive services—financial aid. An informal network of volunteer counselors, based at various colleges throughout New York State, is available to students, primarily for assistance in procedural matters. The main source of direct academic support provided by the program is study guides for each of the tests offered. The program is approved for veterans' and Basic Educational Opportunity Grants. Some opportunities for fee waivers exist for New York residents who qualify as educationally or economically disadvantaged, or who are residents of New York State correctional facilities.

Additional information. Although it is possible to earn the Regents degree entirely by the examinations offered, most people will also use course work and tests from other colleges or testing agencies. This should be taken into account when figuring costs.

NORTH CAROLINA

SHAW UNIVERSITY
Center for Alternative Programs of Education (CAPE)
Raleigh, North Carolina   27611
(919) 755-4905—in Fayetteville area: (919) 484-8119

Philosophy and goals. Provides innovative educational delivery systems for many self-directed, highly motivated persons for whom many existing traditional undergraduate programs are too limited, too prescribed, inflexible, and unadaptable to the life conditions of mature working adults.

Degrees and certificates offered. Bachelor's degrees in the following areas: public administration/criminal justice; business management and accounting; behavioral science; liberal studies.

Accreditation. Accredited by the Southern Association of Schools and Colleges.

Academic calendar. Trimester.

Residency—required contact with program. Students pay by the credit hour and, as such, can determine their own pace. In addition, students may enroll as special students with nonmatriculating status.

Costs. Tuition is charged at the rate of $50.00 per credit hour. In addition, the university has the following fees:

	Required per semester	Optional per semester
Activity		$ 15.00
Athletics		25.00
Insurance	$ 11.50	
Shaw Journal	5.00	
Library	25.00	
Lyceum		15.00
Registration	10.00	
Student Union		20.00
Yearbook	15.00	
	$ 66.50	$ 75.00

Admission requirements. All adults and working students with high school diploma or equivalent are eligible.

Assessment of prior learning. If nonformal, out-of-class learning has occurred and can be documented, measured and/or demonstrated to be equivalent to college-level programs of study, such learning may be recognized and translated into academic credits. Students must apply for life experience credits within the first semester of enrollment. Shaw also accepts both the general and subject examinations of CLEP and the DANTES Subject Standard Test. The Guide to the Evaluation of Educational Experiences in the Armed Forces is used for the evaluation of military courses. Students in the CAPE program may receive credit by taking university-sponsored exemption examinations.

Curriculum—learning options. CAPE has no faculty, majors, or degrees separate from Shaw University but student may pursue studies through the university or through combinations of the following: independent study; specifically arranged seminars; evening classes; weekend classes; daytime classes; courses taken at other accredited colleges and universities; and cooperative education.

Degree requirements. A total of 128 credits is required for the B.A. degree. A student may not earn more than 27 semester hours through a combination of cooperative education and life experience credits. There is no limit to the number of credits a student may earn through national standard examinations (ACT, CLEP). A student may not earn more than 24 semester hours of credits through military schools or through exemption examination credits. A student may not accumulate more than a total of 60 semester hours through one or more combinations of the following alternatives: life experiences; cooperative education; exemption examinations; nationally standardized examinations; and military schools. Each student must be enrolled at Shaw for a minimum of two semesters and complete at least 24 semester hours of credits through either regular class attendance, seminars, or independent study.

Supportive services—financial aid. Specific information on financial aid may be obtained from the Office of Financial Aid. Assistance is available to students through state or federal programs, including BEOG, SEOG, NDSL, and CWS. Veterans are eligible for veterans' educational benefits. In-service persons are eligible for in-service tuition assistance.

OHIO

ANTIOCH COLLEGE
Adult Degree Completion Program
Yellow Springs, Ohio   45387
(513) 767-7331, ext. 275

Philosophy and goals. Purpose is to assist adults in the development of flexible and indivi-dualized programs which are academically sound, personally possible, and which meet Antioch-

Yellow Springs requirements for the degree.

Degrees and certificates offered. Students receive the same B.A. or B.S. degree as students in the residential program.

Accreditation. Fully accredited by the North Central Association of Colleges and Secondary Schools.

Academic calendar. Quarters. Students may apply or matriculate during any quarter in the year.

Residency—required contact with program. Students are encouraged to take classes at the Yellow Springs campus whenever possible. When this is not possible, however, students may complete their course work through independent study. In all cases, adult program students stay in contact with Antioch for planning, conferences, and evaluation.

Part-time enrollment—pace. Students do not have to study for consecutive quarters, but must finish their degree requirements within three years after entrance. Students are not required to take a full load. Counselors and advisers recommend credit load on the basis of the individual's situation.

Costs. The tuition for up to 60 credits is $2,500.00. Students whose programs require more than 60 credits may pay tuition of $50.00 per credit for each credit over 60, or may again pay $2,500.00 for up to 60 credits, depending on which is most advantageous to them.

Demonstrated learning fee of $20.00 for each application form submitted for which the ADCP office has approved and set up the appropriate evaluation session with faculty members. No charge for applications submitted if the college cannot or will not be able to do the evaluation. Each demonstrated learning form is considered applicable to one Antioch course depending on the judgment of the evaluator.

Admission requirements. Applicants must have reached 25 years of age; have completed two years of college (60 credits), or two years at an accredited nursing, business or technical school; have worked or been a homemaker or consistent volunteer in community services for at least two years; not have attended a four-year college full-time in the past two years.

Assessment of prior learning. Students work closely with two assigned advisers, one from the academic department in which the student is majoring and one from the Center for Cooperative Education (CCE). With the assistance of these advisers and, as needed, ADCP committee members, students assess past academic achievement and plan individual programs of study.

Transfer credits from other accredited colleges or universities, and for which they have received a grade of C or better, are accepted as part of degree requirements. Before the preadmissions conferences, the ADCP committee assists applicants to identify past learning relevant to proposed

degree programs and, after consultation with faculty members, advises the applicant on ways to prepare documentation. Evaluation is done through interviews, regular course examinations, faculty-prepared tests covering specific content areas, skill demonstrations, oral examinations, papers, products or portfolios of materials, taped or filmed presentations, and other methods acceptable to the faculty member. Additionally, Antioch accepts CLEP and USAFI credits for transfer.

Curriculum—learning options. Participation is open to adults throughout the United States, largely through independent study, which includes regular courses and tutorials taken independently; reading assignments and papers in conjunction with on-the-job training experiences; preplanned projects such as film-making, painting, musical composition, research, creative writing; student-designed courses. All the foregoing must be supervised and approved by Antioch-Yellow Springs faculty.

Students may also enroll in courses and use facilities of other colleges in the Miami Valley Consortium.

Degree requirements. Adult program students receive the same degree as regular Antioch students and must meet the same degree requirements. To graduate, student needs to complete a minimum of 160 academic credits (divided between general education, a major field, and electives) and eight quarters of work or other nonclassroom activity. Students must obtain 60 credits to meet the general education requirement, 60 in the major field and 40 credits of electives. The eight quarter work requirement is usually met before entrance to the ADCP.

Supportive services—financial aid. The principal sources of support are the student's advisers and counselors in the ADCP Office. Financial assistance available includes BEOG, SSIG, GSL, NDSL, CWS, veterans' benefits.

OHIO UNIVERSITY
Extension Division
Independent Study Program
Athens, Ohio   45701
(614) 594-6721
In Ohio call: 1-800-282-4408

Philosophy and goals. Purpose is to provide a number of flexible ways by which persons capable of pursuing college-level work can earn college credit without some of the limitations imposed by the traditional university structure. Independent study allows an individual to learn at the time, place, and rate suited to his or her own particular needs.

Degrees and certificates offered. Bachelor of General Studies; Bachelor of Arts; Bachelor of Science; Associate in Arts; Associate in Individualized Studies.

Accreditation. Fully accredited by the North Central Association of Colleges and Secondary Schools.

Academic calendar. Quarters.

Residency—required contact with program. The Bachelor of General Studies can be earned entirely through off-campus study. Other degrees may also be earned primarily through independent study, but because of specific degree requirements, the choice of courses within the degree programs may be limited.

Part-time enrollment. Possible.

Costs. Fees (per quarter hour):

Independent study courses	$ 14.50
Independent study projects	17.50
Course credit by examination	7.50
External student application fee	30.00 (one-time fee)

Admission requirements. Open to all who can profit from it and formal admission to the university is not required for enrollment. Admission does not, however, constitute admission to Ohio University or any of its degree programs. Most persons who enroll are high school graduates, but it is not a requirement. Persons interested in pursuing an Ohio University degree, primarily off-campus, through the independent study options may submit an External Student application form. In this form the student provides information about degree goals, past educational experiences, and other data. The application will be evaluated to see if Ohio University can accommodate the goals. This will include an informal evaluation of any previous college work. Ohio University also conducts a College Degree program in selected correctional institutions in Ohio. Financial aid for the incarcerated student is often available to eligible persons. A brochure explaining the program is available upon request from the Independent Study office. To be admitted to the BGS program, a student must have earned 45 quarter hours of credit at a grade point average of 2.0.

Assessment of prior learning. Credit earned at other accredited colleges may generally be transferred if the grade earned is C or better. Credit may be granted for service school courses which are the equivalent of college-level work and for which credit is recommended by the Office of Educational Credit and recorded in A Guide to the Evaluation of Educational Experiences in the Armed Services. In general all published credit recommendations of the Commission on Educational Credit of the American Council on Education are recognized by Ohio University to the extent that they relate to the university programs. Credit may be awarded on the basis of outstanding performance on the CLEP subject examinations, or through the Ohio University Course Credit by Examination program, which allows the student to demonstrate prior college-level learning.

Curriculum—learning options. Student may choose from a number of study options, according to the amount of direction they need. Among the options are:

    a. Independent study courses which are highly structured and involve a tutorial relationship with a faculty member who assists in the selection of textbooks and other learning aids. Generally, a midterm and final exam are required for each course.

    b. Independent study projects, which are based upon regular undergraduate courses at Ohio University. Projects can be created only in topic areas which are not currently available as independent study courses. Arrangements are made on an individual basis, contingent upon the approval of the department in which the course is offered and the availability of a qualified faculty member willing to direct the project.

    The student and faculty member agree upon the learning options, which can include a variety of readings, examinations, papers and projects.

    c. Course credit by examination, in which students receive a brief syllabus which describes the nature of the course, the textbooks and other material to study and the type of examination, for which students prepare on their own; the supervised exam must be taken within six months.

Degree requirements. The Bachelor of General Studies degree is awarded for the satisfactory completion of 192 credit hours with a grade average of 2.0 or above; of these 45 credit hours must be in one concentration area, and 90 must be on the junior/senior level. A minimum of 45 credit hours must be completed while enrolled in the BGS program.

    The Associate in Arts is awarded for the satisfactory completion of a minimum of 96 quarter hours of credit with a minimum 2.0 accumulative grade point average. The 96 credits for the A.A. must include at least 30 credits in arts and humanities courses (some credits in each area), 15 credits in social and/or behavioral sciences and 15 credits in natural sciences and/or mathematics.

    The Associate in Individualized Studies is awarded for the satisfactory completion of a minimum of 96 quarter hours of credit with a minimum 2.0 accumulative grade point average in a self-designed course of study. The student must complete the A.I.S. application outlining an intended course of study and indicate an area of concentration. No minimum or maximum number of credits is required within an area of concentration, with such a determination to be made by resource people in consultation with the student in the development of the program.

Supportive services—financial aid. Counseling and degree planning services are provided throughout the program for individuals earning Ohio University degrees through the External Student Independent Study Program.

    Ohio University and its degree programs are approved for funding by the Veterans Administration. Eligible students who are pursuing their degree by independent study courses and projects will be reimbursed for tuition and fees. The Ohio University independent study courses are listed in the DANTES Independent Study Catalog and tuition assistance may be available to military personnel enrolling in these courses.

UNION GRADUATE SCHOOL
106 Woodrow Street
Yellow Springs, Ohio   45387
(513) 767-7231

Philosophy and goals. It is a UGS premise that a student who sets personal goals enlightened by expert counsel can choose the most effective means to accomplish those goals by receiving informed and dependable feedback on individual progress. Meaningful colloquia with experienced professionals increases the likelihood of satisfaction in learning and of forming the habit of life-long intellectual development.

Degrees and certificates offered. Ph.D. from the Union Graduate School.

Accreditation. UGS is a candidate for accreditation status by the North Central Association of Colleges and Secondary Schools.

Academic calendar. Program operates year-round, but colloquia, which generally begin the student's matriculation, are offered at specific and different times for each of the school's five programs.

Residency—required contact with program. Residency requirements differ for each of the five programs:
    UGS/One students attend either two ten-day or one twenty-day colloquia (offered five times a year in different parts of the country) and are expected to attend two additional weeks of mini-colloquia or similar gatherings; UGS/West students attend one entering residential two-week colloquium (offered three times a year) and three residential one-week seminars, held at three-month intervals, all on the West Coast; UGS/Leadership in Education students are required to attend an initial ten-day colloquium in residence, followed by several mini-colloquia, for a total of a six-week residential requirement; UGS/Center for Minority Studies students fulfill a six-week residency requirement by attending quarterly weekend mini-colloquia and two-week summer colloquia; and Goodwin Watson Institute for Research and Program Development students begin with a two- to three-day planning meeting for orientation. Additional residential time is negotiated in individual learning contracts.
    Students in all programs are required to maintain frequent contact with a core faculty member, and also with two adjunct professors and two student peers who compose the student's educational committee.

Part-time enrollment—pace. Although programs are tailored to individual needs, students are expected to work continuously from the time of admission until the degree is completed.

Costs. Tuition $2,800.00/year
Admission fee   25.00
Tuition is payable in quarterly installments. Students with an M.A. must study for at least one and a half years before earning a degree, and may work for as long as four years. A minimum of 2 years is required for persons without an M.A. Students who are granted "interim status," or a temporary leave because they cannot pursue their

work on a full-time basis, must pay $100.00. Only one six-month interim period is permitted. Students who are granted extensions for work to be completed after the customary four years are assessed the regular $700.00 per quarter. In addition, the student must bear all costs for attendance at colloquia, including transportation, room, and board.

Admission requirements. With few exceptions, entering candidates have progressed beyond the baccalaureate degree, most have earned master's degrees, and many have done additional graduate study. In general, applications include an extensive autobiographical essay describing in some detail the applicant's background, including a description of the applicant's current situation and a full description of educational and professional goals which provides a frank picture of strengths and weaknesses, and explains why these goals cannot be pursued adequately in a traditional doctoral program. Students must also arrange to have all college and postcollege study transcripts forwarded to the school, as well as three recommendations. Some students may be asked for interviews.
    Each of the five programs has somewhat different criteria and procedures. Additional information and application forms should be requested from the different programs at the following addresses: Union Graduate School/One and Union Graduate School/Leadership in Education: 106 Woodrow Street, Yellow Springs, Ohio 45387.
    Union Graduate School/West: 717 Market Street, Suite 616, San Francisco, California 94103.
    Goodwin Watson Institute for Research and Program Development: 2331 Victory Parkway, Cincinnati, Ohio 45206.
    Union Graduate School/Center for Minority Studies, c/o Coppin State College, 2500 West North Avenue, Baltimore, Maryland 21216.

Assessment of prior learning. Prior learning, demonstrated through transcripts, the autobiographical essay, and meetings with core faculty during the initial colloquium, is used to help determine the nature and content of the individual study program.

Curriculum—learning options. UGS/One and UGS/West allow study in many fields; UGS/One is primarily for students east of the Rockies, and UGS/West is primarily for students west of the Rockies. The Leadership in Education Program is designed for persons engaged in any aspect of education. The Goodwin Watson Institute for Research and Program Development is for people with special interests in research and in effecting change in institutions of higher learning and other areas of society. The Center for Minority Studies is for students interested in study, research, and internships concerned with the history, culture, and/or problems of disadvantaged minorities living within the United States and its territories. Each of the programs is run somewhat differently, but the programs do share certain basic similarities. Individual study plans are devised and revised by students in frequent consultation with their education committees. Study plans are comprised of three parts:

independent studies, which involve participation in colloquia, selected reading lists, and other forms of traditional and/or nontraditional study to broaden and deepen a student's learning; internship, usually of one year's duration, in which a student works closely with a professional or professionals in one or two fields, or possibly does independent study, but definitely completes a project relating theoretical knowledge to practical situations; and a project demonstrating excellence, which must represent a significant contribution to our culture.

Learning agreements are certified by the learner's committee.

Degree requirements. Students must complete their study plans and project, and submit their work in full to program committee for appraisal. Students must work in program for a minimum of one year (those with only a B.A. two years) and a maximum of four years.

Supportive services—financial aid. The student's core faculty adviser and educational committee are the main resources. In addition, students are expected to meet with each other with some frequency, both formally and informally. A limited amount of financial aid is available in the form of National Direct Student Loans and College Work-Study funds. Information is available from the financial aid administrator of the UGS program unit in which the student intends to enroll.

Additional information. Enrollment is over seven hundred.

OKLAHOMA

FLAMING RAINBOW UNIVERSITY
University Without Walls
14 South First Street
Stilwell, Oklahoma   74960
(918) 774-3644
406 East Downing Street
Talequah, Oklahoma   74464
(918) 456-5662

Philosophy and goals. An independent member of the Union for Experimenting Colleges and Universities; focus is on the development of an educational institution that could answer the needs of the American Indian community. An academic process has been evolved that offers personalized learning in a culturally distinct environment. This means offering a range of learning that includes basic skills and the latest individualized educational techniques.

Degrees and certificates offered. Bachelor of Arts from the UECU.

Accreditation. Full state accreditation.

Academic calendar. Semesters. Semesters are extended to six-month cycles to allow for the use of multiple delivery systems, such as consecutive rather than concurrent course work. The fall semester runs from July through December, and the spring semester from January through June.

Residency—required contact with program. It is possible to design a program of study that requires minimum contact with the program. However, because of the unique nature of Flaming Rainbow, students are encouraged to maintain regular contact when possible.

Part-time enrollment—pace. All students are viewed as full-time enrollees. A full-time enrollee is defined as a student who completes no less than four courses in a given semester.

Costs. Tuition is $700.00 per semester or $1,400.00 annually. The only additional fee charged to students is an annual library fee of $20.00.

Admission requirements. Any person at least 18 years of age or possessing a high school diploma/GED certificate may apply. No attempt is made to block enrollment because of previous academic failure at any level. Individual attention is given to the academic needs of each student from the time the enrollment process begins. A formal decision by an admissions committee will be transmitted to the applicant indicating:

a. acceptance to Flaming Rainbow;

b. provisional acceptance as a special student, including the specific special conditions for admission and continued matriculation;

c. refusal to accept the applicant, giving the reasons why Flaming Rainbow cannot meet his/her learning needs.

Assessment of prior learning. The method or process for assessment of prior learning is divided into four categories:

a. General information from student via personal interview, in which short- and long-term goals and aspirations are discussed;

b. formal educational data, including elementary, secondary, and previous college credit. All information must be validated by official documents;

c. practical work experience data, including all paid and unpaid work experience. If possible, this information will be verified by immediate supervisor or personnel department;

d. education and/or knowledge gained via practical living experiences shown by CLEP, ACT, or other formal tests, and through a qualitative interview approach.

The maximum number of allowable credits is 20 units; however, this maximum will only be granted in exceptional cases.

Curriculum—learning options. The educational process at Flaming Rainbow utilizes a variety of delivery systems, including seminars, workshops, classes, self-directed study, and individual work with faculty.

Lower Divison
First year: 1 unit, learning to Learn I.
Emphasizes communication skills, study skills,
learning to take effective notes, learning to
use library resources, and assists the student
in making the transition into an academic situation;
10 units, Exploratory Studies. An investigation
of a number of academic disciplines utilizing
various learning modes and following individual
interests. Provides an overview of many disciplines
and a basis for future indepth studies.
Second year: 10 units, Interdisciplinary Studies.
Interdisciplinary approach to meeting the breadth
expectation of a postsecondary education in the
arts and humanities, social sciences, behavioral
sciences and natural sciences; 1 unit, Learning
to Learn II. This marks the transition to
upper-division studies and orients the student
to the methods of self-directed learning.

Upper Division
Third year: 10 units, area of concentration.
Projects during the year are designed to fulfill
depth expectations for the area in which the
student is specializing.
Fourth year: 10 units, Senior Studies. Student
must provide a qualitative and quantitative
demonstration of the performance and competency
abilities in the area of concentration. This can
range from major research project to a program of
intensive reading and study in the major field.
Students' long- and short-term educational
objectives are articulated in a learning agreement.

Degree requirements. The unit system of value for
work completed is based on a minimum of 42 units
for graduation. One unit is the equivalent of
3 semester credit hours; 42 units equal the 126
credit hours required for graduation at traditional
institutions.

Minimum time in residence is twelve months
for students who transfer from other institutions
of higher education with three or more years of
transfer credit.

Supportive services—financial aid. Flaming
Rainbow employs a full-time financial aid officer.
The university participates in NDSL, CWS, FISL,
BEOG, SEOG, Tuition Aid Grant Program (Oklahoma),
and Bureau of Indian Affairs Scholarship.

Additional information. The institutional objective
for Flaming Rainbow over the next five years is
to become a national Indian university. Its
purpose is to provide postsecondary services for
people of diverse cultural groups, especially
to the low-income, and educationally underserved
American Indian of eastern Oklahoma, while
functioning as a model for the National Indian
University.

OKLAHOMA CITY SOUTHWESTERN COLLEGE
External Directed Studies, Inc.
4700 N.W. 10th Street
Oklahoma City, Oklahoma 73127
(405) 947-2331

Philosophy and goals. Designed for that segment
of student population that, because of various
commitments, finds itself immobile or otherwise
unable to take advantage of a campus experience.

Degrees and certificates offered. A.A. in
business administration, business management,
religious institution management, technical
management, and sociology; A.S. in pre-teaching,
law enforcement, and pre-law.

Accreditation. Fully accredited as a two-year
college by the North Central Association of
Colleges and Secondary Schools and Oklahoma
State Regents for Higher Education.

Academic calendar. Semester.

Residency—required contact with program. Students
may complete their degrees entirely through
independent study.

Part-time enrollment—pace. Students are allowed
to proceed at their own pace.

Costs. Tuition is $25.00 per credit, plus a
course fee of $10.00 for books and cassettes.

Admission requirements. Submission of
enrollment application form, along with summary
of all military and civilian work that possibly
could receive college credit; transcripts from
each civilian college or university attended.

Assessment of prior learning. OCSC will accept
work completed at accredited institutions, either
on campus or through external programs. Work
is acceptable provided the student has an overall
2.0 (C) on the 4.0 scale. Learning attained
through service schools as recommended by the
American Council on Education is acceptable,
as well as credits earned through the Community
College of the Air Force.

Parts 1, 2, 3, 4, and 5 of the CLEP general
examination will be evaluated at 6 semester hours
each if passed with a percentile score of 25
or higher. CLEP subject examination will be
evaluated at 3 semester hours per subject if
passed with a percentile score as recommended
by E.T.S. DANTES subject examinations will grant
credit for courses, group study, and end-of-course
tests. The minimum acceptable percentile score
will be 25. However, in each case, the Course
Review Board will determine course transferability.

GED general examinations pertain to Old
College Level GED; 6 semester hours are granted
per section passed. Acceptable scores are as
follows:

Test number one	55
Test number two	60
Test number three	61
Test number four	57

or an overall average of 60 on all four tests.

Curriculum—learning options. Students follow a
prescribed program for completion of the degree.
Home study courses are the only learning options
other than assessment of previous learning.
The courses in the EDS program are structured
around a text and a linearly programmed guide.
The guides are divided into modules, with each

module pretested, posttested, and bearing behavioral objectives. In addition, audio cassette tapes accompany each course and parallel the module on which the student is studying.

Module evaluations, provided in each course, must be remitted to the college, examined by the students' assigned professor, and returned to the student before the final course examination is written by the student.

Degree requirements. To obtain an Associate of Arts or Science degree, 64 semester hours are required. Of these, 12 of the last 21 hours must be earned through Oklahoma City Southwestern College. This requirement may be satisfied internally or externally. In addition, students must complete the prescribed course sequence and requirements of their degree program.

Supportive services—financial aid. Students in the EDS have access to all the support services of OCSC. The program is approved for veterans.

UNIVERSITY OF OKLAHOMA
Bachelor of Liberal Studies
College of Liberal Studies
1700 Asp Avenue
Norman, Oklahoma   73037
(405) 325-1061

Philosophy and goals. The purpose is to provide an academic program for adult students who because of job, family, or other circumstances, cannot pursue a baccalaureate degree in the traditional manner. The BLS Specialty Option is built on the core curriculum of the Bachelor of Liberal Studies, with the addition of special studies in a selected field of interest. The programs are directed to the needs of employees who seek to know more about their field and at the same time earn a college degree; they are not intended to meet preemployment needs of younger job seekers. A Master of Liberal Studies program is designed for the person who has a B.A. in a special field or a general liberal arts degree and desires broader liberal learning at the graduate level.

Degrees and certificates offered. B.L.S., Specialty Option Program, Criminal Justice Studies, Education Studies, Management Studies, Paralegal Studies, Women's Studies, Upper Division Option. Master of Liberal Studies.

Accreditation. Fully accredited by North Central Association of Colleges and Schools.

Academic calendar. Admission and enrollment for the programs can occur at any time of the year.

Residency—required contact with program. BLS: one three-week seminar per year. One four-week seminar the final year. B.L.S./Upper Division Option: two-day introductory seminar; three-week comprehensive area seminar; four-week inter-area seminar. M.L.S.: One-week introductory seminar, three-week colloquium, three-week advanced seminar.

Part-time enrollment—pace. Students proceed at their own pace in each area of independent study and complete a comprehensive exam.

Costs. B.L.S.	In-state	Out-of-st
Total four-year cost	$2,160.00	$4,275.00
B.L.S. Upper Division Option		
Total four-year cost	1,270.00	2,500.00

Fees include the use of assigned books. There is a deferred monthly payment plan for students enrolled in independent study.

M.L.S. program		
Total two-year cost	975.00	1,900.00

Books are not included in M.L.S. costs.

A record maintenance of $50.00 is charged for maintenance of records in all programs, after the first year.

Admission requirements. B.L.S.: high school graduates are admissible. B.L.S. Upper Division Option: is available to applicants who have an associate's degree or who have completed 60 or more college hours. M.L.S.: requires admission to the Graduate College of the University of Oklahoma. Admission applications provided by the College of Liberal Studies.

Assessment of prior learning. Placement tests allow students to enter each area at their own ability levels. Prior college credit, advanced standing examinations, and CLEP scores may be applied toward advanced standing in B.L.S. and permits possible exemption in some phases.

B.L.S. Upper Division Option: Assessment of prior learning is applicable to meet requirements.

M.L.S.: not available.

Curriculum—learning options. The B.L.S. combines guided independent study and three-week seminar in three areas of study—humanities, natural sciences, and social sciences—plus a final inter-area which includes independent study in an area. Students are expected to complete one area of study in a year; however, some complete degree requirements in shorter or longer periods.

B.L.S. Specialty Option Program: students comple 3 units in the specialty along with study in B.L.S. independent study. A unit consists of a study guide, reading list, and job-related project. For a specialty option there are 10 to 15 units, of which the student will select and complete 9. The liberal studies curriculum is partially defined by a core book list. Progress is evaluated by a comprehensive examination.

B.L.S. Upper Division Option: liberal studies curriculum is the same as in the basic B.L.S. program. Independent study is individually tailored to the student's prior academic achievement. A two-day introductory seminar, guided independent study, a three-week comprehensive area seminar focusing on one of the three basic areas; inter-area independent study which includes critiquing specified books and writing a study in depth; a four-week seminar on an interdisciplinary theme. Evaluation includes performance on a comprehensive exam at the end of a study phase in the comprehensive area and the inter-area.

M.L.S.: Students can pursue specific interests in individualized programs planned for their needs and objectives concentrating in one of the three broad areas—humanities, natural sciences, social sciences. With the flexibility of the curriculum, students may pursue reading and research related to their career interests. One-week introductory seminar; directed reading—approximately one year of assigned readings by faculty adviser; colloquium—three weeks, pursues a theme or problem and leads to development of master's thesis topic. Advanced study of about one year, with faculty director; master's thesis; advanced seminar—three weeks; an interdisciplinary theme is explored and there is a final review of the thesis by a faculty committee.

Degree requirements. Candidates for B.L.S. degrees must earn 124 credit hours by the completion of each of the phases described. Candidates for the M.L.S. degree must earn 32 credits by completing each of the phases described.

Supportive services—financial aid. Faculty advisers are the main source of contact for each student, although additional counseling is available if needed.

Students in the program are eligible for the following financial aid programs: BEOG, SEOG, NDSL, CWS, GSL, state-sponsored financial aid, and veterans' benefits.

PENNSYLVANIA

ELIZABETHTOWN COLLEGE
Center for Community Education
Elizabethtown, Pennsylvania   17022
(717) 367-1151

Philosophy and goals. Established in 1973 to meet the needs of adults through the incorporation of a broad range of learning experiences and recognition of the value of self-directed education.

Degrees and certificates offered. Bachelor of Liberal Studies; Bachelor of Professional Studies; Associate of Arts; and Associate of Science.

Accreditation. Fully accredited by the Middle States Association of Colleges and Secondary Schools. Provisional accreditation status from the National Association of Schools of Music.

Academic calendar. Students may enroll at anytime.

Residency—required contact with program. Major form of contact is appearance before an evaluation committee.

Part-time enrollment—pace. Candidates pursue the requirements for consideration at their own pace.

Costs. The comprehensive fee for prior learning assessment is the equivalent of one semester of full-time tuition. For the 1977-78 academic year, this is $1,500.00. The comprehensive fee becomes due in segments as follows: $500.00 upon enrollment in the program, $500.00 accompanying submission of the completed dossier, and $500.00 following action by the evaluation committee. Non-refundable application fee is $25.00.

The candidate is responsible for the cost of any examinations employed in the documentation of learning and any course work or other learning experiences used to satisfy the requirements of the evaluation committee.

Admission requirements. Upon receipt of the completed application information, the Center for Community Education will review the application and will, within 30 days, advise the applicant in writing regarding admission to the program. A high school diploma or equivalent is required.

Assessment of prior learning/Curriculum—learning options. Since the Center for Community Education itself offers no instruction, learning done prior to enrollment is treated in the same way as learning done after enrollment. After enrollment the candidate assembles information and compiles a detailed dossier of all prior learning. Detailed instructions for the content and format of the dossier will be forwarded following enrollment. The completed dossier should be submitted within nine months following enrollment. After a preliminary review by the Center staff, the completed dossier is evaluated for credit by evaluation committee.

Credit for courses completed with a grade of C or better at an accredited college or university are transferred directly. Course work at non-accredited institutions may be accepted on an individual basis.

Other structured learning, such as professional and technical school courses, military and government training, business and industrial in-house programs, seminars, workshops, and correspondence courses is not documented in terms of academic credit. These experiences are evaluated on an individual basis with respect to their content and method of instruction.

Learning may also be demonstrated by examination. Six semester hours of credit are awarded for a satisfactory score on each of the CLEP general examinations, and either three or six semester hours are awarded for passage of each CLEP subject examination, depending on its scope. Other standardized examination programs will be considered on an individual basis.

Also, special examination in certain topic areas can be constructed and administered by the Elizabethtown College faculty upon arrangement with the Director of the Center.

When adequate evidence of learning is present, six semester hours are awarded for each year of full-time work in the major area of study, and two semester hours for each year of full-time work not related to the major. Avocational learning may not be specifically credited but will be considered as it serves to meet the educational goals of Elizabethtown College.

Degree requirements. Approximately 145 semester hours is required for a baccalaureate degree, and approximately 70 semester hours are required for an associate's degree. Because of the highly individual character of each degree program, "the evaluation committee may approve small deviations from these requirements."

A maximum of 60 semester hours of credit from work and/or life experience may be counted toward the baccalaureate degree, and no more than 30 semester hours may be counted toward an associate degree.

Each degree program has three required components: a major area of study, a liberal distribution of learning in areas of general education, and a body of learning which meets remaining credit hour requirements for graduation. The evaluation committee has the responsibility to establish the specific requirements and to confer the degree.

Supportive services. Center staff are the major source of support for the student.

NORTHAMPTON COUNTY AREA COMMUNITY COLLEGE
College at Home Program
3835 Green Pond Road
Bethlehem, Pennsylvania 18017
(215) 865-5351

Philosophy and goals. College courses leading to a certificate or associate's degree, or taken for general interest.

Degrees and certificates offered. Associate's degree in accounting, business administration, child care education, liberal arts, education, and general education. Certificates in architectural technology, child care education, typing.

Accreditation. Fully accredited by the Middle States Association of Colleges and Secondary Schools.

Academic calendar. Semesters and courses can begin every day of the year subject to the availability of an instructor. The time period alloted to complete a course is sixteen weeks.

Residency—required contact with program. It is possible for students in the CAHP to complete programs without classroom attendance, but frequent contact with faculty members is strongly encouraged. Course arrangements are made on an individual basis by personal consultations, telephone conferences, cassette exchanges and mailings.

Part-time enrollment—pace. The program is designed for part-time enrollment.

Costs. For residents of sponsoring school districts (Bangor, Bethlehem, Easton, Nazareth, Northampton, Pen Argyl, Saucon Valley, and Wilson) and for other Pennsylvania residents who have made special arrangements through their local community college, the tuition is $20.00 per credit. For other Pennsylvania residents who are not served by a community college, or who have not made special arrangements with one, tuition is $40.00 per credit. For out-of-state students, cost is $60.00 per credit.

For all students, fees are as follows:

Application fee (nonrefundable)—$10.00; transcript of academic records (first transcript free, each additional copy—$1.00); college comprehensive fee for all students (nonrefundable) —$2.00 per credit hour.

Admission requirements. Admissions are limited to those who are unable to attend regular, on-campus courses and to those who are self-motivated. Application is made through the Admission Office. Previous school record is considered, but a high school diploma is not required. Personal interviews are required to determine why regular attendance is not possible and if the applicant possesses sufficient motivation to study at home.

Assessment of prior learning. The College Level Examination Program and many departmental challenge exams are offered. All credit is granted after successful completion of six credits at NCACC. A maximum of 30 credits will be granted for CLEP, challenge examinations, Advanced Placement Exams, or any combination thereof.

Previous college experience can be applied toward a degree program at NCACC. Transcripts will be evaluated by the records office to determine whether credit can be received.

Curriculum—learning options. Courses are the same as those taken by on-campus students. Students work independently and establish individualized instruction plans to meet learning goals. Students work at their own pace, in their own homes, completing courses within a 16-week period, and are encouraged to take one course at a time, registering for another upon completion of the first course.

Each degree program contains a general education core consisting of a minimum number of semester hours in the fields of humanities, social science, math and sciences.

Letter grades are determined on the basis of achievement. Course examinations can be arranged by mail.

Degree requirements. A minimum of 60 semester hours of credit are required, of which 15 must be taken at NCACC, either through the CAHP or on campus. Of the last 15 hours prior to receiving an associate's degree, 9 must be taken through NCACC, the remainder of the credit requirement can be completed elsewhere and in other ways.

Supportive services—financial aid. Tutorial services are available at no charge upon recommendation of an instructor. This can be arranged at the campus, at an associated community based learning center, or in the home, if necessary.

A learning resources center located on campus can be reached by telephone and materials may be borrowed through the mail. Materials include books, cassettes, slides and instructional kits.

Cassette equipment and slide viewers are available on campus and at several community based learning centers, and can also be borrowed for use at home.

Financial aid is available on a limited basis. A brochure on financial aid for part-time students can be obtained from the Financial Aid

Office. Veterans Administration benefits can be applied towards CAHP fees. However, only tuition and fees are reimbursable. No monthly stipend is given.

Additional information. Nearly 1,200 students began CAHP courses in 1974-78.

UNIVERSITY OF PITTSBURGH
External Studies Program
Pittsburgh, Pennsylvania   15260
(412) 624-3333

Philosophy and goals. Established in 1972 to meet the educational needs of adults in the southwestern Pennsylvania area whose time and mobility are limited by work or family obligations. The program enables those who can't attend classes on a regular basis to earn college credits at home at the same pace as students enrolled in on-campus evening classes. It also provides an alternative to traditional classroom instruction for those who prefer more independence in their study.

Degrees and certificates offered. Bachelor of Arts and Bachelor of Science degrees.

Accreditation. Fully accredited by Middle States Association of Colleges and Secondary Schools.

Academic calendar. Trimester. Terms begin in September, January, and May.

Residency—required contact with program. Each course requires attendance at three on-campus meetings during the 15-week term. These workshops are held on the Oakland Campus of the University of Pittsburgh on Saturday morning or afternoon, depending on courses selected. At these sessions students meet with instructors and engage in specific learning activities.

Part-time enrollment—pace. Most students are enrolled on a part-time basis. A minimum of one course per year is necessary to avoid re-enrollment fees.

Costs. Application fee: $15.00 (nonrefundable)
Tuition for part-time students (fewer than 12 credits) is:
Pennsylvania residents $ 51.00 per credit.
Nonresidents   102.00 per credit.
Tuition for full-time students (12 credits or more) is:
Pennsylvania residents $ 655.00 per term
Nonresidents   1,310.00 per term
For the spring term only, full-time tuition is computed on a per-credit basis.

Admission requirements. Students who wish to earn a bachelor's degree must satisfy the following criteria for admission:
   a. Must be high school graduates or have passed the General Educational Development (GED) test.
   b. Students who have attended another

college or university are required to be in good standing, with a cumulative quality point average of 2.00 or better.
   c. Applicants who intend to pursue a program leading to a bachelor's degree, but who do not meet the criteria required for admission as degree students, may be admitted as degree provisional students. The provisional student may not register for more than two courses per 15-week term. Upon completion of 12 to 18 credits with a quality point average of 2.00 or better, the student is admitted as a degree candidate.

Assessment of prior learning. A maximum of 90 credits of acceptable work taken by a matriculated student at another four-year institution will be approved for transfer. Scores on the CLEP general examinations may be submitted for evaluation for advanced placement after admission.

Curriculum—learning options. A specially-prepared Study Guide is coordinated with the textbooks and gives students guidance while learning on their own. Majors are available in economics, psychology, public administration, and social sciences area of concentration.

Degree requirements. To earn a degree students must take at least 120 credit hours. The last 30 credits, or the work of the senior year, including at least 15 credits in the major, must be taken in the School of General Studies.
   The 120 credit hours must be distributed among the academic areas indicated below:

ACADEMIC AREA	CREDITS REQUIRED
Communications	9
Languages, math, logic	6-8
Lower-Level Understandings	
Humanities	12
Social sciences	12
Natural sciences	12
Upper-Level Understandings	
Humanities, social sciences,	
natural sciences	9
Major Areas of Study	Variable
Electives	Variable

Supportive services—financial aid. Students have access to all the University of Pittsburgh facilities and services. A newsletter published six times a term is the major communications link between the staff and students. It provides program and course information as well as articles of special interest.
   Students who enroll for 6 or more credits are eligible for financial aid including BEOG, SEOG, NDSL, and GSL. External Studies courses are approved for benefits under the G.I. Bill.

RHODE ISLAND

ROGER WILLIAMS COLLEGE
Open Division
Old Ferry Road
Bristol, Rhode Island   02809
(401) 255-1000

Philosophy and goals. Designed to provide a degree program with only minimal interference with students' employment, family, and personal commitments. It seeks to serve people who have determined that a traditional academic structure is unsuitable, undesirable, or unavailable to them.

Degrees and certificates offered. B.A. or B.S.

Accreditation. Fully accredited by the New England Association of Schools and Colleges.

Academic calendar. Fall and spring semesters.

Residency—required contact with program. Students are expected to maintain a negotiated amount of contact with their facilitators. Students are also required to participate in a minimum of eight classroom courses, taken either at Roger Williams College or another institution.

Part-time enrollment. Possible.

Costs. Tuition:

1 course	$ 253.00
2 courses	506.00
3 courses	759.00
4 courses	1,012.00
Full-time	1,265.00

Students who register for more than one course must also pay the following:

Student activity fee	$20.00
Athletic fee	5.00
Health fee	5.00

Assessment of prior learning $50.00

Admission requirements. Admission is normally limited to people who have a record of successful previous college attendance and/or a record of creditable employment experience. Students without previous college experience may be required to take advanced placement examinations (such as CLEP) and to enroll in classroom courses prior to enrollment in external forms of study. People without previous college attendance and/or creditable employment experience are discouraged from applying.

Assessment of prior learning. Academic credit may be awarded for any prior or current life and work experience which (1) represents college-level skills or competencies, and (2) can be properly documented, verified, and related to educational objectives. The evidence for this documentation may be supplied by any of the following: formal but noncredit educational programs (certificates, official descriptions, etc.); products of the experience (reports, articles, films, etc.); job descriptions, sufficiently detailed; third party documentation of accomplishments and proficiency (supervisory ratings, awards, licenses, external or internal examinations); student's written and/or oral analysis of the epxerience; or display of skills and talents before an expert. An adviser for credit documentation will provide help or clarification in preparing credit documentation request.

Students may receive credit for work previously completed at other colleges or universities. Also, credit may be granted from the CLEP tests or from similar tests. Military training programs are credited if such programs can be shown to be the equivalent of college-level study.

Curriculum—learning options Students help draft and design their own programs of study. Programs are usually combinations of study which may include tutorials, independent studies, directed readings, internships, classroom courses, lectures, conferences, employment or volunteer service, travel. Open Division students may utilize the regularly-scheduled classroom courses at the college from the day programs, the continuing education programs, or the summer sessions, as well as classroom courses offered at other colleges and universities.

An external course (independent study or directed readings) in which the student meets periodically with an instructor can be arranged for students who find it difficult to attend classroom courses or who wish to study a subject not available in the classroom.

Degree requirements. A total of 38 units of credit (equivalent to 38 courses) are required for graduation. Of the 38, 2 approved units in the social sciences, 2 in the natural sciences, and 2 in the humanities/fine arts; beginning in 1978, 1 unit from each division of the college, plus a course in functional writing, 8 of these courses must be standard classroom courses, and 10 courses must be completed while enrolled in the program.

Supportive services—financial aid. The facilitator and program committee are the main source of guidance provided by the program. The program does employ an adviser to assist students in the preparation of credit documentation. Students have access to all support services of Roger Williams College, including financial aid. They are thus eligible to apply for BEOG, SEOG, NDSL, CWS and GSL.

The Open Division is also approved for veterans, and veterans may receive 12 months of full-time financial benefits so long as the student is continuously enrolled and meets the minimum classroom attendance requirement.

TEXAS

BAYLOR UNIVERSITY
Criminal Justice Program
Waco, Texas   76703
(817) 755-1611

Philosophy and goals. Provides for the working man or woman an educational opportunity not limited by the traditional handicaps imposed by duty assignments and inflexible academic schedules. Conceived and designed as a curriculum guided study program, it will train professionals in the field of criminal justice. Specifically, the program prepares individuals for leadership roles in police administration, police personnel management, advanced criminal investigation, juvenile procedures, and corrective penology.

Degrees and certificates offered. Bachelor of Science in Criminal Justice.

Accreditation. Fully accredited by the Southern Association of Colleges and Schools.

Academic calendar. Semester.

Residency—required contact with program. Students participate in intensive classroom-in-residence periods which include 90 hours of lecture, discussion, group problem-solving, intensive class work, and examination in addition to individual study.

Part-time enrollment. Part-time study is generally not possible.

Costs. Tuition and fees for the Advanced Program in Criminal Justice are as follows: Application fee $25.00 (this is a one-time fee and is non-refundable); tuition per semester hour $55.00

Admission requirements. Consideration will be given to the applicant whose academic preparation, work experience, and/or personal qualities give promise of success in the program. Each candidate who has completed 64 semester hours in an approved Law Enforcement Education Program and who has satisfied the general requirements for admission to Baylor University shall be admitted. Official transcripts of all college work must be received for evaluation before formal application for admission is made to the Office of Admission of the University.

Assessment of prior learning. Assessment of previous learning is not possible.

Curriculum—learning options. Academic competence is gained primarily through a series of inter-disciplinary courses evolving from the social sciences, humanities and law. The internship requirement for the program is met by weekly in-service occupational activity with a law enforcement agency or department. This inservice requirement is necessary, but does not receive college credit per se.

Learning is divided into study units, each of which ends with intensive classroom seminars. The seminar session is preceded by preparatory reading and study equivalent to that normally accomplished during the traditional three-hour or one-hour semester course. Curriculum study guide materials and assignments are placed in the hands of the student and are to be completed before actual participation in the seminar session. The assignments do not involve correspondence lessons, but rather are preparation for this period of instruction, discussion and examination. Also, the student will have taken study progress examinations each six or seven weeks during the semester in preparation for the seminar and final examination.

Degree requirements. Each candidate is required

to complete the planned program of 60 semester credit hours, which includes directed readings, research papers, 540 clock hours of intensive in-residence class study, examinations, and such other requirements as are outlined in the program. The student shall maintain a grade point average of 2.5 for the 60 hours of work.

Supportive services—financial aid. LEEP assistance is available to those who qualify. The program is characterized by opportunity for individual counseling and tutorial assistance.

DALLAS BIBLE COLLEGE
8733 La Prada Drive
Dallas, Texas   75228
(214) 328-7171

Philosophy and goals. The Dallas Bible College's philosophy of education is based on an evangelical Christian philosophy of life.

Degrees and certificates offered. Associate of Arts in Biblical Studies; Bachelor of Science in Biblical Studies.

Accreditation. Fully accredited by the American Association of Bible Colleges.

Academic calendar. Students may enroll at any time during the year.

Residency—required contact with program. Contact with the program may be conducted primarily by mail, phone, or cassette tape, but some resident courses are required, as is in-service participation in a teaching or a preaching ministry at the student's church.

Part-time enrollment—pace. Students may enroll at anytime during the year and study at their own rate, attempting to finish at least one lesson a week.

Costs. Tuition is $20.00 per semester hour in addition to costs for textbook and tapes. Time payments may be arranged for tuition totaling $30.00 or more.

Admission requirements. Degree applicants must be at least 25 years of age and have completed 32 semester hours of transferable college credit. Applicants must obtain an application kit which includes:
    a. diagnostic test materials;
    b. guidelines for preparation of self-evaluation and for preparing a model of competencies;
    c. guidelines for the program of study suggested by the student.

Assessment of prior learning. Assessment of prior learning is not possible at Dallas Bible College.

Curriculum—learning options. Students are required to study Biblical studies, Christian vocational studies, or general education in the form of prescribed independent study courses. Elective credits can be taken in regular course work, guided research or research problem (thesis), guided reading, independent study, practicum and seminar.

Supervised exams are given with each college credit course to measure students' progress. Usually there will be one exam per semester hour of credit course. Students designate a responsible nonrelated adult who receives the exam in the mail and administers it to the student.

Degree requirements. A total of 64 semester hours is required for the A.A.B.S. and 130 for the B.S.B.S. degree. Biblical studies ranges from 48-74 semester hours, Christian vocation studies from 20-40, general education studies 32-50 hours, elective studies are limited to a maximum of 20 hours, and 32 credits of previous college work is required for acceptance to the program.

Supportive services—financial aid. The program is not approved for veterans and offers no financial aid.

SAINT EDWARD'S UNIVERSITY
New College
3001 South Congress Avenue
Austin, Texas   78704
(512) 444-2621

Philosophy and goals. Designed to service a population formerly deprived of college opportunities, with an educational program which is adapted to their life situation.

Degrees and certificates offered. Bachelor's degree in Liberal Studies.

Accreditation. Fully accredited by the Southern Association of Colleges and Schools. Students whose degree plan includes teacher certification or social work certification will also be awarded certification by the appropriate certifying agencies.

Academic calendar. Continuous. Students may enroll at any time.

Residency—required contact with program. The student is not required to live on campus but must take three required hours—the New College Seminar and Colloquium which are taught on St. Edward's campus. Students are expected to maintain regular and continuous contact with the New College program.

Part-time enrollment—pace. Students must be regularly engaged in learning activity on a continuous basis with a minimum of 9 hours completed satisfactorily each year.

Costs. Admission fee (nonrefundable) $ 15.00
Records Fee (one time, nonrefundable)   25.00
Readmission fee (nonrefundable)   15.00
Graduation fee   35.00
Tuition:

Tuition Downpayment for the New College
Seminar and Colloquium   201.00
Tuition for individualized learning
arrangements   (credit hour)   67.00
Tuition for traditional classes at
St. Edward's University   (credit hour)   67.00
Challenge Exams   (credit hour)   10.00
Assessment of prior learning
(submitted through the portfolio method)
Initial assessment fee   100.00
Fee scale based on credits granted
approximately $20.00 credit hour.

Admission requirements. Students may be admitted to the program if they meet the following requirements: are at least 25 years of age; have graduated from high school or earned a high school equivalency certificate; have a demonstrated ability to do college work; are willing to take the primary responsibility for learning and attaining a college degree; have the time to engage in learning activities on a regular and continuing basis until the college degree is achieved; and have completed all the required application procedures.

Assessment of prior learning. Prior learning is assessed only after the student has enrolled in NC and taken the New College seminar, through CLEP, ACT subject exams, challenge exams taken at SEU, transfer credit, military course work, and the assessment of prior learning outside the classroom submitted through the portfolio method.

New College accepts up to 90 hours of transfer credit with grades of C or higher from any accredited institution provided those fit within an approved student degree plan. New College accepts no more than 66 hours from one or more junior colleges.

New College will accept up to 30 credit hours from the CLEP General Examination. A score above the twenty-fifth percentile can earn six hours credit on the various subsections. Any previous course work in an area covered by the CLEP for which credit has been earned will disqualify a student from earning any credits in that section of the exam.

Curriculum—learning options. The New College curriculum design designates both areas of study and levels of competency. It emphasizes six areas of liberal studies with a seventh focusing on a major concentration of knowledge in depth. These areas of study are interfaced with four broad levels of competency.

The New College offers a variety of ways to learn and obtain college credit: independent studies, field studies, internships, traditional classes at St. Edward's and other accredited institutions, CLEP, ACT subject exams, challenge exams, taken at SEU, transfer credit, military course work and portfolio assessment of prior learning. The student degree plan is a written statement of the student's program to meet degree requirements. Each student with the assistance of an adviser designs his/her own personalized degree plan to meet his/her educational goals.

Degree requirements. To be eligible for a bachelor's degree in liberal studies, students must meet the

following degree requirements: successful fulfillment of an approved degree plan conforming
to the New College Curriculum Design. Successful
completion of 120 credit hours including:
successful completion of a minimum 30 credit
hours from New College, St. Edward's University;
successful completion of the New College Seminar;
successful completion of the New College Colloquium;
fulfillment of all graduation requirements and
procedures.

The New College Seminar and Colloquium are
the only three required hours. The remaining
117 are selected by the student and arranged
in the degree plan design.

Supportive services—financial aid. New College
faculty are the principal source of support.

Students are eligible to apply for BEOG,
SEOG, NDSL, CWS, GSL and veterans' benefits.
New College also has available a limited amount
of institutionally based financial aid.

UTAH

BRIGHAM YOUNG UNIVERSITY
Special Degrees for Adults
Division of Continuing Education
172 FB
Provo, Utah   84602

Philosophy and goals. Designed to assist the
student "to obtain the techniques needed for
continuing his learning all the days of his life,
to develop varied interests and to capitalize on
these interests in meeting the problems he faces
in the modern world, to know the sources and the
approaches needed to acquire knowledge and to
apply that knowledge in the service of mankind,
to continue the development of the whole person."

Degrees and certificates offered. AIS (Associate
of Independent Studies) and BIS (Bachelor of
Independent Studies).

Accreditation. Fully accredited by the Northwest
Association of Secondary and Higher Schools.

Academic calendar. Program operates year-round.
Five of six seminars required for the BIS degree.
are offered only in summer, the first is offered
twice yearly.

Residency—required contact with program. Each
of six seminars for the BIS require two weeks on
campus, as do each of three seminars for the AIS.
Students are expected to contact advisers at
least once a month.

Part-time enrollment—pace. Most adults will be
studying on a part-time basis.

Costs. Tuition $3,000.00
Application   15.00
Admission fee   50.00
Special fee payments are available on request.
These figures do not include the costs of

housing and food during the seminars. However, a
substantial tuition reduction may be achieved if
a student qualifies to have certain areas of study
waived.   (See Assessment of prior learning.)

Admission requirements. The program is open to
anyone who has a high school diploma or who is at
least twenty-one years old and is approved by a
BIS counselor. Applicants must agree to abide by
the BYU Code of Conduct and to commit themselves
to high standards of Christian morality.

In order to apply and register, one must
complete an application form, admission forms,
submit transcripts of high school and/or college
credits, submit Code of Conduct properly executed,
submit a letter of recommendation from one's own
bishop, pastor, or church administrator, take any
diagnostic tests of ability and previous learning
required by the counselor, and submit application
and admission fees.

For application forms, address the Department
of Special Degrees.

Assessment of prior learning. Areas of study may
be waived on the basis of satisfactory scores in
the CLEP, previous college work, up to sixty-four
semester hours of credits, and by special
examinations. Counselors work with students and
applicants to evaluate all pertinent criteria to
determine specific student programs and requirements.

Students with 64 semester hours or more of
approved college credits may request transfer
acceptance of the credits for the BIS program.
Similarly, 32 semester hours may be transferred
for consideration in the AIS program.

Curriculum—learning options. The program is
designed to allow students to proceed at their
own pace. The average time required for completion of the BIS degree requirements is 3 to 6
years.

The BIS program consists of a "Preparation
Phase" (4 to 6 months) concerned with "How to
Think" and "How to Communicate"; a "Growth
Phase" in four 6 to 12 month parts: Man and the
Meaning of Life: scriptures, Church history,
philosophy, and world religions together with
"learning adventures" in applying knowledge to
practical situations; Man and Society: personality,
history, family, social order, politics, economics,
Utopia, and race relations; Man and Beauty:
literary, theater, visual, and auditory arts;
and Man and the Universe: physics, astronomy,
mathematics, chemistry, geology, botany, and
zoology; and the "Closure Phase" in which
the student is expected to carry out an approved
project relating the skills and knowledge acquired
in his or her studies to some exciting problem
or objective most relevant to his needs. Each
of these six study sequences is followed by a two
week on-campus seminar. Evaluative procedures are
built into each area of study. Students are never
failed. They may either pass or be asked to
restudy and retest. Students are not dropped,
although they may wish to withdraw.

For the AIS program, the studies are similar;
however, only two of the three areas ("Society,"
"Beauty," and "the Universe") are selected for study
by the student, and there is no major final project.

Degree requirements. Successful completion of the various areas of study, the seminars, and the final project as described in Curriculum—learning options (see above) are required for the BIS. The requirements for the AIS are similar, and the differences are as indicated in Curriculum/learning options.

Supportive services—financial aid. The adviser is the key person who counsels the student. The BIS degree program is approved for benefits by the Veterans Administration.

VERMONT

COMMUNITY COLLEGE OF VERMONT
94 Main Street, P.O. Box 81
Montpelier, Vermont   05602
(802) 828-2401

Philosophy and goals. The program is founded on the conviction that the highest purpose of education is to foster self-reliant learners—people who have learned how to learn. Such people can assess what they have learned in the past and decide what they wish to learn in the future; they can plan to reach their goals; they can act on the plan; and they can determine when they have achieved the plan.
    Underlying this approach is the conviction that we learn both by doing and reflecting on what we have done. Learning is going on all the time. As we come to realize this and learn to channel it constructively, we are learning how to learn; we are becoming more self-reliant.

Degrees and certificates offered. Associate's degree.

Accreditation. Fully accredited by the New England Association of Schools and Colleges, Inc.

Academic calendar. Open admission.

Residency—required contact with program. Community College of Vermont operates primarily on a course model. However, learning outside the classroom is encouraged as are on-the-job training, apprenticeships, and independent study programs. Courses are offered at varied locations throughout the state.

Part-time enrollment—pace. Students wishing a degree may proceed at their own pace on a full or part-time basis.

Costs. Lifelong Learning Program Costs per course:

	Resident	Non-Resident
0-12½ contact hours	$25.00	$50.00
More than 12½ up to 25 contact hours	35.00	70.00
More than 25 up to 37½ contact hours	40.00	80.00
(Courses exceeding 37½ contact hours may require additional tuition)		
Independent Studies		
If CCV provides the instructor	$70.00	$140.00
If student provides the instructor and CCV approves	25.00	50.00

Degree Program Costs per semester:

	Resident	Non-Resident
Full-time (150 contact hours)	$200.00	$400.00
3/4 time (112½ contact hours)	150.00	300.00
1/2 time (75 contact hours)	100.00	200.00
1/4 time (37½ contact hours)	60.00	120.00

Admission requirements. A member of the Vermont State Colleges System, the college is open to any resident of the state, regardless of age, sex, financial situation, geographical location of previous educational experience. Students call the nearest site office and request interviews. On the basis of this meeting with a trained counselor, students are offered the learning situation which best fits their special circumstances.

Assessment of prior learning. Assessment of prior learning is done as part of each student's overall learning plan. The portion of prior learning that might be applied to each student's degree program is determined individually.

Curriculum—learning options. Students design their own learning program built on a framework of ten broad areas of competence: self-awareness, cultural awareness, interpersonal relationships, manual and physical competence, analytical competence, communication, community relations, creative competence, relationship with the environment, and knowledge. Students identify what they have learned from life experiences as a basis for a plan to help them accomplish their own educational, personal, and occupational goals. Because of this approach, a student may select almost any area of concentration, depending upon his or her own needs.

Degree requirements. To receive the degree, students must demonstrate that, given their own goals, they are competent as necessary in the ten fundamental competency areas listed above.

Supportive services. Each student receives help in a group or individual setting in identifying goals, developing a study plan, carrying out the plan, and demonstrating that the plan is accomplished. Local Review Committees of community people work closely with each student to guide and validate.

GODDARD COLLEGE
Adult Degree Program
Plainfield, Vermont   05667
(802) 454-8311

Philosophy and goals. The program is designed to provide learning opportunities through independent study and field work for adults who cannot attend college on full-time basis. Learning is defined as "the outcome of activity an individual undertakes to solve or resolve a problem, overcome an obstacle, answer an important question or achieve something deeply needed."

Degrees and certificates offered. B.S. and Vermont Teacher Certification available.

Accreditation. Fully accredited by New England Association of Schools and Colleges.

Academic calendar. The academic year is divided into two six-month semesters (called cycles), which are continuous from date of enrollment. Twelve possible enrollment dates throughout the year, coinciding with residency sessions.

Residency—required contact with program. Each cycle begins at a two-week required resident session, and is concluded six months later at the next required residency. During these sessions, each student works with an adviser to evaluate the past semester's work and plan a study program for the coming cycle, and to take intensive short courses. Other contact with the program is generally through correspondence with faculty.

Part-time enrollment. Not possible, but since each cycle is six months long, students are expected to spend an average of at least 20 hours per week in their studies.

Costs. Tuition $1,200.00 per semester (includes room and board during residency sessions); Application fee $20.00. Upon acceptance, $100.00 deposit required. Remaining tuition, room, and board due upon registration.

Admission requirements. ADP is for persons 21 years old and over. The typical student has had some college or professional experience, but those able to demonstrate their readiness and ability to do independent study may be admitted. Admission is based primarily on the written application and on transcripts of past high school and college work. Interviews or visits to the college are not required, but applicants are encouraged to visit Goddard During an ADP resident session.

Assessment of prior learning. Advanced standing is granted on the basis of previous college work, scores on the CLEP general exams, and the evaluation of prior life experiences. Each 15 semester hour unit of college work in LAS subjects at grade C or above are transferable as one semester of study in the ADP.

Students with less than 1 year of transfer credits can earn up to two semesters through acceptable scores on the CLEP General Tests.

Advanced standing can also be gained through favorable evaluation of educational life experience. Each student can, regardless of advanced standing gained through transferred credit or CLEP tests, present a petition to the ADP Dean containing persuasive evidence about personally valuable, high quality, extraordinary education endeavors. Among these may be college studies not taken for credit or studies in noncollege institutions. When a petition for educational life experience credit is acted on favorably, the student is usually granted one semester of advanced standing.

Curriculum—learning options. The major forms of learning are independent study and field work Students can use resources in their own communities, such as lecture series, libraries and museums, as well as courses at other colleges. Most students, however, rely primarily on correspondence

with Goddard faculty. The ADP faculty advise students and sponsor work in the social sciences, humanities, fine arts, education, and creative writing. Additional members of the regular Goddard faculty are called on according to the particular needs of ADP students.

Learning experience gained on-the-job can be part of ADP study. Since ADP emphasizes a broad-based liberal education, many students plan studies related to, but extending beyond, their normal job responsibilities.

Degree requirements. Eight cycles (6-month semesters) must be completed satisfactorily. A minimum of three of these cycles must be completed while enrolled in the ADP.

Supportive services—financial aid. Preadmission counseling is available to help students decide whether the program is suited to their needs. Once enrolled, the major source of guidance is the adviser and faculty.

ADP students also have access to the services available to regular Goddard students and are thus eligible to apply for federal and other financial assistance. Approximately 50 percent of the ADP students receive financial assistance of some kind.

GODDARD COLLEGE
The Graduate Program
Plainfield, Vermont   05667
(802) 454-8311

Philosophy and goals. Education is a process of growth in awareness which begins within the individual and extends into the world; it is to change and to be changed. Effective education can take place wherever the learner is, through application to a task.

Degrees and certificates offered. M.A. in many areas and M.F.A. in writing from Goddard College.

Accreditation. Accredited by the New England Association of Schools and Colleges.

Academic calendar. Program operates year-round. Admission on the first of each month.

Residency—required contact with program. The M.A. program is organized into three parts: Division I for students in New England and within 150 miles of Boston, New York, Philadelphia, Washington, D.C., Los Angeles, and San Francisco (California centers may also serve students in other Western states); Division II for students in the South, New York State, the Midwest, and Europe; and the Goddard-Cambridge Graduate Program in Social Change. For all programs, regular regional meetings are held to supplement and support students' individual resources. In some regions, clusters of students meet weekly for specialized and interdisciplinary workshops, seminars, and other discussions. Other students meet in small groups to work collectively on joint projects or to pursue overlapping interests. Topical seminars may be organized in the regions or on the Goddard campus to focus on a theme of vital interest to a number of students. Students are strongly encouraged to attend all relevant local meetings, regional seminars, and occasional colloquia at Goddard. Division II cooperates with the Goddard Summer Program to offer programs that begin with summer residency at Goddard to be followed by independent study elsewhere (for example, programs in social ecology, learning disabilities, art therapy, theater/music/dance, new artisans, and community media). The Goddard-Cambridge program offers project-oriented group study in and around Cambridge, Massachusetts, in such areas as imperialism, American social and cultural issues, and feminist studies, often involving both research and action components.

The M.F.A. program in creative writing requires intensive twelve-day residence periods at Goddard in February and August, followed by individually designed six-month writing and reading projects.

Part-time enrollment—pace. Students are expected to devote the major share of their time for at least a year to the program.

Costs. Tuition:

Division I and some Division II students $2,900/year
Students in Europe, Oregon, Colorado,
  Idaho, Montana, New Mexico, Utah,
  Washington, and Wyoming   3,150/year
Goddard-Cambridge students   2,700/year
Application fee   20.00

Additional costs may include travel expenses and housing for colloquia.

Admission requirements. Applicants should have received their B.A.s from accredited institutions. Applicants must file an application form together with the application fee, have three letters of recommendation and transcripts of all previous college study forwarded to the program, and must compose an essay which serves as a preliminary draft of the study plan. Such an essay should include discussion of the proposed scope of the project, including goals, reasons for undertaking the study, previous work in the field, and time-frame expectations; methods, including readings and field work proposed, skills to be developed, anticipated effects of the study, organization of time in the program, records of progress, means and frequency of communication with field and core faculty, planned summarization of the work, and the form the final product will take (such as book, series of essays, film, extensive paper, or any other means you might propose); and recommended criteria for the evaluation of your studies. Applications may be deferred, if room is not available, until room becomes available.

A personal interview with the regional core faculty is essential for admission, for when the core faculty member is convinced that the applicant can undertake a worthwhile program of study, the offer of admission is made.

Assessment of prior learning. No advanced standing is given.

Curriculum—learning options. The program seeks to encourage diversity and experimentation. In general, the goal is to facilitate planned

experience, reflection upon that experience, and modifications of future action in light of that reflection. The student is expected to arrange for field faculty supervision and to consult with the field faculty adviser and the core faculty member to develop a preliminary study plan. Field faculty advisers may be professors employed at other institutions, independent writers, psychologists, physicians, artists, community organizers, and are selected by the core faculty member and student jointly. The finalized study plan is used as the basis for a contract, in which the plan of study and means for evaluation of the project are delineated.

Degree requirements. Requirements vary with individual student study contracts. Final evaluations are made in a committee meeting which includes the student, core and field faculty advisers, and other consultants when appropriate. Reactions of fellow students to a final presentation at a regional seminar or colloquium will also be sought when possible. An important part of the total procedure is the student's own written evaluation of the work. Committee members submit written evaluations to the core faculty, and the core faculty decides whether or not to award the M.A. degree.

Supportive services—financial aid. The regional core faculty member is the student's primary source of support.

Federal Law Enforcement Education Program funds are available for qualified students, and the graduate program is approved for benefits by the Veterans Administration.

VIRGINIA

GEORGE MASON UNIVERSITY
Bachelor of Individualized Study
Office of Extended Studies
4400 University Drive
Fairfax, Virginia   22030
(703) 323-2436

Philosophy and goals. Designed for the mature, highly motivated person ready to assume the responsibility for his or her own self-growth.

Degrees and certificates offered. Bachelor of Individualized Study.

Accreditation. Fully accredited by the Southern Association of Colleges and Schools.

Academic calendar. Semester.

Residency—required contact with program. While most students do participate in some types of on-campus activities to complete their degrees, it is possible for a student to design a program that would require minimum contact with the university.

Part-time enrollment—pace. It is possible for students to proceed at their own pace.

Costs.

Credit Hours	In-State	Out-of-State
1	$ 32.00	$ 62.00
2	64.00	124.00
3	96.00	186.00
4	128.00	248.00
5	160.00	310.00
6	192.00	372.00
7	224.00	434.00
8	256.00	496.00
9	288.00	558.00
10	320.00	620.00
11	352.00	682.00
12 through 17	384.00	744.00
For each additional hour over 17 add:	32.00	62.00

	In-State	Out-of-State
Application fee	$ 10.00	$ 10.00
Tuition, full-time (12-17 semester hours) per semester	384.00	744.00
Tuition, part-time (11 semester hours or less) per semester, per hour	32.00	62.00
Laboratory breakage deposit	5.00	5.00
Graduation fee	15.00	15.00
Special registration fee	15.00	15.00

Admission requirements. Program is open to persons 25 years of age or older who have indicated their commitment to adult continuing education by accumulating 30 semester hours of college-level credit acquired at any regionally accredited institution.

At least 15 of the 30 semester hours required for acceptance into the program must be of conventional classroom instruction; the remaining 15 hours of the initial 30 may have been earned by CLEP subject examinations, USAFI, correspondence, television, or other nontraditional modes of imparting and measuring knowledge, and independent study administered by a regionally accredited institution of higher learning. The hours presented for acceptance, however, may not include credits awarded by other colleges or universities for prior learning experiences by means other than by examination. Knowledge claimed on the basis of prior learning experience must be validated by George Mason following acceptance into the program. Persons seeking acceptance must be able to show a 2.000 grade point average (g.p.a.) on a 4.000 scale on work presented for acceptance but may include in the graded transfer work hours of D off-set by higher grades. If necessary, the 30 hours required for acceptance may be selected from a larger number of courses taken in order to show the requisite 2.000 g.p.a. on entry credits. The applicant must also seek undergraduate admission to George Mason University through the Admissions Office. Concurrent with admission applications to the university, a student's application for acceptance into the BIS program will be evaluated based on a personal counseling session.

Assessment of prior learning. Students must have at least 30 semester hours of credit as prerequisite to admissions. In addition to generous transfer provisions, students may earn credits for prior learning experiences. More than 80 percent of the credits required for the degree can be earned for learning done prior to enrollment.

Curriculum—learning options. In addition to day and evening courses available at GMU, students may utilize correspondence courses, television courses, independent study, and courses at other schools, in developing an individualized program. Program should provide the student with general education competencies as well as concentration in competencies of specific disciplines.

Degree requirements. The BIS degree requires a total of 120 semester-credit-hours or the equivalent, with a 2.000 g.p.a. on a 4.000 scale on all graded course work completed within the Consortium. In the event a student has accumulated more than 120 credit-hours, he/she may select that combination which produces the highest g.p.a.

Supportive services—financial aid. George Mason University's Counseling Center provides specialized services for student development including counseling for personal adjustment, social skills, and communication enhancement, marriage and couples counseling, educational and career counseling and psychological testing for understanding how one functions as a person. Individual counseling and group workshops for personal growth and development are also available. Minority students may wish to contact the Center's Counselor for Minority Students.

The principal source of support is the student's adviser. Assistance is available to students through all major state and federal programs including BEOG, SEOG, NDSL, CWS, etc. Veterans are eligible for veterans' benefits.

WASHINGTON

FORT WRIGHT COLLEGE
Link Program
West 4000 Randolph Road
Spokane, Washington 99204

Philosophy and goals. Enables students to gain degrees by their college level learning on the job or by courses taken at an institution that does not grant degrees, as well as by conventional course work.

Degrees and certificates offered. B.A. or B.S. degree program for the mature learner.

Accreditation. No information available.

Academic calendar. Semester.

Residency—required contact with program. A minimum of 12 semester hours of credit in residence are required.

Part-time enrollment—pace. Students may proceed at their own pace. All examinations or other credits are recorded as they are completed.

Costs. Tuition (as of 1976) was $55.00 per credit hour for each course completed at Fort Wright College, and $20.00 per credit hour for approved equivalency credits.

Admission requirements. In that the Link Program is essentially noninstructional, students must have accumulated sufficient past learning to be considered for the program. Applicants must also file Fort Wright College application forms with the Admissions Office. In addition, the following are required:
    a. letters of recommendation from two former or present employers or business associates;
    b. veterans must file a copy of DD 214;
    c. personal résumé;
    d. forward transcripts.
Applicants are then accepted according to regular Fort Wright procedure.

Assessment of prior learning. After admittance, the program coordinator contacts the student and arranges an interview during which the coordinator assists the candidate in composing a statement of objectives and the area of concentration which is to be pursued. In light of these factors and general college requirements, a possible series of nontraditional credits is drawn up, with hoped-for credits assigned to each activity. A limit of 60 semester hours of experiential credit is allowed. Only 60 semester hours of credit may be accepted from a junior or community college.
    For each proposed credit equivalence, the student will prepare in writing, on forms provided by the coordinator, a summary of what was learned, how it was learned, and what evidence can be submitted as documentation of the experience. These justification papers are ordinarily due within six weeks of receipt of the learning plan.
    The coordinator then distributes copies of these learning experiences with appropriate documentation to the members of a preview board consisting of three or four faculty members and the major adviser. This group examines the learning plan carefully from every standpoint—college requirements, major requirements, distribution of electives—and makes recommendations to the review board. They also decide whether or not the student fulfills the college competency in written English.
    The review board presents to the student the findings of the preview board, compares the learning plan with the purpose the student has for entering the program, and allows the input of the professional associate before the learning plan is officially accepted.

Curriculum—learning options. Information not available.

Degree requirements. Degree candidates must complete a major of 10 to 12 courses and have some work in each of four fields: philosophy and theology, history or sociology, fine arts, science or mathematics. Seventy-two hours of credit are required for the degree, with a minimum of 12 semester hours of credit to be completed in residence at Fort Wright. To earn a degree the student must give evidence of proficiency at least equivalent to the average college graduate majoring in the same field. In addition, the student must meet the specific requirements for the major he/she has chosen and present a sufficiently wide range of electives to fill out a well-rounded education.

Supportive services—financial aid. Information not available.

WESTERN WASHINGTON UNIVERSITY
Human Services Program
Bellingham, Washington   98225
(206) 676-3190

Philosophy and goals. A two-year, upper-division, off-campus learning program. The curriculum is interdisciplinary, systems oriented, and based on concepts from social science and organizational development perspectives. Curricular goals stress the knowledge needed for effective work in human service activities. The curriculum is designed to use field experience as a laboratory throughout the two-year period.

Degrees and certificates offered. Bachelor of Arts.

Accreditation. Fully accredited by the Northwest Association of Schools and Colleges.

Academic calendar. Quarters.

Residency—required contact with program. Students are allowed a maximum of 36 combined credits of field work. The remaining credits necessary for the degree are obtained through Core courses, Seminars, and Problem Series workshops offered at "in-field" locations.

Part-time enrollment—pace. The program is designed as a two-year upper division program, and students are normally expected to graduate after their second year. A small percentage complete the program in three years.

Costs. Tuition cost for the 1978-79 Academic Year was $197.00 per quarter for a full-time student.

Admission requirements. Applicants to the Human Services Program may be either:
    a. Salaried employees who work in agencies and institutions which fit the human services category and who would like to complete their B.A. degree; or
    b. persons who have, or can obtain, volunteer or fellowship placements with agencies or institutions which fit the human services category.
    Preference will be given to those applicants who have completed two years of college or university study including the general education requirements (sciences, mathematics, communications). Candidates who have not completed their general education requirements must do so as soon as possible on entering the program.

Assessment of prior learning. No information

available.

Curriculum—learning options. The learning modes used to complete the degree program are distributed in the following manner:

Core group	24 credits
Seminars	18 credits
Problem series	12 credits
Field work	36 credits
Total	90 credit hours

The field placement with a human services agency provides a maximum of 6 credit hours per quarter, which are integrated with 9 classroom credit hours to provide the full-time human services student with 15 credits per quarter. Since the field placement is the work experience accompanying academic study, a student must sustain a relationship between classroom credits and field placement credits.

The core courses provide knowledge and problem solving methods for human services organizations and activities. The roles of the various participants and organizations are examined. Problem solving techniques and conceptual analysis are applied in specialized program areas. These courses are categorized into tracks for individual student emphasis. The problem series offers an opportunity for students to specialize in areas not available through courses in the regular course curriculum. All students are required to take one section each year during the Winter quarter. Students may take up to two additional sections by contract with their core group instructor.

Degree requirements. To earn a baccalaureate degree through the Human Services Program, participants must complete 180 quarter credits, including:

    a. completion of the general university requirements as stated in the university catalog;

    b. completion of credits in general electives;

    c. ninety (90) credits in the Human Services curriculum, usually within two academic years (6 quarters), including 36 field placement credits.

Supportive services—financial aid. The principal source of support is the student's adviser. Assistance is available to students through all major state and federal programs including BEOG, SEOG, NDSL, CWS, etc.

EASTERN WASHINGTON UNIVERSITY
General Studies Degree Program
Cheney, Washington 99004
(509) 359-2397

Philosophy and goals. Designed to meet the needs of people interested in earning Bachelor of Arts degrees and who are skilled and experienced in technical, professional or paraprofessional specialities, but would like to add a liberal arts education.

Degrees and certificates offered. Bachelor of General Studies.

Accreditation. Fully accredited by the state legislature and the Northwest Association of Secondary and Higher Schools.

Academic calendar. Quarters.

Residency—required contact with program. The primary instructional mode is classroom instruction. As an upper division program, it is assumed that students will be able to complete a percentage of their program through transfer credit. Courses are available in the evening.

Part-time enrollment—pace. Students may proceed at their own pace.

Costs.	Resident	Non-Resident
Undergraduate	$206.00/qtr.	$661.00/qtr.
Graduate	228.00/qtr.	752.00/qtr.
Undergraduate (part-time)	21.00 cr./ hr.	21.00 cr./ hr.
Graduate (part-time)	23.00 cr./ hr.	23.00 cr./ hr.

Admission requirements. Each applicant must provide evidence of professional or technical skills and experiences; certificates, college or school transcripts, letters from training or work supervisors, union memberships, licenses, or personal résumés. Training alone without related experience usually will not be considered adequate preparation for entry into this degree program. Persons who have little or no college credit at time of application will be required to take either the Washington precollege test or the College Board Scholastic Aptitude Test (SAT) and submit scores for evaluation. Those who have earned at least 30 academic college credits prior to application and whose grades are superior may be exempted from the test requirement.

Assessment of prior learning. Students may apply appropriate credits from other regionally accredited colleges or universities. Upper-division courses taken elsewhere will be counted as part of the 60 required for degree. CLEP and USAFI exams are also accepted.

Curriculum—learning options. Students must take a prescribed sequence of <u>classroom</u> courses. Other courses are available to students with approval of the program adviser.

Degree requirements. All EWU graduates are required to complete the following general requirements:

English composition	10 quarter credits
General education	to total not less than 55 quarter credits
Humanities	15-20 quarter credits
Social sciences	15-20 quarter credits
Science and/or mathematics	15-20 quarter credits
Special option	0-5 quarter credits

At least 60 credits must be in upper-division courses (numbered 300 or above) and at least 45 credits must be earned at EWU.

Supportive services—financial aid. The principal

source of support is the student's adviser. Assistance is available to students through all major state and federal programs including BEOG, SEOG, NDSL, and CWS.

WEST VIRGINIA

REGENTS BACHELOR OF ARTS DEGREE PROGRAM
West Virginia
See below for addresses of various campuses.

Philosophy and goals. The program is designed for adults with distinctly different needs; it can be tailored to such needs and is particularly appealing for those who have completed some college work.

Degrees and certificates offered. B.A. in Liberal Arts. There is no major or minor field of specialization in the program.

Accreditation. Each institution participating in the program is fully accredited by the West Virginia Board of Regents.

Academic calendar. The program operates on a standard fall, spring, summer semester system.

Residency—required contact with program. There is a residency requirement of 15 semester hours at one institution in the state system. Upon completion of the residency requirement the student may choose from courses offered at any of the accredited institutions in the system.

Part-time enrollment—pace. There is no prescribed timetable for completing the program.

Costs. Tuition: course fees and registration fees will be determined according to the established fee schedules of each institution.
　　Application fee: none.
　　Course equivalent credit: $50.00 per evaluation, regardless of the number of credit hours awarded.

Admission requirements. A high school diploma or equivalent certificate is required. Applicants submit an application to the sponsoring institution and can arrange for an interview. They must provide complete transcripts as well as any test scores. Applicants' high school class must have graduated at least four years prior to application.

Assessment of prior learning. Upon admission to the program the student may earn credit in several ways:
　　CPEP, CLEP, College-Level GED, USAFI, and similar testing results.
　　Transfer credit or correspondence credit from accredited institutions.
　　Credit based on work and or life experience, based on an evaluation of documentation submitted to the program coordinator. Credit is awarded only for those experiences that learning and skills

comparable to the outcomes of courses of study at post-secondary levels. There is no upper or lower limit of credit awarded by this method.

Curriculum—learning options. The program expects the same level of academic quality from students as from those enrolled in more traditional degree programs. Poor scholarship in early years should not discourage applicants who have demonstrated the ability to acquire and use knowledge. Course prerequisites and grading standards will be the same as those for regular program students. Letter grade and pass/fail option is available.

Degree requirements. A total of 128 semester hours is required, 36 of which must be distributed as follows: communications (6 hours), humanities (6 hours), natural science (6 hours), social sciences (6 hours), and general education electives (12 hours). Upper-division semester hour requirement is 40; electives, 52, to be chosen from the cooperating schools curriculum. Grade point average is 2.0.

Supportive services—financial aid. The program coordinator is available to students to discuss completion of admissions documents, course enrollment matters, assessment for work and life experiences. Any correspondence with the colleges should be addressed to the program coordinator of that particular institution.

Additional information. The following are the participating members of the Regents B.A. Degree Program:
West Liberty State College
West Liberty, West Virginia　(304) 336-8068
Fairmont State College
Fairmont, West Virginia　26554　(304) 367-4000
West Virginia University
Morgantown, West Virginia　26506　(304) 293-0111
Shepherd College
Shepherdstown, West Virginia　25443 (304) 876-2511
Bluefield State College
Bluefield, West Virginia　24701　(304) 325-7102
Concord College
Athens, West Virginia　24712　(304) 384-3115
Glenville State College
Glenville, West Virginia　26351　(304) 462-7361
West Virginia State College
Institute, West Virginia　25112　(304) 766-3000
West Virginia Institute of Technology
Montgomery, West Virginia　(304) 442-3071

WISCONSIN

UNIVERSITY OF WISCONSIN-EXTENSION
Department of Engineering and Applied Science
The Professional Development Degree Program in
　Engineering
432 North Lake Street
Madison, Wisconsin　53706
(608) 262-2061
OR

Civic Center Campus
929 North Sixth Street
Milwaukee, Wisconsin   53203
(414) 224-4181

Philosophy and goals. To provide engineers and scientists with a flexible plan for continuing education, based upon personal objectives and needs and designed to keep them competitive in their field, now and in the future.

Degrees and certificates offered. Professional Development Degree (P.D. in Engineering).

Accreditation. Fully accredited by the North Central Association of Colleges and Secondary Schools.

Academic calendar. Semester.

Residency—required contact with program. While it is possible to obtain the degree with a minimum of contact, some special workshops, evening classes, or institute work have been designed as learning options for the program. However, each student's program is individually designed and may be constructed to minimize classroom attendance.

Part-time enrollment—pace. The 120 Continuing Education Units (CEU) required must be completed within a seven-year time period, but otherwise students proceed at own pace.

Costs. There is no registration fee.
     Institutes, workshops, seminars: fees for these 2- and 3-day programs range from $125.00 to $275.00 and usually cover notebooks and materials, one evening dinner, lunches, and refreshments at breaks.
     Short Courses: fees run from $350.00 to $600.00 depending on course length (1-week, 2-week), type of course, costs of prepared notes or texts, and perhaps use of laboratory facilities, computers, and special materials.
     Special programs: some programs are offered at fees lower than usual, depending on needs of particular segments of state people and their relative ability to pay. Typical are refresher programs or programs relating to municipal and state personnel.
     Independent study (correspondence): fees will vary in relation to number of course lessons or credits. Generally, students may expect to pay approximately $5.00 per unit. The cost of any required textbook is additional, as well as a registration fee of $1.00 for each course.

Admission requirements. At least a bachelor's degree in engineering, or a science degree with background that is acceptable to the administrative committee. Acceptance in the program is not influenced by any previous grade point average.

Assessment of prior learning. Most of the Continuing Education Units (CEU) should be earned through University of Wisconsin studies. However, up to 60 CEU (not more than one-half of the program requirements) can be transferred from other accredited colleges and universities; from documented courses and programs acceptable to the P.D. degree joint administrative committee; and they must be earned within the seven-year maximum time period that precedes the P.D. degree award date.

Curriculum—learning options. The program makes CEU available to the candidate from all of the various continuing engineering study offerings:
     Institutes; seminars, workshops, conferences; short courses; evening courses; independent study; guided individual special study projects; as well as residence courses undertaken on campus or at more remote locations via audio network, and independent study/correspondence courses.
The curriculum is distributed among four broad principal segments: technical updating; technical advancement/upgrading; professional electives; and outside interest electives.
A guided individual study project is an essential, required part of the candidate's program. It is to be established and evaluated under faculty guidance. This must be a study project of some significance, but there can be wide latitude of choice. Requirements for completion include the submittal of a report as evidence of individual study capability. It is recommended to candidates that about 20 CEU be earned through the special study work.

Degree requirements.

		CEU required
a.	Technical updating (refreshers, fundamentals)	Not more than 24
b.	Technical advancement/upgrading (new technology and applied science)	At least 36
c.	Professional electives (supplementary technical, managerial, and business topics)	About 36
d.	Outside interest electives (humanities, language, science, general broader knowledge)	About 24
	Total CEU for degree	120

The use of CEU follows the accepted national standard for evaluating and granting credit for continuing education efforts. A 3-credit one-semester undergraduate course, for example, is equal to 14.4 CEU.

Supportive services—financial aid. The principal source of support is the student's adviser. Assistance is available to students through all major state and federal programs including BEOG, SEOG, NDSL, and CWS.

UNIVERSITY OF WISCONSIN—GREEN BAY
University Without Walls
Green Bay, Wisconsin   54302
(414) 465-2643

Philosophy and goals. Aim is to work toward noncompetitive systems, nonhierarchical learning situations, learning for active participation in social change, integration of life, values, work, learning, the rational and the nonrational.

Degrees and certificates offered. B.A. and B.S. from the University of Wisconsin—Green Bay.

Accreditation. Fully accredited by the North Central Association of Colleges and Secondary Schools.

Academic calendar. Learning continues on a year-round basis, but the standard UWGB calendar is used to help structure UWW studies.

Residency—required contact with program. All applicants attend a three-day admissions workshop (see Admission requirements.) Students also must meet with faculty advisers both to formulate and to evaluate learning contracts, and must maintain contacts with those advisers at rates specified within the contracts.

Part-time enrollment—pace. Possible. Student proceeds at own pace, but must file a progress report for time extension should a project continue beyond the beginning of a new term.

Costs. Vary, depending on curriculum. Generally, costs are comparable to traditional UWGB tuition and fees.

Admission requirements. Applicants send transcripts of all previous school work to the UWGB Admissions Office, together with an application form and a description of reasons for entering program, future plans, work previously done, intellectual development, education, interests, directions, and goals. Applicants are then invited to the three-day admissions workshop, in which the program and its procedures are fully explained. Students meet with each other and with advisers, and applicant is interviewed. At the end of this process, a mutual decision about admission is made by the applicant and the UWW staff.

Assessment of prior learning. Up to 93 credits may be granted for prior learning experiences, including transfer credits and credits based on CLEP examinations. In addition, a freshman testing program can earn the student up to 18 credits, and special examinations may be arranged to prove competence in meeting specific degree requirements. Finally, life experience may be documented and submitted for credit assessment.

Curriculum—learning options. UWW students fulfill the same requirements as UWGB students, but the heart of the UWW program is the learning contract. Learning contract experiences may be formulated freely, but should be intended to achieve educative equivalence with standard course offerings, and must be satisfactory both to a faculty adviser, who will supervise and evaluate the student's efforts, and to departmental chairpersons. Students plan their programs in consultation with a UWW adviser, but responsibility for initiation, development, structuring and sustaining a course of study is the student's. In addition to the learning contract, credits can be earned through UWGB courses, courses at other universities, TV and media courses, extension courses, and extension correspondence courses; although students may complete a program strictly on the basis of prior learning and learning contracts, they are encouraged to combine these techniques with traditional classroom methods.

Concentrations are offered in communication-action, growth and development, human adaptability, humanism and cultural change, managerial systems, modernization processes, nutritional systems, population dynamics, regional analysis, science and environmental change, urban analysis, and personal concentration. Personal concentration, again, is student-initiated and must receive faculty approval.

Degree requirements. Through a combination of the means described above, a UWW student must fulfill the equivalent of a standard UWGB course of study. Students must demonstrate proficiency in English; earn 5 credits in each college of the university (community sciences, environmental sciences, human biology, and creative communication); participate in or develop contract equivalents for the interdisciplinary freshman, intermediate, and senior university seminars; fulfill necessary preparatory studies or "tool subjects" requirements; earn 30 credits toward a concentration or major; and articulate an academic plan. A minimum of 124 credits must be earned, with 31 upper-level credits earned in association with the UWW program.

Supportive services—financial aid. The UWW adviser is the student's chief source of guidance.

UWW students are eligible for the same state and federal financial aid programs as UWGB students.

Glossary

Accreditation: see Regional Accreditation.

Advanced Standing (related term: assessment of prior learning): Advanced standing is credit awarded for prior learning, usually on the basis of tests or course work. It implies that the student has already begun working toward the institution's degree. A student with significant learning experiences may, for example, begin a program as a second-year student rather than a first-year student.

Adviser (related terms: mentor, facilitator, facilitator/adviser, program adviser): Although the function of the adviser will vary from program to program, in general he or she is the person responsible for helping students devise, carry out and evaluate study programs. Advisers may offer academic vocational, and in some cases personal support. They seldom offer direct instructional services, but provide students with suggestions for locating learning resources on their own. In some programs, however, faculty members who are sponsoring independent study projects will serve also as advisers.

Advisers will usually have faculty status or other professional qualifications, although they will not necessarily be trained counselors.

Assessment of prior learning (related terms: assessment of past learning, advanced standing, assessment of critical life experience, assessment of educational life experience, special assessment): Assessment of prior learning is the process by which a program will determine which aspects of students' prior learning experiences are applicable to their degree. It involves an analysis of all work done at other schools and colleges; independent learning assessed by testing agencies such as CLEP or USAFI (see below); and learning experiences which have never been evaluated, such as independent reading, professional experience, development of specific products, or participation in specific action projects. The student is responsible for submitting documentation of his or her learning. The process is usually coordinated by the student's adviser and conducted by an assessment committee.

Authorization: Authorization refers to approval or licensing of a school of state bodies, such as the state legislature or state board of higher education, and/or to accreditation by a regional association (see Regional Accreditation), or a professional association, such as the National League for Nursing.

Basic Educational Opportunity Grant (BEOG): A federal grant program which makes funds available to eligible students attending approved colleges, community/junior colleges, vocational schools, technical institutes, hospital schools of nursing, and other post-high school institutions.

In academic year 1978-79 (July 1, 1978 to June 30, 1979) you may apply for a basic grant if you are an undergraduate student enrolled on at least a half-time basis in an eligible program.

Beginning with the 1978-79 academic year, you can apply for a basic grant by completing one of several different forms. You should contact the financial aid office at the school(s) you are considering to determine which form to use.

Regardless of the form you use to apply for a basic grant, be sure to follow the instructions on the form carefully. Within 6 weeks of submitting the form, you will be notified as to whether you are eligible.

Submit the notification to your school, which will calculate the amount of the basic grant you are eligible to receive. (You may submit the notification to more than one school.) The amount of your award will be based on determination of eligibility and the cost of attendance at your school. During the 1978-79 academic year, the awards will range from $200.00 to $1,600.00.

College-Level Examination Program (CLEP): sponsored by the Educational Testing Service in Princeton, New Jersey, and offers standardized tests in a variety of subject areas. There are five general exams, which cover the content a first or second year college student would be expected to have learned in the following areas: English composition, mathematics, natural sciences, social sciences, and humanities.

In addition, the program offers tests in specific subject areas, such as American history, hematology, or statistics, which cover information similar to that which might be learned in a standard undergraduate course. All external degree programs, and most colleges, award advanced standing on the basis of acceptable scores on CLEP tests. Tests are multiple choice and cost $20.00 apiece.

For more information, contact CLEP, College Entrance Examination Board, 888 Seventh Avenue, New York, New York   10019.

College Work-Study Program (CWS): provides jobs for students who have great financial need and who must earn a part of their educational expenses. You may apply if you are enrolled at least half-time as a graduate, undergraduate, or vocational student in an approved postsecondary educational institution.

The educational institution which participates in College Work-Study arranges jobs on campus or off campus with a public or private nonprofit agency, such as a hospital. If you are found to be eligible, you may be employed for as many as 40 hours a week.

In arranging a job and determining how many hours a week you may work under this program, the financial aid officer will take into account: your need for financial assistance; your class schedule; and your health and academic progress. In general, the salary you receive is at least equal to the current minimum wage. Maximum hourly wage rate depends on the job and your qualifications.

Apply through the financial aid officer at your school. He is responsible for determining your eligibility and arranging the job.

Competency-Based Learning: As it is used in this book, competency-based learning is learning in which the focus is upon the learning of skills which have broad application rather than just the memorization of facts, to which we refer as "information-based" learning. Competency-based learning is not presented as an alternative to information-based learning, but as an important component of learning which demands equal attention.

Cooperative Assessment of Experiential Learning (CAEL): initiated by the Educational Testing Service in 1973, CAEL was a research and development effort designed to explore issues related to the assessment of learning that was done in nontraditional settings and under the sponsorship of nontraditional educational institutions. During its four-year existence, CAEL coordinated the activities of over 250 member colleges in the development of procedures by which such learning could be evaluated.

Council for the Advancement of Experiential Learning: the new name under which CAEL (see above) operates since becoming an independent organization.

Curriculum: in the traditional sense, curriculum refers to either the general course offerings or the content of specific courses offered by a college. Although some external degree programs do offer courses, in most cases the areas of study are defined by the student. Thus, in this book, curriculum refers also to the kinds of opportunities that are available to students for developing study programs in specific areas.

Defense Activity for Nontraditional Education Support (DANTES): was started in 1974 to continue and expand the services offered by the United States Armed Forces Institute (USAFI) in providing education assistance to enlisted men and women. Among the services currently available are the administration of CLEP tests, dissemination of information about nontraditional study options, distribution of free books and study guides for examinations, information related to the assessment of prior learning, and planning and advising assistance. For more information, write: DANTES, Ellyson Center, Pensacola, Florida.

Experiential Learning (related term: field work): experiential learning, in this book, refers to learning which occurs outside the confines of a traditional classroom. It is learning in which immediate attention is on the application and testing of theory rather than on the theory itself.

External Degree Study (related term: extended degree): in its purest sense, external degree study is study which can be completed without ever having to set foot on a college campus; study which is therefore external of a college. There are only three major programs in this country in which this is possible. A number of programs, however, come close to offering this option, and these are also usually referred to as external degree programs. The following definition of an external degree program is currently being employed by the National Institute of Education:

An external degree program is a formalized but external sequence of studies leading to a particular college-level degree. In descriptive terms, it is a program emphasizing minimal classroom coursework and minimal residence requirements. It generally allows considerable transfer credit for prior documentable learning obtained through a variety of sources (e.g., work experience, life experience, coursework taken in other institutions, in military settings or in places of employment) and emphasizes individually designed, self-directed study. Faculty contact often is only advisory in nature (rather than instructional). Traditional grades are often not a part of the system of evaluation and award of credit or evaluation may be accomplished in several ways (e.g. through critique of the portfolio of the student's work, through letter of report testifying on progress by a tutor or other supervisor, through narrative evaluation of a completed project by the faculty adviser or through tests and examinations). Transcripts may be entirely narrative (i.e., with no grades or course titles) or may combine grade evaluation with narrative sections about work completed.

The schools described in Section II are those which fit the above definition. The major criterion for including a school was the amount of credit that could be earned for prior learning and the portion of the program that can be completed through off-campus study. Also included are programs which award considerable credit for life experience and allow for a great deal of off-campus study, but do not define themselves as external degree programs. The major difference between such programs and other programs which would call themselves external degree programs seems to be the amount of emphasis which is placed on the small amount of campus contact which is required.

Federal Financial Aid Programs: see Basic Educational Opportunity Grant, College Work-Study Program, National Direct Student Loan Program, Veterans' Benefits, Guaranteed Student Loans.

Federally Insured Student Loan (FISL): See Guaranteed Student Loan.

Field Work (related terms: off-campus learning, field experience, learning, action-oriented learning, practicum, experiential learning): field work refers to learning situations in which the student learns by doing. Its purpose is to enable the student to understand and develop skills in the practical application of knowledge usually learned in the classroom. Field work can be student-initiated, or can involve participation in the ongoing activities of an existing organization such as a school, a social service agency, or a business.

Guaranteed Student Loans (GSL, related term: FISL) enable students to borrow directly from lenders in order to finance educational expenses. While the bulk of these loans is made by commercial lenders, some states and educational institutions also are lenders. The loans are insured by the federal government or guaranteed by a state or private nonprofit guarantee agency.

You may apply for a GSL loan if you are already enrolled, in good standing, and making satisfactory progress, or have been accepted for enrollment at least half-time, in an eligible college, university, or professional school, or an eligible vocational, technical, trade, business, or home study school.

The maximum you may borrow as an undergraduate is $2,500 per academic year. Graduate and professional students may borrow up to $5,000.00 per academic year. (In some states the maximums are less.) The total you may borrow for undergraduate or vocational study is $7,500.00. The total for graduate and professional students is $15,000.00 including any amount borrowed for undergraduate study.

Graduate students enrolled in health professions schools located in the United States may borrow larger amounts.

The interest rate is 7 percent. In most cases, the federal government will pay the interest for you until you must begin repaying the loan.

The Loan Must Be Repaid. The loans may be canceled in certain extreme instances such as the death of the student borrower, but there are no other means of loan cancellation. Payments normally begin between nine and twelve months after you graduate or leave school, and you may be allowed to take up to ten years to repay the loan.

Students normally obtain detailed information and application forms directly from lenders or from the financial aid office of their educational institution. It is possible, also, to obtain this information and applications from state guarantee agencies or from the appropriate regional office of the U.S. Office of Education.

Independent Study: refers to any type of study in which the student covers material on his or her own, without participation in formal classroom activities. Content areas may be defined by the student (usually in coordination with a faculty member or adviser), may be geared toward passing a standardized proficiency test, or may be completely structured by a faculty member.

Internship (related term: field work): a type of field work in which the student contracts with an agency or organization to undertake certain work responsibilities in exchange for the opportunity to become familiar with the activities of a specific work environment.

Learning Contract: in this book, a learning contract is a plan to complete a learning project over a specified time period. In most adult-oriented degree programs, the term is used in a similar way and contains the same components, although the terms by which they are labeled may differ somewhat. It also implies an agreement between a student and an adviser or faculty member which spells out the work the student will do over a set period of time and the services the adviser or faculty member will provide. It specifies the mode of learning, the skills and knowledge the student hopes to gain, the amount of time that will be spent, the methods that will be used to

evaluate it, and the amount of credit that will be awarded upon successful completion.

National Direct Student Loan Program (NDSL): is for students who are enrolled at least half-time in a participating postsecondary institution and who need a loan to meet their educational expenses.

You may borrow up to a total of: $2,500.00 if you are an undergraduate student who has already completed two years of study toward a bachelor's degree. (This total includes any amount you borrowed under NDSL for your first two years of study); $10,000.00 for graduate study. (This total includes any amount you borrowed under NDSL for your undergraduate study.)

Repayment begins nine months after you graduate or leave school for other reasons. You may be allowed up to ten years· to pay back the loan. During the repayment period you will be charged 3 percent interest on the unpaid balance of the loan principal.

No payments are required for up to three years while you serve in the Armed Forces, Peace Corps, or VISTA.

Apply through the financial aid officer at your school. He can also tell you about loan cancelation provisions for borrowers who go into certain fields of teaching or specified military duty.

Orientation Sessions: workshops or meetings designed to familiarize a new or prospective student with the policies and procedures of the particular program, with the learning options that will be available, and with the demands and expectations that are associated with external degree study.

Postsecondary Education: commonly used in reference to all formal educational experiences a student engages in after high school. It is often used as a substitute for the term higher education, which refers only to studies in colleges and universities.

Program Adviser: see Adviser.

Regional Accreditation: (related term: authorization): the process by which an institution receives recognition that it is offering its students the educational opportunities implied by its objectives. Schools apply for accreditation through a nationally recognized regional accrediting commission.

The commission is responsible for coordinating accrediting teams composed of professional educators who have expertise relevant to the educational opportunities offered by the applying institution. Each team undertakes an ongoing investigation of an institution's policies and procedures. The entire process, which may take three to four years, consists of five steps: (1) establishment of criteria, (2) a self-evaluation study of the program by the institution seeking accreditation, (3) evaluation of the institution by competent authorities to determine whether it meets the established criteria, (4) publication of a list of institutions that meet the criteria, and (5) periodic reviews to ascertain whether accredited institutions continue to meet the criteria. Institutions accepted by an accrediting agency or association as meeting its criteria are said to be accredited or approved. One of the best available methods of ascertaining the general standing or quality of an institution of higher education in the United States is to examine its accreditation status.

Institutions with liberal arts and general programs and, in some cases, those with special programs may be accredited by one of six regional accrediting associations. Regional accreditation applies to the entire institution. It indicates that each constituent unit is achieving its own particular aims satisfactorily, although not necessarily all on the same level of quality.

Schools must generally be approved or accredited by a particular state before receiving regional accreditation. If a school has regional accreditation, it can usually be assumed that it is also approved by the state in which it operates.

Residency (related term: campus contact): the term residency is used in different ways by different programs. Throughout this book, the term is used in reference to either the time period a student actually spends living on campus (for adult-oriented programs this is applicable only during one- or two-week intensive residency sessions), or the amount of campus contact a student must have, either through meetings with an adviser or attendance at courses and workshops.

This is different from the use of the term "residency" by some schools, who use the term to refer to all the learning in which a student engages while enrolled in the school. By this definition, no distinction is made between learning which occurs on campus and learning which occurs off campus, just so long as the student is registered in a specific degree program.

Residency Sessions: short-term on-campus stays in which students review their past semester's work with their adviser, make plans for the next semester's work, and participate in planned activities. These activities may be courses or lab work directly related to the students' studies, may be designed to interest students in new areas, may be for the purpose of providing remedial help (such as developing study skills), or may be for pure entertainment. In many external degree programs, residency sessions are the main source of contact with other students.

Institutions which operate residency sessions build their entire programs around them, and attendance is a must.

Self-Directed Learning: learning in which the major responsibility for designing and directing studies lies with the learner.

Sponsored Learning: refers to any learning activity which is being carried out for credit or some type of formal recognition from an organization created to provide educational services (schools, colleges, training programs) or to evaluate learning (CLEP, USAFI, etc.).

Supplemental Educational Opportunity Grant Program (SEOG): for students of exceptional financial need who without the grant would be unable to continue their education. You are eligible to apply if you are enrolled at least half-time as an undergraduate or vocational student in an educational institution participating in the program. Graduate students are not eligible. If you receive an SEOG, it cannot be less than $200.00 or more than $1,500.00 a year. Normally, an SEOG may be received for up to four years. However, the grant may be received for five years when the course of study requires the extra time. The total that may be awarded is $4,000.00 for a four-year course of study or $5,000.00 for a five-year course.

If you are selected for an SEOG, your educational institution must provide you with additional financial assistance at least equal to the amount of the grant.

Apply through your financial aid officer, who is responsible for determining who will receive an SEOG and the amount.

Union for Experimenting Colleges and Universities (related term: University Without Walls): developed from the work of a consortium of seven colleges which was formed in 1964 for the purpose of developing innovative alternatives to traditional higher education.

Today, the UECU is itself a university, offering a degree which is in the candidate stage of obtaining regional accreditation. Among the programs operated by the UECU are the University Without Walls program, and the Union Graduate School. The University Without Walls program involves more than twenty-five colleges throughout the country. Each of these colleges may be connected with the UECU either as a center, which means that the college is essentially owned by the UECU and offers the UECU degree, or as an affiliate, which means that the program is run by the institution sponsoring it, under its own educational policies.

United States Armed Forces Institute (USAFI): introduced during WWII, USAFI existed as an agency offering courses and examinations to those serving in the military. Although the subject examinations and courses offered by USAFI are still applicable toward college degrees at many colleges, most of the services of that agency are now provided by a new agency, DANTES (see separate description).

Unsponsored Learning: refers to skills or knowledge which are developed on one's own or through professional or volunteer experience, and have never been assessed by an educational organization.

Veterans' Benefits: monthly education benefits are available to veterans who have served in the military between January 31, 1955, and January 1, 1977, and to the dependents of deceased or disabled veterans, or to a service person forcibly detained or missing in action.

Benefits currently range up to $311.00 per month for full-time study, with additional allowances for dependents. Part-time study is possible.

Financial need is not taken into account, but veterans must be attending a school which is approved by the Veterans Administration. Contact the closest VA office to learn of special requirements placed on nontraditional study programs.

Notes and References

Introduction

1. K. Patricia Cross, "The Adult Learner," Current Issues in Higher Education (Washington, D.C.: American Association of Higher Education, 1978).

Chapter 1: New Options for Older Learners

1. Office of Noncollegiate Sponsored Instruction, New York State Department of Education, A Guide to Educational Programs in Noncollegiate Organizations (Albany, N.Y., 1974).

2. Commission on Educational Credit, American Council on Education, A Guide to the Evaluation of Educational Experiences in the Armed Forces (Washington, D.C.: American Council on Education).

3. Bureau of Labor Statistics, U.S. Department of Labor, Dictionary of Occupational Titles (Washington, D.C.: Government Printing Office).

4. Harold D. Dunkel, Whitehead on Education (Columbus: Ohio State University Press, 1965).

5. Cyril O. Houle, "Deep Traditions of Experiential Learning," in Morris Keeton et al. Experiential Learning: Rationale, Characteristics, and Assessment (San Francisco: Jossey-Bass, 1976), p. 29.

6. National Center for Educational Brokering, Educational & Career Information Services for Adults: 1978 Directory. National Center for Educational Brokering, Washington, D.C., 1978. ($2.00)

7. Richard Bolles, What Color Is Your Parachute? A Practical Manual for Job-Hunters & Career-Changers, 18th ed. (Berkeley: Ten Speed Press, 1977), p. 43. (Can be obtained from publisher, P.O. Box 7123; Berkeley, CA 94707, $5.95.)

Chapter 2: Planning Your Learning Experience

1. Robert A. Mager, Goal Analysis (Belmont, CA: Fearon Publ./Leon Siegler, Inc., 1972).

2. Dr. Mardelle S. Grothe, quotations from unpublished materials. For further information, write to Dr. Mardelle S. Grothe, Route 2, P.O. Box 580, Lincoln, MA 01773.

3. Malcolm Knowles, Self-Directed Learning: Guidelines for Students & Teachers (New York: Association Press, 1975).

4. Harold T. P. Hayes, "The Pursuit of Reason," New York Times Magazine, Sunday, June 12, 1977, p. 77.

5. Ibid., p. 78.

6. Thomas Taylor, The Ticket-of-Leave Man (1863) in George Rowell, ed., Nineteenth Century Plays (Oxford: Oxford University Press, 1972).

7. Related by artist Rafael Ferrer in a slide presentation of his work at the University of Wisconsin.

8. Gregory Bateson, Steps Toward an Ecology of Mind (New York: Ballantine, 1975).

9. Edward De Bono. The Use of Lateral Thinking (London: Pelican Books, 1967).

10. Arthur W. Chickering, "Developmental Change as a Major Outcome," in Morris Keeton, ed., Experiential Learning: Rationale, Characteristics, and Assessment (San Francisco, Jossey-Bass, 1976), p. 85.

11. H. B. Gellat and Gordon Miller, Decisions and Outcomes (College Entrance Examination Board, New York, 1971).
    Note: Although the exercises and information in this book are useful for adults, many of the examples are targeted toward high school students. Adults who are interested, however, might also benefit from the Leaders' Guide to Decisions and Outcomes, which is available as a supplementary text.

12. Irving L. Janis and Leon Mann, Decision-Making (New York: Free Press, 1977).

13. Gail Thain Parker and Gene Hawes, College on Your Own (New York: Bantam Books, 1977).

Chapter 3: Degree Requirements, Grades, and Credits

1. Marcel Proust, Swann's Way (New York: Random House, 1928).

2. Brochure of Minnesota Metropolitan State University.

3. Cooperative Assessment of Experiential Learning (CAEL), Suite 208, American City Building, Columbia, Maryland 21044.

4. Aubrey Forrest, A Student Handbook for Preparing a Portfolio for the Assessment of Prior Learning (CAEL Working Paper #7, Princeton: Educational Testing Service, 1975).

5. Ibid., p. 3.

6. Ibid., p. 24.

7. See Chapter 1, note 2.

8. See Chapter 1, note 1.

Chapter 4: Jobs, Graduate School, and Lifelong Learning

1. Richard Bolles, What Color Is Your Parachute? A Practical Manual for Job-Hunters & Career-Changers, 18th ed. (Berkeley: Ten Speed Press, 1977) p. 43.

2. Ibid.

3. David Riesman, Nathan Glazer, Reuel Denny, _The Lonely Crowd: A Study of the Changing American Character_ (Garden City, N.Y.: Doubleday reprint, 1953).

4. Ibid., p. 36.

5. The statements are adapted from a simulated board game entitled "Operation Parachute," which precedes the text of _What Color Is Your Parachute?_

6. Bolles, _Parachute?_, p. 111.

7. Ibid., p. 112.

8. Ibid., p. 113.

9. Song by Stanley Incompetini, "Catch-22 Job Search Blues" (Winsted, Conn., unpublished song lyric).

10. James O'Toole, _Work, Learning, and the American Future_ (San Francisco: Jossey-Bass, 1977).

11. Laure N. Sharpe and Carol P. Sosdian, _A Study of the Negotiability and Acceptability of External Degrees: Survey of Graduates_ (Bureau of Social Science Research under contract from the National Institute of Education, Washington, D.C.: 1977).

12. Ibid., p. 98.

13. Ibid., p. 95.

14. Ibid., p. iv.

15. Dr. Mardelle S. Grothe, in conversation.

16. O'Toole, _Work_, p. 5.

17. See Note 11, above.

18. Ron Gross, _The Lifelong Learner_ (New York: Simon & Schuster, 1977).

Chapter 5: Costs and Financial Aid

1. Willis L. Johnson, _Directory of Special Programs for Minority Group Members: Career Information Services, Employment Skills Banks, Financial Aid Sources_ (Maryland: Garret Park Press, 1976).

2. Roland Turner, _The Grants Register_.

Section II

1. The institutions described in Part I were located through the following sources:

Alfred Munzert, _National Directory of External Degree Programs_ (Machias, N.Y.: Hemisphere, 1976).

John Nero and Wayne Blaze, w. Barbara Lazarus Wilson, _External Degree Study: A New Route to Careers_ (Newton, Mass.: Education Development Center, 1975).

Laure N. Sharp and Carol P. Sosdian, _Guide to Undergraduate Degree Programs in the United States_ (Bureau of Social Science Research Under Contract with The National Institute of Education, Washington, D.C.: 1977).

2. The following directories can be useful in locating additional learning resources:

Douglas Dillenback and Susan Wetzel. _The College Handbook_ (New York: CEEB (updated regularly).

James Cass and Max Birnbaum. _Comparative Guide to American Colleges_, 8th ed. (New York: Harper & Row, 1977).

National University Extension Association, _Guide to Correspondence Study_ (Washington, D.C.: National University Extension Association, 1977).

National University Extension Association, _Directory of On-campus, Off-campus, Part-time Degree Programs for Adults_ (Washington, D.C.: NUEA, 1977).

Frances Coombs Thompson. _The New York Times Guide to Continuing Education in America._ (New York: Quadrangle Books, 1972).

Wayne Blaze, et al., _Guide to Alternative Colleges & Universities_ (Boston: Beacon Press, 1974).

Ewald Nyquist, Jack Arbolino and Gene Hawes, _College Learning Anytime, Anywhere._ (New York: Harcourt Brace Jovanovich, 1977).

Ron Gross, _The Lifelong Learner_ (New York: Simon & Schuster, 1977).

Gail Thain Parker and Gene Hawes, _College on Your Own._ (New York: Bantam, 1977).

3. Office of Education, Bureau of Student Financial Aid, _Student Financial Aid, 1977-8 Handbook_ (Washington, D.C.: U.S. Department of Health, Education and Welfare, 1977), pp. 3-4.

Index

Basic Educational Opportunity Grant (BEOG), 38, 125
Bateson, Gregory, 15
Baylor University, 110
Bemidji State University, 78
Bluefield State College, 120
Bolles, Richard, 10, 29, 30
Brigham Young University, 113
Bureau of Social Science Research, 31, 33
Business administration and management, 46, 53, 63, 64, 67, 69,
        75, 76, 87, 89, 90, 93, 97, 100, 105, 122. See also
        Student-designed studies

CAEL (Council for the Advancement of Experiential Learning),
        9, 23-26, 30, 126
California State College: at Bakersfield, 46; at Dominguez
        Hills, 47; at San Berardino, 47; at Sonoma, 46; at
        Stanislaus, 46
California State Polytechnic University, Pomona, 47
California State University: at Fresno, 46; at Fullerton, 47;
        at Hayward, 46; at Long Beach, 47; at Los Angeles, 47;
        at Northridge, 47; at Sacramento, 46
Campus Free College, 50
Career planning, 13, 18
Central Michigan University, 75
Central YMCA Community College, 57
Chaminade University of Honolulu, 56
Chicago State University: BEOG program at, 60; University
        Without Walls at, 60
Chicago TV College, 9
Chickering, Arthur, 15
Clarke, Arthur C., 11
Classics. See Liberal arts and sciences; Student-designed
        studies
College Level Examination Program (CLEP), 7, 16, 18, 125
College of St. Rose, 89
College on Your Own (Parker), 17, 18
College Placement Council, 31
College Work-Study Program (CWS), 38-40, 125-126
Columbia Union College, 71
Commerce, 63. See also Business; Student-designed studies
Communications. See Liberal arts and sciences; Student-
        designed studies
Community College of Baltimore, 72
Community College of Vermont, 114
Community services/community development, 19, 23, 78, 80,
        82, 90, 93. See also Student-designed studies
Competency-based education, 5, 7, 23, 25, 30, 126
Computer science, 93. See also Business; Engineering;
        Student-designed studies
Concord College, 120
Consortium of California State Universities and Colleges, 45
Cooperative Assessment of Experiential Learning, see CAEL
Correspondence study, 75, 77, 85, 115, 122. See also Student-
        designed studies
Costs, 37, 43
Council for the Advancement of Experiential Learning, see CAEL
Counseling: and human services, 118; and rehabilitation, 19.
        See also Student-designed studies
Credentials, 31
Credit for learning from life experiences, 6, 8
Criminal justice, 54, 78, 100, 111. See also Law; Student-
        designed studies
Cross, K. Patricia, xi
Crystal, John, 27, 30

Dallas Bible College, 111
DeBono, Edward, 15
Decision making, 15, 16
Defense Activity for Nontraditional Education Support (DANTES), 126

Department of Labor, 7
Depaul University, 58
Divide and Conquer, 14, 18
Doctoral degrees (PhD, EdD, DA), 47, 53, 56, 81, 103
Drafting, 72. See also Student-designed studies

Eastern Washington University, 119
Economics. See Liberal arts and sciences; Student-designed
        studies
Education: community college faculty, 53; early childhood, 46;
        general, 106; leadership, 103; pre-teaching, 105;
        special, 18; teacher certification, 114
Education brokering, 10, 40
Educational Testing Service, 23
Eliot, Thomas Stearns (T.S.), 21, 23
Elizabethtown College, 107
Empire State College, 37
Employers, attitudes of, 31, 32
Engineering (technology), 19, 53, 63, 121. See also Student-
        designed studies
English literature, 18. See also Liberal arts and sciences;
        Student-designed studies
Enrollment, nationwide, 32
Environmental planning, 46. See also Liberal arts and sciences;
        Student-designed studies
Experiential learning, 6, 8, 9, 31, 126
External degree study, 5, 6, 7, 18, 126

Fairmont State College, 120
Fashion merchandising, 76. See also Business; Student-
        designed studies
Federally Insured Student Loan (FISL), see Guaranteed Student
        Loans
Financial aid, 37, 38, 39, 43, 126
Fine arts. See Illustration; Master of Fine Arts; Student-
        designed studies
Flaming Rainbow University, 104
Florida International University, 52
Fort Wright College, 117
Framingham State College, 73
Friends World College, 91

Gellat, H. B., 16
George Mason University, 116
Glenville State College, 120
Goal analysis, 13, 14, 18
Goal Analysis (Major), 13
Goal-setting, 13, 18
Goddard College: adult degree program at, 7, 114; graduate
        program at, 115
Governors State: BEOG Program at, 60; University Without
        Walls at, 61
Graduate School Admissions Tests, 32, 33
Graduate study, 32, 33
Grants, 38-40
Gross, Ron, 34
Grothe, Mardelle, 13, 32
Guaranteed Student Loans (GSL), 39, 40, 126-127

Harper College, 62
Hawkshaw Approach, 14, 18
Health, 46, 53, 122. See also Student-designed studies
History. See Liberal arts and sciences; Student-designed
        studies
Hofstra University, 92
Holistic planning, 6, 9
Hope, Bob, 14
Hospitality, hotel, and restaurant management, 53, 63, 76.
        See also Student-designed studies

Howard University, 51
Humboldt State University, 46

Illustration, 97. See also Student-designed studies
Independent study, 127
Indiana University (all branches), 67
Inner-directed character, 29
International College, 47
International University, 81
Internship, 127
Invitational mood, 14

Janis, Irving L., 16
Job market, 30, 32
Job searching, 29

Kansas State University, 69
Kelly, George, 14
Knowles, Malcolm, 13
Koko dodge, 15, 18

LaSalle Extension University, 62
Law: paralegal, 106; prelaw, 105. See also Criminal justice;
        Student-designed studies
Learning contract, 14, 30, 127
Liberal arts and sciences (includes humanities, social
        sciences, sociology, psychology), 45, 46, 50, 54,
        56, 64, 65, 66, 67, 69, 72, 74, 76, 78, 80, 82, 86, 87,
        89, 90, 91, 93, 97, 100, 101, 102, 105, 106, 108, 109,
        110, 111, 112, 113, 115, 117, 118, 119, 120, 122
Liberal studies. See Liberal arts and sciences; Student-
        designed studies
Libraries, 9
Lifelong Learner, The (Gross), 34
Lifelong learning, 34
Loans, 38-40
Lonely Crowd, The (Riesman), 29

Mager, Robert, 13
Master of Arts (MA), 46, 47, 75, 80, 81, 115
Master of Business Administration (MBA), 19, 81, 97
Master of Fine Arts (MPA), 81, 97, 115
Master of Liberal Studies (MLS), 106
Master of Science (MS, MSSc), 50, 81, 97
Materials management, 82, 104. See also Student-designed
        studies
McCook Community College, 85
Meditation, 8
Merchandising, 76. See also Business; Student-designed
        studies
Metropolitan State University, 79
Miller, Gordon, 16
Minnesota Metropolitan State University, 7, 23
Minorities, 31, 40
Morain Valley Community College, 63
Mundelein College, 64
Music therapy, 18. See also Student-designed studies

National Direct Student Loan (NDSL), 38-40, 127
National Institute of Education, 31
New England College, 86
New York Institute of Technology, 93
New York State Department of Education, 6, 9, 25
New York Times Magazine, 15
New York University, University Without Walls at, 94
Northampton County Area Community College, 108
Northeastern Illinois University, 64
Northwood Institute, 76
Nova University, 53
Nursing, 54, 57, 99. See also Student-designed studies